Albert Bierstadt

Gordon Hendricks

ALBERT BIERSTADT

PAINTER OF THE AMERICAN WEST

Harrison House

Published by *arrangement with* Harry N. Abrams, Inc.,
in association with the Amon Carter Museum of Western Art

то Philip F. Purrington

Half-title page: Albert Bierstadt at about forty-two.
Collection Mrs. Orville DeForest Edwards,
Dobbs Ferry, New York

1. *(frontispiece) Camping in the Yosemite.* 1864.
Oil on canvas, 34×27″ (86.4×68.6 cm.).
The Timken Art Gallery, The Putnam Foundation,
San Diego, California

Margaret L. Kaplan, Managing Editor
Nai Y. Chang, Art Director
Ruth Wolfe, Editor
Robin Fox, Book Design
Lisa Pontell, Picture Editor

This 1988 edition published by Harrison House/Harry N.
Abrams, Inc., distributed by Crown Publishers, Inc., 225 Park
Avenue South, New York, New York 10003.

Printed and Bound in Japan
ISBN 0-517-66284-1
h g f e d c b a

Contents

Preface

I N 1962, WHILE RESEARCHING a biography of Eadweard Muybridge, "the father of the motion picture," I discovered that Muybridge and the landscapist Albert Bierstadt knew each other, were friends, and that evidently some of Muybridge's photographs were used by Bierstadt in his work. It turned out that the painter had used the photographs only as *aides-mémoire* and had in no discoverable instance literally transcribed them. But the two were in San Francisco for the same two-and-a-half-year period in the full flush of their careers, had many friends in common, and the painter had praised the photographer as an artist. I therefore decided that to learn as much as I could about Eadweard Muybridge I must find out more about Albert Bierstadt.

I then turned to what I expected would be a well-researched mass of scholarly work on nineteenth-century American art and was surprised and disappointed to learn that if I wanted to know anything more about Albert Bierstadt, I would have to find it out myself. I also discovered that the many new facts concerning the painter that I had found, chiefly in San Francisco newspapers contemporary with his visits, were entirely new to art historians. Many of these items pinpointed the artist's movements into, around, and out of the city; his work schedule and the names, exact dates, and scenarios of his works; his exhibitions and the critical reactions to these; and his social life among the elite of the Bay area. I decided to publish part of what I had found; Dr. H. W. Janson, editor-in-chief of *The Art Bulletin,* agreed that I should; and the result was an article in the September, 1964, issue entitled "The First Three Western Journeys of Albert Bierstadt."

Since the appearance of this article, accompanied by a check list of 281 works I believed to have been produced as a result of these western trips, I have been the unintentioned but not unwilling center of Bierstadt expertise.

In March, 1970, a précis of the article appeared in *Auction,* and as a result I was asked by Mitchell Wilder, director of the Amon Carter Museum of Western Art in Fort Worth, Texas, to prepare a full-length biography of the artist and to help organize an exhibition of his work. The museum has supported my work on the biography, and the exhibition was held at the Amon Carter Museum in 1972 and subsequently traveled to the Corcoran Gallery, Washington, D.C.; the Whaling Museum, New Bedford, Massachusetts; the Pennsylvania Academy of the Fine Arts, Philadelphia; and the Whitney Museum of American Art, New York City.

Besides having the fullest cooperation and support—both moral and financial—from Mr. Wilder and the Amon Carter Museum, the museum's Curator of Collections, Peter Hassrick, has been a constant, enthusiastic collaborator, and both men have lightened a work load made considerably heavier because of the relatively early deadline for the exhibition.

I am also particularly grateful to various relatives of the artist and his first wife, who were generous of their time and efforts: Mrs. Leon Bascom, Mrs. Orville DeForest Edwards, Mrs. Ralph Rooks, and Dr. and Mrs. Albert Morton Turner.

Others who have helped make it possible to do the work are: The American Philosophical Society, Walter Ames, Marjorie Arkelian, Joseph Baird, Jack Bartfield, E. Maurice Bloch, Enid Boyce, Morton Bradley, Marion Brophy, Guido Castelli, Larry Curry, Barbara Denyer, Tom Dunnings, Lew Ferbraché, J. O. Forbes, Milton S. Fox, Robin Fox, Philip C. Gifford, Aurilla Gladding, James Gregory, John Howat, David Hunt, Jack Jackson, H. W. Janson, Martin Liefer, Laura Luckey, Joyce Mayer, Mrs. Jacob McBean, Sutherland McColley, Lawrence Nahm, Maria Naylor, Helen Olsson, R. F. Petersen, Lisa Pontell, Philip F. Purrington, E. P. Richardson, Leigh Robinson, Julia Sabine, Elizabeth Morris Smith, Joseph W. Snell, Frank H. Sommer, Marcy Spiegel, James Steed, Beatrice Taylor, Evan Hopkins Turner, Robert Vose, Ruth Wolfe, and Rudolph Wunderlich.

I have tried, in this book, to make the story of Bierstadt's life and work as interesting, coherent, and relevant as I could. There has been a rush of new interest in the American heritage, and Albert Bierstadt was a major figure in the history of nineteenth-century art of this country. I hope that this work will, with a minimum of error, supply a need for facts concerning him.

Gordon Hendricks
New York City
February, 1974

Introduction

MODERN ART HISTORIANS HAVE NOT TREATED Bierstadt kindly. Virgil Barker called him "a professional Americaneer in paint," "heavy-handed," and an artist whose pigment was "repellent in its dull monotony."[1] But Bierstadt did not promote America so self-consciously, and although he helped people to love the West and be proud of it, he himself loved it and was proud of it as few men have been since. His work was, indeed, occasionally heavy-handed, but it is rarely repellent and often attractive and exhilarating. Barker makes the excellent point, however, that, like the classical German academic, Bierstadt occasionally lost sight of the whole in his effort to combine accurate details. Often, however, his synthesis was successful, and sometimes it achieved a transcendent statement of the fresh wilderness, a wilderness pausing only momentarily to allow itself to be recorded by this violator from the outside world.

Edgar P. Richardson is not at all condescending. He wrote that Bierstadt's large canvases, such as *The Rocky Mountains*, "captivated the public by their grandiose size and profusion of skillfully observed detail."[2] He goes on to say that "one misses in Bierstadt's works the deep passion of Church's vision of nature." But Bierstadt's public, during his lifetime and today, are frequently captivated by the passion that this art historian misses. They lost themselves among the Rocky Mountains and continue to do so because the artist was able to transmit to them his own love of nature. What he showed them rarely existed in the combination that was before them. But by making a "composition" such as Thomas Cole did, he often elevated and exhilarated them and made them proud of their country and its West. He also made them want to go there. In the same way, Cole celebrated the newly found glories of the Catskills forty years earlier. Richardson is correct in deploring Bierstadt's lack of control over the hot, bright colors he sometimes used and in saying the artist's detractors are occasionally snobbish. He closes by writing that Bierstadt was "a first-rate second-rate artist." This is strictly true: Bierstadt was no Eakins or Homer or Stuart or Copley. Unfortunately, however, the phrase is glib, a slogan, a catch phrase. "Second-rate" is used to denote inferiority, and covers, in general use, the worst and most patronizing that can be said about an artist. Richardson is not patronizing, but he has given those who are, a tool with which to dismiss, in one breath, some of the finest painting of American romantic landscape art.

Today, after twenty years, the same art historian has altered his view. "If I

9

were writing the chapter now," he writes me, "I would concentrate on the marvelous freshness of eye shown in Bierstadt's sketches from nature. He was a remarkable observer of air, light and the feeling of a place—all set down with superb skill in his sketches. . . . Bierstadt was one—and one of the best—of those who discovered the grandeur of the American West and made our nation aware of it. When those big dramatic pictures do not come off, they are dreadful. When they do, they have an excitement for us still after one hundred years: what must they have meant when all this was totally new, to the eyes of his own time!"

A third writer, James Thomas Flexner, gives a careful, accurate analysis of Bierstadt's style and skillfully points out his weaknesses and the reasons for his success; but he errs in his supporting data and thus undermines his conclusions. He leaves us with a sense that Bierstadt has been dismissed. He closes his section on the artist by quoting an appraisal made by John F. Weir in 1876, long after the artist's best work had been done. Weir wrote that Bierstadt's works were "vast illustrations of scenery . . . carelessly and crudely executed," a "lapse into sensationalism and meretricious effects, and a loss of true artistic aim."[3] To the extent to which this was true of Bierstadt in 1876, it takes no account of the artist's previous twenty years. Weir himself speaks of the artist's "*loss* of true artistic aim," recognizing that he once had it. Flexner leaves us with the impression that he never had it.

Whatever is said about Bierstadt now, much worse was said during his lifetime. Whatever his failures—and Eakins and Stuart had failures, too—his successes envelop us with the beauty of nature, its sunlight, its greenness, its mists, its subtle shades, its marvelous freshness. All of these Bierstadt felt deeply. Often he was able, with the struggle that every artist knows, to put his feelings on canvas. When he succeeded in what he was trying to do—to pass along some of his own passion for the wildness and beauty of the new West—he was better than Frederick Church, and as good as any landscapist in the history of American art.

NOTES: 1   Virgil Barker, *American Painting* (New York: Bonanza Books, 1950), p. 587.

2   The quotations in this paragraph are from Edgar P. Richardson, *Painting in America* (New York: T. Y. Crowell, 1956), p. 230.

3   James Thomas Flexner, *That Wilder Image* (New York: Bonanza Books, 1962), p. 299.

One

Birth, Childhood, Youth

1830-1853

NOTE FOR CAPTIONS: Titles are those supplied by owners, even if I believe these to be incorrect. Dubious titles are followed by: [correct title?]. Whenever possible, I have placed what I believe to be the correct title in brackets following the "official" title; when I have been unable to do so; I have written: [incorrect title]. The dating is my own and sometimes differs from the owners'; see introduction to Check List (p. 325) for further explanation of the dating. —G.H.

2. J. Murday. *The "Hope."* c.1840. Oil on canvas, 19 × 26″ (48.2 × 66 cm.).
The Whaling Museum, New Bedford, Massachusetts

"I HAVE AGAIN LOADED the Hope with Whale oil for Bremen & placed the cargo under the care of my Brother & directed him on his arrival at Bremen to consult with you for a better Market. Should it appear that Bremen is as good as any other market he will deliver the cargo to you . . . thee may control the Cargo in going to any other Port if it should be thought best on thy arrival at Bremen—things seem so unsettled on the Continent of Europe makes it necessary to provide accordingly." [1]

These words, written on April 2, 1831, by George Howland, a New Bedford ship owner, to his agent in Bremen and to his brother, the captain of the *Hope* (Fig. 2), begin the American story of the painter Albert Bierstadt.

Four days later the *Hope* set out for a ten months' voyage from home port. When she got to Bremen, her agent and her captain decided that she should try another port, and as a result she sailed back to Rotterdam. There, at the mouth of the Rhine, she took aboard a family of seven from Düsseldorf, some one hundred miles up the river. The family was that of Henry Bierstadt (Fig. 4), and the youngest of Bierstadt's six children on board the *Hope* was Albert, just turned two years. The Bierstadts came from Solingen, a few miles inland from Düsseldorf, and Albert had been born in that town on January 7, 1830.[2]

The *Hope*'s owner was worried about the "unsettled" conditions in Europe. These were caused by the aftermath of the Napoleonic Wars. Düsseldorf had become the capital of the Napoleonic grand duchy of Berg in 1805, and in that year Henry Bierstadt, aged twenty, began his army service. In 1815 the city was transferred to Prussia, and Bierstadt was discharged. Two years later he married the artist's mother, Christina (Fig. 5), then twenty-four. Their first child, Charles, was born two years later, followed by Anna Helen in 1822, Edward in 1824, Anne Wilhelmine in 1826, John in 1828, and finally Albert, in 1830. John died the year before Albert was born, and the family must have been glad to have a new son to replace him. Family tradition has it that Christina did not want to bring up her children in the warlike atmosphere of her country. In this feeling she was joined by thousands of other parents of the time and place. And, like the others, her choice of America was typical.

Family tradition again places the date of the arrival of the *Hope* in New Bedford as February 22, 1832. The *Hope*'s records show only a wharfage fee, and the local newspapers, curiously, show no such arrival. But the wharfage fee is at an appropriate time, and there is no reason to think that the date was pulled out

13

3. The Bierstadts' house at Acushnet Avenue and Mill Street, New Bedford, Massachusetts, photographed before 1941. The Whaling Museum, New Bedford, Massachusetts

of the hat. Howland's account books show expenses charged to the setting up of a new cooperage shop soon after the arrival, and it seems reasonable to think that the new cooper was Henry Bierstadt. That was his business later. It might also explain the occasion for the emigration: Howland needed a good cooper—it was an essential part of the whaling business—and he may have thought that Bierstadt was the man for the job. Henry's sons Edward and Charles, who later became photographers, followed their father into the woodworking business.

But it was different for young Albert. Exactly how and when it was different is a matter of uncertainty, and again the historian must depend on family tradition. Until 1850, when the artist was twenty, there is nothing specific to link him with his later career as a painter. Further, little is known about his early life. He attended the local public schools, and a fellow student remembered that he was clumsy, "always stumbling up the aisles—never knowing his lessons, and a boy who no one thought would ever amount to anything."[3] But such a beginning is "remembered" for many of the world's famous men. And it is difficult to square clumsiness or slowness with Albert Bierstadt.

The young Bierstadt has been said to have worked for a local cake decorator, but there is no support for such a theory. The story that he worked in a frame shop is a more likely one. If this is so, perhaps this is how he first came into contact with paintings, and how he first became interested in art as a career. In New Bedford he was not without acquaintances among the artistic fraternity. William A. Wall was perhaps the leading luminary in that field, with William Bradford and Albert Van Beest not far behind.[4] Another was J. W. Stock, a portrait painter from Springfield, Massachusetts, who offered his work to New Bedford's citizens in 1846. There was moral support, at least, for art in New Bedford during the artist's youth. With prosperity, there as elsewhere, the "luxuries" of life became attractive, and, there as elsewhere, painting was thought to be a luxury. It was "the divine art" to a local paper in 1845,[5] and Bierstadt's family, though naturally concerned that their son should have a secure living, must have shared this opinion. Their European background would have also encouraged this view of an artist's career. They would be glad if he could, but could he? It was difficult even for the best.

The Bierstadts' house in New Bedford, from perhaps 1835 onward, was at the northeast corner of Acushnet Avenue and Mill Street (Fig. 3). Henry Bierstadt's cooperage was evidently at the rear, at 58 Ray Street. When the family

15

4. Henry Bierstadt, the artist's father. c.1851. Daguerreotype, possibly by Peter Fales. Collection Albert Morton Turner, Orono, Maine

5. Christina Bierstadt, the artist's mother. c.1851. Daguerreotype, possibly by Peter Fales. Collection Albert Morton Turner, Orono, Maine

came to New Bedford they were said to have been one of the first three German families in town. The Acushnet Avenue house was in a good residential section. It was also successively the site, before the Bierstadts moved in, of the first Methodist meetings in New Bedford in 1795 and of a tavern. A prayer stool from the Methodist days is still in New Bedford's Whaling Museum. According to local legend, Mrs. East, the wife of the builder of the house, used to climb through a scuttle on the roof and shout announcements of meetings across the river to the residents there. A hearty woman, even for a whaling port.

Bierstadt's artistic career began, in recorded history, with the publication on May 13, 1850, of an offer to teach monochromatic painting:

MONOCHROMATIC PAINTING,

AT LIBERTY HALL.

A. BIERSTADT is prepared to give instructions in this new and beautiful art. By his mode of teaching his pupils are enabled to execute good pictures at their first attempt, far superior to their own expectations. His room is always open for the reception of visitors who desire to see specimens of the scholars and his own make. Terms $3 for 24 hours, and warrants every picture the scholars make worthy of a frame.[6]

He was said to have published a flyer on June 6, offering to "take one more Class in this beautiful Art,"[7] which may or may not suggest that the advertisement had been a draw.

By now the artist had a studio. He also began to exhibit, and before he left for training abroad in 1853, he had works in at least three separate shows. The first of these was in New Bedford itself in 1851, when he exhibited some of his work in John Hopkins's store in the Ricketson Block. Hopkins was later to be the artist's principal local supporter (see Chapter 2). The second occasion was an exhibition at the New England Art Union in Boston in 1851, in which he had a crayon drawing titled simply *The Landscape*. The third showing was in the Massachusetts Academy of Fine Arts in 1853, where he exhibited a painting he called *The Old Mill*.[8]

The 1851 New Bedford exhibition called forth a local patron. The

16

Hathaway family had been in the shipping business for some time, and a Mrs. Hathaway now began to buy from young Bierstadt. She continued to do so for some years (see Chapter 2). On August 14, 1851, he gave her a receipt for a picture and frame. The picture was called *Ruins of Carthage,* and the amount for both was twenty-five dollars.[9]

In 1851 the artist also made a debut as a producer. On July 1, he announced that he had "made engagements with Geo. Harvey, Esq., for the use of his *truly splendid Pictures*"[10] of American scenery. These were to be shown in Concert Hall by use of the Drummond light, a dissolving lantern that enabled the operator to blend one picture into the next without interruption. The Harvey of Bierstadt's exhibition was, of course, the George Harvey whose magnificent watercolors of Ohio, Michigan, and Canada were celebrated throughout the East. In September Bierstadt brought Harvey's pictures back for several shows in Liberty Hall, this time in partnership with Peter Fales, a local daguerreotypist. Both visits drew crowds. During the September showing, a local reporter was "agreeably disappointed"[11] to find the show even better than he had thought it would be. He was fascinated with the grotesque effects of the dissolving lantern:

> The dissolving of one picture into another sometimes develops the most grotesque conjunction of objects. A lady daintily tripping over dry ground is suddenly plunged to the ankles in a brawling stream; or a man sitting securely upon a prostrate log is transferred to the back of an ox. . . . The proprietors, Messrs. F. & B., seem determined to place these views before the public in a creditable manner, and if they do, they will verily reap their reward.[12]

The previous December Bierstadt's partner Fales had himself been associated with a member of the Hathaway family in introducing locally "a new German method of drawing," which enabled a student "in one hour to . . . sketch with facility and accuracy."[13] All of which is tantalizingly close to Bierstadt's claim of six months earlier—"pupils are enabled to execute good pictures at their first attempt."

In 1853 Bierstadt painted *A Cavalier,* showing the head of a man in perhaps fifteenth-century costume (Fig. 6). It has been called a self-portrait, but evidently it is not. It may have been painted before the artist left for Europe, to show Johann Peter Hasenclever, with whom he expected to study, an example of what

6. *A Cavalier.* 1853? Oil on wood, 18 × 13″ (45.7 × 33 cm.).
Collection Ellen R. Lempereur, Weston, Massachusetts.
It has been suggested that this is a self-portrait,
but evidently it is not

he could do. Or it may have been painted in Düsseldorf immediately after he arrived; it was later described as showing the Düsseldorf palette.[14] The difference between *A Cavalier* of 1853 and the artist's next portrait, *Martha Simon* of 1857, painted after the European experience, is striking (Fig. 28).

Other works, sold at auction in 1870, could also belong to Bierstadt's pre-European career. One was in monochrome: *Marine, Moon Rising;* three more were in crayon: *Chowder Party, Entrance to New Bedford Harbor,* and *Virginia Water;* and two more were evidently a combination of crayon and watercolor: *Mount Hope from Fall River* and *Round Hill Light House, Buzzard's Bay.*

For all his relatively substantial local success, Bierstadt knew he would never be a really good artist until he had better training. Such training, he thought, was not available to him in New Bedford or anywhere else in America. He had few financial resources, however, and it is said that a local gentleman, Captain William G. Blackier (Fig. 7), decided to sponsor the artist's European study.

7. Chester Harding (attr.).
Captain William G. Blackler. 1830–35.
Oil on canvas, 24½ × 19½"
(62.2 × 49.5 cm.).
The Whaling Museum,
New Bedford, Massachusetts

NOTES:

1 From the manuscript books of George Howland, in The Whaling Museum, New Bedford, Massachusetts.

2 Although all the descendants agree that the town was Solingen, *The New Bedford Daily Mercury* (sometimes called *The New Bedford Mercury*), in an 1897 reprise of the artist's career, gave the place of his birth as Eberfeldt.

3 From a lecture given in Fairhaven, Massachusetts, in 1921 or 1922, by Mrs. Elwin G. Campbell, whose teacher went to school with Bierstadt. Manuscript in the Millicent Library, Fairhaven.

4 Wall (1801–1885) had essentially a New Bedford reputation, with little celebrity outside his native town. Bradford (1823–1892) became famous for his Arctic scenes and shared a patron, Legrand Lockwood, with Bierstadt. Van Beest (1820–1860) was Bradford's teacher and shared a studio with him. He sometimes signed his name alongside Bradford's to a painting on which they both had worked.

5 *The New Bedford Daily Mercury,* June 6, 1845.

6 *The New Bedford Daily Standard* (sometimes called *The New Bedford Daily Evening Standard*), May 13, 1850. Monochromatic painting was common as a beginning technique for a worker in oils. Different tones of the same color—generally black or gray—were used exclusively. The

19

student could thus be trained in values before he began to use colors. It was a good method: inadequate work in values often resulted in poor color work. The art historian Henry T. Tuckerman wrote that Bierstadt began to paint in oils in 1851. However, since it would have been difficult to do monochromatic painting in another medium, say crayon, chalk, or even watercolor, it seems likely that the year was 1850 rather than 1851.

7   From a transcription in Richard Shafer Trump, "Life and Works of Albert Bierstadt," (Ph.D. diss., [Columbus] Ohio State University, 1963), p. 23. Dr. Trump has pointed out a number of references that I have found useful. He wrote that this Bierstadt flyer was in the New Bedford Free Public Library, but I did not find it there. There is no reason to doubt its authenticity.

8   The first of these exhibitions is said to have been reported in a clipping loaned to Trump (see previous note) by the Whaling Museum, New Bedford; I have not seen it. The second exhibition is documented in *Catalog of Paintings now on Exhibition* (Boston: New England Art Union, 1851) in the library of the Boston Museum of Fine Arts; the third, in *Catalog of the First Semi-Annual Exhibition of Paintings* (Boston: Massachusetts Academy of Finé Arts, 1853) in the library of the Boston Athenaeum.

9   *Ruins of Carthage* is unlocated; the receipt is in the Henry Francis du Pont Winterthur Museum, Winterthur, Delaware.

10   *The New Bedford Daily Standard,* July 1, 1851.

11   *The New Bedford Daily Mercury,* September 9, 1851.

12   *Ibid.*

13   *Ibid.,* December 24, 1850.

14   From a catalogue of the Edward Bierstadt sale of April 27, 1905.

Two

Study in Europe

1853-1857

8. Study for *Sunshine and Shadow*. 1855.
Oil on paper, 19 × 13″ (48.2 × 33 cm.).
The Newark Museum, Newark, New Jersey.
Gift of J. Ackerman Coles, 1920

IN 1853 DÜSSELDORF WAS THE MECCA for most young American art students wanting to study in Europe. Bierstadt, a native of the area and a relative of one of the city's shining artistic lights, Johann Peter Hasenclever, was naturally drawn there. Departure lists for 1853 do not show his name. We can only assume that the money he is said to have been given for his trip—by Captain William G. Blackler and others in New Bedford—was not enough for a cabin, and steerage, where Bierstadt must have traveled, was beneath notice.

Evidently he went first to Liverpool, as the overwhelming majority of Atlantic travelers did at this time, and took the railroad to London. It is beyond credibility that the young, eager artist did not stay in London for at least a few days to see the art treasures there. A slight indication that London was his first stopping place may be his early sketchbook, which was manufactured and sold in that city.

It was repeatedly stated during Bierstadt's lifetime and consistently since that he went to Europe in 1853[1] and came back in 1857, but his first chroniclers were careless in making his stay only three years, and subsequent ones merely followed the error. Only Virgil Barker, in *American Painting*, has squarely faced facts and said the artist had four years in Europe.

It is said that Bierstadt went to Düsseldorf expecting to study with Hasenclever, his mother's cousin, and that when he got there he discovered that the artist had died. According to one authority Hasenclever died on September 16, 1853, and according to another, on December 16. If the latter is correct, Bierstadt could not have gotten to Düsseldorf before December 16; if the former, any time after September 16.

By January 3, 1854, Bierstadt was making plans for travel outside Düsseldorf when the weather got warmer. On that date he had written the U.S. legation in Berlin, and two days later the legation secretary answered him:

Your letter of the 3rd just came duly to hand. I am instructed by Mr. Vroom to inform you that a passport given at this Office is considered valid by the Authorities throughout Germany only for the purpose of the return of the bearer to the United States. Hence it would be useless to send you one. In place of it, I am instructed to send you the enclosed paper, which is more in the nature of a personal request and guarantee. I am instructed to advise you that your best course will be to write immediately to the State Department at Washington, requesting a regular passport. . . . It is to be regretted that in spite of repeated remonstrances our State and City Authorities will continue to involve travellers in difficulties by the issuing of passports which foreign authorities are not bound to recognise.[2]

This correspondence indicates that the artist was surely in Germany when he wrote his letter of January 3: a letter could not have come to Berlin in only two days from a more distant place.

The three principal sources for our knowledge of the artist's life in Europe, besides his works themselves, are Worthington Whittredge's *Autobiography,* Sanford S. Gifford's letters and journals, and the published account of the life of William Stanley Haseltine.[3] Haseltine got to Düsseldorf in 1855 and Gifford in 1856, so we are left until those years with Whittredge's memory.

It seems clear, however, that when Bierstadt got to Düsseldorf and found that Hasenclever had died, he sought out Whittredge and Emanuel Leutze. Whittredge (Fig. 9) wrote that the young Bierstadt brought with him studies he had made back home and asked the two men to help persuade Andreas Achenbach to teach him. They thought the work was so poor—and they could not bear to tell him so—that they told him that Achenbach, under no circumstances, took pupils. Leutze is said to have remarked when Bierstadt had gone, "Here is another waif to be taken care of."[4]

Leutze was wrong. Bierstadt was carefully independent:

But Bierstadt was not made to be a waif. He soon proved that he was not likely to be a charge upon anybody. He refused to drink beer or wine, and if invited to dinner managed to get around all such invitations in a polite way, especially if they looked in the least as if they required dinners to be given in return. He had no money to spend in that way and preferred to be thought unsociable rather than impoverish himself by giving costly dinners.[5]

Evidently in April, 1854—and it was for this travel that he must have wanted a passport—Bierstadt packed up his spare belongings and was off into the Westphalian countryside. Whittredge recorded the trip:

9. Emanuel Leutze. *Worthington Whittredge*. 1856.
Oil on canvas, 57⅞ × 40½″ (147 × 102.9 cm.).
The Metropolitan Museum of Art, New York City

After working in my studio for a few months, copying some of my studies and a few others which he borrowed, he fitted up a paint box, stool and umbrella which he put with a few pieces of clothing into a large knapsack, and shouldering it one cold April morning, he started off to try his luck among the Westphalian peasants where he expected to work. He remained away without a word to us until late autumn when he returned loaded down with innumerable studies of all sorts, oaks, roadsides, meadows, glimpses of water, exteriors of Westphalian cottages, and one very remarkable study of sunlight on the steps of an old church which some years afterwards was turned into a picture that gave him more fame than anything he had ever painted. It was a remarkable summer's work for anybody to do, and for one who had had little or no instruction, it was simply marvellous. He set to work in my studio immediately on large canvases composing and putting together parts of studies he had made, and worked with an industry which left no daylight to go to waste.[6]

The study of sunlight on the steps of the church is now in the Newark Museum (Fig. 8). It was used for a larger composition of the artist's third year in New York, *Sunshine and Shadow* (Fig. 81), which was, indeed, one of his most celebrated paintings, even if it did not give him "more fame than anything he ever painted."

Whittredge goes on to describe Bierstadt's working methods:

There was a window in my studio out of which he could see the sky and watch the clouds, so he made for himself a set of chalks of such tints as he needed and every day he made studies of skies, after I had got through with my day's work and sometimes before I got up in the morning. The pictures which he painted were dispatched to New Bedford as soon as possible after they were done, were sold there and his pockets soon had money in them.[7]

One of the paintings which the artist worked up in Düsseldorf in the winter following his 1854 trip into bucolic Westphalia was one he dispatched on March 23, 1855, to his New Bedford patron Mrs. Hathaway. A letter that the young painter sent to her has been preserved:

10. Andreas Achenbach. *The Shore, Scheveningen.* 1849. Oil on canvas, 17½ × 23½″ (44.4 × 59.7 cm.).
Saint Johnsbury Athenaeum, Saint Johnsbury, Vermont

11. *Westphalian Landscape.* 1855. Oil on canvas, 26 × 34½″ (66 × 87.6 cm.).
Webb Gallery of American Art, Shelburne Museum Inc., Shelburne, Vermont

12. *Approaching Storm*. 1854. Oil on canvas, 16⅜ × 20½″ (41.6 × 52.1 cm.).
Arnot Art Museum, Elmira, New York

The picture which you had the kindness to order from me is now on its way to America, where I hope it will arrive in good condition. The view is near Limburg, Westphalia near the river Ruhr which can be seen in the distance and on the hill which rises from its surface stands the ruins of an old Castle which formerly belonged to Charles the tenth, it was destroyed in the thirty years war by the Franch [sic], you can see the hill on which it stands much better than the Castle owing to the great distance in the foreground—I have represented an old farmhouse among the trees which is so characteristic of Westphalia. The woman crossing the bridge in the immediate foreground has just returned from the forrest [sic] where she had been collecting dried leaves to be used as bedding for the animals. The custom of caring [sic] things on the head is common all over Germany. If this picture should not prove perfectly satisfactory, I do not wish you to take it but will paint you another. I trust, however, that you will find this much better than any of my former pictures and that others will like it, and be the means of my disposing of more of my pictures in New Bedford. In a few months I shall have some large pictures on the way, and I hope I shall find some purchasers for them in New Bedford, thanking you a thousand times for your kindness I remain with the highest esteem

Your ob't servant
Bierstadt.[8]

Mrs. Hathaway's painting is now in the Shelburne Museum's Webb Gallery of American Art (Fig. 11). Another painting, of the same farmhouse from the other side, is in the Arnot Art Museum in Elmira, New York (Fig. 12).

Mrs. Hathaway's painting may have been one of six Bierstadt sent to be exhibited at Hopkins's store in New Bedford in August, 1855. A delightful painting of a blue sky with a stream and a rowboat (Fig. 13) may also have been in this group. *The New Bedford Daily Mercury* received the paintings enthusiastically:

MR. BIERSTADT'S PAINTINGS—We have made several visits to the store of Mr. Hopkins, for the purpose of enjoying the beautiful paintings recently sent home by Mr. Bierstadt. It seems but yesterday

13. *Westphalia*. 1855. Oil on canvas, 43 × 58½″ (109.3 × 148.6 cm.).
Private collection. (Formerly in Swain School of Design, New Bedford, Massachusetts.)

15. Cover of Bierstadt's European sketchbook, showing experimentation with signature. 1853–plus. Addison Gallery of American Art, Phillips Academy, Andover, Massachusetts

that Mr. Bierstadt left here for the purpose of pursuing his studies at the Art School of Dusseldorf, and now we have a most satisfactory evidence of his progress in the shape of six finished and beautiful performances. Mr. Bierstadt's painting is in the style of the modern German artists, minute and elaborate, but we think these pictures very free from mannerism. The "View on the Weser" is particularly good, and there is a very effective moon-light scene. The still water in his pictures is very successful, but he has been less happy with water in motion, which, professors of painting to the contrary notwithstanding, does not run in a nutmeg grater pattern. We have been, we repeat, several times to see these charming pictures, and we shall continue to go as long as they are exhibited, as well as advise our friends to go also. We have a right to be proud of Mr. Bierstadt, for he is a New Bedford boy, by education, if not by extraction, and we can safely predict for him a successful and distinguished future if he continues to improve as he has done.[9]

Not all Bierstadt's fellow citizens concurred. According to Worthington Whittredge, when another New Bedford newspaper reporter saw the artist's work, he decided that it was too good to be Bierstadt's and said so in print. He also suggested that it was the work of Whittredge. Bierstadt's mother sent the clipping to Whittredge and asked if the report was true and if her son really had talent after all. If he did not, she wanted him to come home. Whittredge gives an account of what happened then:

As I had never touched the pictures, nor Leutze either, we felt this to be such an unjust accusation that we went to work at once to correct the editor and set the people right in New Bedford, first endeavoring to make his mother happy by assuring her that her son certainly had talent and would succeed. Then we drew up a paper which we signed stating that the pictures were the genuine work of Bierstadt, that we had never had anything to do with them, beyond a little criticism common to the profession. With this paper in our pockets we went that night to the "Malkasten" where as usual were assembled a large number of artists among whom were Achenbach and Lessing, seated around a long deal table with their mugs of beer and schoppens of wine. Anything new from America was always interesting to this company, especially as many of them had their works then on exhibition in New York, and when Leutze told the fate of Bierstadt, it struck Bierstadt that if Achenbach and Lessing would sign this paper, it would be a great gratification to his mother. After the paper was translated to them, they added their names without any hesitation. The Germans generally know the names of their artists, and these two names were doubtless remembered by the old people, and when they saw them attached to a rather flaming document about their son's abilities, it may be believed that it gave them a great deal of pleasure. The letter was soon sent to New Bedford and appeared in the various newspapers there, the offending editor apologizing sufficiently, he thought, by admitting it to his newspaper without comment. The pictures after that were soon sold.[10]

Fragments of the very letter that Bierstadt's friends produced that night still exist in the Winterthur Museum, although Whittredge is apparently wrong in saying that Lessing signed the letter. Although in four pieces, the closing seems complete, and contains the names of only Leutze, Achenbach, J. B. Irving, and Haseltine. It is possible, of course, that Whittredge, like Leutze, may have written a separate note. The fragments begin:

pictures, which he painted while in Dusseldorf, were painted in my studio, where Mr. Whitredge [sic] his teacher had his rooms. I am therefore quite qualified

of Alberts abilities, and oppose simple truths—to injurious misrepresentations no matter from what motive the [sic] may have arisen I would be obliged to you for the name of the artist who published such—Yours very resp

E. Leutze

Dusseldorf—I know nothing which Albert Bierstadt lacks to become an honor to his profession and his country, but a little judicious encouragement

16. Bierstadt's European sketchbook, page 14. 1853–plus. Addison Gallery of American Art, Phillips Academy, Andover, Massachusetts

33

17. Bierstadt's European sketchbook, page 9.
1853–plus. Addison Gallery of American Art,
Phillips Academy, Andover, Massachusetts

are ready to declare the same and you will find their names in coroboration [*sic*] of this below.

A. Achenbach

[J.] B. Irving, Jr.
Charleston So. Car.

William S. Haseltine
Philadelphia

The Malkasten mentioned by Whittredge must have been a place of fond memories for Bierstadt; later he gave the name to his splendid home overlooking the Hudson River. In Düsseldorf the Malkasten was a gathering place for artists, and in it was a permanent exhibition of their work. It had been founded by Leutze and Achenbach, among others, some years before, and supported a fund from which the artists could bórrow without having to pay interest. Sanford Gifford's description mentions some of its other activities:

> Their rooms are decorated with frescoes, &c. There is a theatre belonging [*sic*], where comical plays and operas, composed and conducted by the artists, are performed often. It is a place where they congregate in the evening to sup, smoke, talk, drink beer, play billiards, and amuse themselves in various ways.[11]

Leutze had introduced euchre to the club, and the stakes were two-and-a-half cents. "A true brotherhood seems to reign among them," Gifford added. "They are very natural and free in their intercourse with each other, [but] with all their love of social relaxation they are very industrious, and are very early risers."[12]

On November 11, 1855, Bierstadt was in Salzburg, possibly at the end of a long summer's excursion. Perhaps during the same trip he also visited nearby Berchtesgaden. A sketchbook he used during these trips through the German provinces is now in the Addison Gallery of American Art in Andover, Massachusetts (Figs. 14–18). The cover bears interesting evidence of the artist's early indecision as to how to sign his name.

With the North German winter waxing cold, Bierstadt ran low on funds. Either he wrote his New Bedford friends about his plight or they surmised it. In any case, they resolved to try to help him. Three of the previous summer's six paintings were still in Hopkins's rooms, and Hopkins and others decided to try to sell them for display in the new public library. "To complete his education abroad," *The Mercury* reported, "he is now in need of funds."[13] One John B. Congdon was put in charge of the fund raising, and *The Mercury* hoped that New Bedford's "generous citizens" would "remember and liberally assist Mr. Bierstadt." Two weeks later the *Mercury* reporter went up to Boston to see the paintings at the Athenaeum. He came back with the impression that Bierstadt had "no superior in landscape, among late American artists."[14] New Bedford's citizens did, in fact, come through, and several of the artist's paintings found their way onto the library walls (see Chapter 3).

In the summer of 1856—perhaps in June—Bierstadt, his purse replenished from home, went up the Nahe River to a village called Kim. He was accompanied by Whittredge, Haseltine, Horace Howard Furness, Irving, Enoch Wood Perry (who was later to visit Yosemite with Bierstadt), and others. Whittredge had visited Kim the preceding March and had liked it very much. We know from Gifford that they were there no later than June 19. Besides making sketches, they went fishing, celebrated the Fourth of July with true nineteenth-century restraint, and had a generally good time. They all had nostalgia for Kim for the rest of their lives.

The next month, including July 27, when Gifford saw them there, the group was at Lake Lucerne. Walking along the lake one fine evening Gifford met Bierstadt for the first time. They had a very pleasant evening. "They are going to spend several weeks on the lake," Gifford wrote.[15] While there Bierstadt made studies for *Lake Lucerne,* his first official exhibition painting. At Kusnach, also on Lake Lucerne, he made studies for a picture he later called *The Bernese Alps, as Seen near Kusnach.* A canvas which I believe to be this painting is extant (Fig. 19), as is a smaller oil of Lake Lucerne (Fig. 20).

While at Brunnen-on-Lucerne, Bierstadt and Whittredge stayed at an inn called Weissen Ross, "an humble inn but a good one," Whittredge wrote.[16] A painting of a nearby cottage has come down to us (Fig. 21). He recounts an adventure with goats:

> To get from the "Weissen Ross" to the path along the cliffs we had to cross a strong hewn slab that bridged the distance some fifty feet from one tall rock to another, and which was some twenty feet above the

18. Bierstadt's European sketchbook, page 15. 1853–plus. Addison Gallery of American Art, Phillips Academy, Andover, Massachusetts

19. *Bernese Alps, as Seen near Kusnach* [correct title?]. 1859. Oil on canvas, 42 × 71″ (106.7 × 180.3 cm.). Hammer Galleries, New York City. Kusnach is not in the Bernese Alps

20. *Lake Lucerne, Switzerland.* 1856.
Oil on paper mounted on canvas, 13⅛ × 18⅝″ (33.3 × 47.3 cm.).
Collection Jo Ann and Julian Ganz, Jr., Los Angeles

21. *Cottage near Lake Lucerne* [correct title?]. 1856.
Oil on paper, 11½ × 13½″ (29.2 × 34.3 cm.).
Whereabouts unknown

water. The slab was about eighteen inches wide, without a railing, rather a ticklish thing to cross! One day the scene we wanted to paint was best viewed from the middle of this slab, and we resolved to sit down upon it one behind the other with our sketch boxes before us and our legs dangling over the sides. It was afternoon. The shades of evening were fast approaching. The curfew bell was being tolled. We were in desperate haste to catch the fleeting effects of the scene, when I heard a singular clattering of feet, upon the slab behind me, and looking around encountered the nose of an old goat and saw a large herd behind him. I called to Bierstadt and explained the situation. He said the goats would have to wait, and I thought so too and hurried to put in the final touches to my picture, when suddenly the fore goat, who had got tired of waiting leaped over my back, landed between me and Bierstadt, made another leap over him and went on home without so much as a single snort. This was the signal for the rest of the herd and they all followed in regular succession, as if they had been drilled to such performances all their lives.[17]

They took the boat to Flüelen, where they began their ascent of Saint Gotthard, which they would have to cross to get to Italy. They went up in a "great lumbering diligence," and stopped on the top for refreshments before starting down. In Italy they stopped on Lake Maggiore and visited Isola Bella. Then to Genoa and to Leghorn by a "little chunky steamer." They were both seasick on the choppy sea. From Leghorn they went to Florence, "the cradle of the Renaissance." At Florence, Whittredge seems to have parted company with Bierstadt, for after that his narrative is nothing but "I," "I," "I." It has been said on uncertain authority, it seems to me, that Bierstadt got to Rome in November, 1856. If he got there at approximately the time Whittredge did, then November is not a bad guess.

Gifford's "European Letters" mention Bierstadt in Rome for the first time in an account of a visit Gifford made to the artist and his companion, Ludwig, "a young painter of Western American Indians," on March 13, 1857. From then on, Gifford fills in the remainder of Bierstadt's stay in Europe pretty well. On March 17, the three, with William H. Beard, went to Monte Mario, sketched donkeys and sheep, and returned to Rome by a walk of six or eight miles. On March 22, they were again together, and on the twenty-fifth with Virgil Williams (whom Bierstadt was to see years later in California), the three visited the Grotta Ferrata, Frascati, the ruined Villa Borghese, and were back to Rome by 6:30, where Bierstadt, Whittredge, Beard, and Gifford spent the evening together. Other evenings together followed regularly. On March 29, Bierstadt exhibited a painting of the Wetterhorn he had painted since he got to Rome, and Gifford thought it one of the best in the exhibition.

On Easter Sunday, Bierstadt and Gifford went to St. Peter's to see the papal benediction. They were with ladies, who were jostled by a French abbé. When Gifford remonstrated, the abbé retorted, *"Je ne presse pas les dames. Je suis français!"*—"I am not pushing the ladies! I am French!"

In Rome there was also a German artists' club, and many hours were spent there helping with costumes for a pantomime of the siege of Troy to be presented at Cerbara on April 22. When the day came, Bierstadt did not go along. Visits to the Palazzo Doria, the Forum (where they sketched water buffalo), the Colosseum, the Villa Salust, the Church of the Cappuccino, and the illumination of St. Peter's were on their schedule for the Sunday after Easter. Then sketching in the Campagna (Figs. 22 and 23); visits to the Cafe Nuovo in Rome (and undoubtedly to the Cafe Greco); and with Enoch Wood Perry, the U.S. Consul in Rome and later a good friend of Bierstadt in California, to visit the sculptor Thomas Crawford, who was then living in Rome. There they saw William Page's portrait of Mrs. Crawford. On May 5, Bierstadt went with Gifford, Whittredge, and Beard to visit Peter Cornelius, who had founded the Dusseldorf Academy of 1821.

By May 24, they were in Naples, on the first excursion of their southward journey from Rome, and Bierstadt sketched the bay (Fig. 24). In the evening they went to the San Carlo Opera and heard *I Puritani*. The two planned to spend a month in Capri, and in Naples Bierstadt tried to get his trunk out of customs:

> Bierstadt finds it will cost $20 or $30 and an infinite deal of trouble to get his trunk out of the custom house. The officials seem to be all a set of swindling sharpers. Seeing they were bent on robbing us to the utmost, B. determined to disappoint them by not taking the trunk out—sending it to England instead. Six or eight men had been engaged two days

22. *Olevano.* 1856 or 1857. Oil on canvas mounted on panel, 19 5/32 × 26½″ (48.6 × 67.3 cm.). Saint Louis Art Museum, Eliza McMillan Fund. A study for Fig. 23

making an inventory of the contents. One man could have done it in an hour. They were in a splendid rage when they found themselves cheated out of their prey. . . . Our sketch boxes and a couple of guide books of mine we could not get then. The boxes were to be re-examined and duties paid on every half used tube of color and every stump of a brush.[18]

In Naples they bought colors and were off toward Capri by donkey at 5 A.M. on the twenty-seventh. They visited Ischia, the Sybil's Cave, and were back in Naples by 5:30 P.M. They took the railroad immediately to Portici and ascended Vesuvius at midnight. At sunrise the next day they sat on the warm lava, roasted their eggs and sausages in the hot fissures, and drowned both eggs and sausages in the Lachryma Christi they had bought on the way up.

They visited Pompeii, returned once more to Naples, and left there the next day for Capri, this time in earnest. At Capri they registered at the Hotel Pagano (where they were charged sixty-four cents a day) and were promptly propositioned by three "bronze sirens" who had come over with them on the boat. On the first of June and regularly until they left Capri on the twenty-sixth, the two sketched on the Piccola and Grand Marinas. (A sketch in the Boston

40

23. *Italian Village Scene (Olevano)*. 1860. Oil on canvas, 30 × 48″ (76.2 × 121.9 cm.).
Butler McCook Homestead, Antiquarian and Landmarks Society, Inc., of Connecticut, Hartford

24. *Mount Vesuvius and the Bay of Naples.* 1857.
Oil on paper, 6¼ × 13¼″ (15.9 × 33.7 cm.).
M. Knoedler & Co., New York City

25. *The Bay of Salerno* [correct title?]. 1858.
Oil on canvas, 22 × 36″ (55.9 × 91.4 cm.).
Vose Galleries of Boston.
Bierstadt painted three Italian bays at this
time; this bay is most likely Salerno

26. *Fishing Boats at Capri.* 1857. Oil on paper mounted on canvas, 13½ × 19½″ (34.3 × 49.5 cm.).
Museum of Fine Arts, Boston. M. and M. Karolik Collection

Museum is dated June 14, Fig. 26.) Their lunch was brought down from the hotel every day on the head of a brown-skinned girl with bright eyes and a chubby face. They thought she had "a killing way" of saying *"Addio"* when she left. Every day they bathed in the bright sea.

They left Capri on the morning of June 26 for Sorrento. There was a storm, and they had to land at Massa and walk to Sorrento. They then traveled fifteen miles over the mountains to Amalfi, where they stayed at the Albergo dei Cappuccini. Again they sketched and bathed in the sea. Visits to Ravello, Salerno, and Paestum were next:

> We reached Paestum just as the last rays of the sun were gilding the magnificent ruins of the temples. . . . There is no decent place to stay in Paestum. . . . When we reached the ferry of Sitarus, Bierstadt discovered he had lost his sketch book, thinking he might have dropped it on the road, he walked back four miles. He was fortunate enough to find it at the osteria at Paestum where we had stopped for a moment. . . . B. is a strong and rapid walker, and the man [who insisted on accompanying him on his walk back] had to run all the way to keep up with him. The day was very hot, and by the time they got back the poor devil was ready to drop with exhaustion. Of course he wanted to be paid . . . and all the cut-throats about said, "Yes, the poor fellow had worked hard and ought to be paid."[19]

At La Cava, six miles from Salerno, they stayed at "a princely hotel" that presented them with "a princely bill." At Salerno, Bierstadt made studies for a painting of the bay (Fig. 25). At Nocetta they sketched the ruined church of Santa Maria Maggiore, and at noon on July 1 took the boat back to Naples. Four days later Gifford sailed for Leghorn, apparently leaving Bierstadt behind.

This is the last we know of Bierstadt until *The New Bedford Daily Mercury* announced on September 3, 1857, that he had gotten back home. He had sent his trunk full of the precious results of four years' work to London, and he probably took a steamer, possibly from Naples, to the north. How or exactly when he got to Liverpool for his trip back across the Atlantic is unknown. We do not know, as a matter of fact, exactly when he arrived. Again the passenger lists failed to mention the returning hero.

44

NOTES: 1 Worthington Whittredge, the Cincinnati artist, said Bierstadt made the trip in 1852, but his *Autobiography* (see note 3) is innocent of documentation for this point.

2 O. Jennings Wise to Bierstadt, January 5, 1854, Henry Francis du Pont Winterthur Museum, Winterthur, Delaware.

3 The Whittredge *Autobiography* has been edited by John I. H. Bauer and published in the *Brooklyn Museum Journal*, volume for 1942, pp. 5–68. The original manuscript is in the Archives of American Art, New York City. The Gifford material is also in the Archives. The Haseltine book, *William Stanley Haseltine* (London: Frederick Muller, 1947), was written by his daughter, Helen Haseltine Plowden. Mrs. Plowden presumably has—or had—charge of her father's now unlocated manuscripts.

4 Whittredge, *op. cit.*, p. 26.

5 *Ibid.*

6 *Ibid.*

7 *Ibid.*, p. 27.

8 Richard Shafer Trump, "Life and Works of Albert Bierstadt" (Ph.D. diss., [Columbus] Ohio State University, 1963), p. 212.

9 *The New Bedford Daily Mercury*, August 4, 1855.

10 Whittredge, *op. cit.*, pp. 27–28.

11 Sanford R. Gifford, "European Letters," vol. 1, June 5 1856, entry, Archives of American Art, New York City.

12 *Ibid.*

13 *The New Bedford Daily Mercury*, February 7, 1856.

14 *Ibid.*, February 23, 1856.

15 Gifford, *op. cit.*, July 27, 1856, entry.

16 Whittredge, *op. cit.*, p. 32.

17 *Ibid.*

18 Gifford, *op. cit.*, May 25 and June 25, 1857, entries.

19 *Ibid.*, July 1857, entry.

Three

Back in America
First Exhibitions 1857-1859

27. *Spear Fishing* [*Lake Lucerne?*]. 1857–58. Oil on canvas, 31½ × 49″ (80 × 124.5 cm.). The Los Angeles Athletic Club

Although his name was not on the lists of arriving passengers in Boston or New York, and the New Bedford papers did not list the names of passengers, Bierstadt must have gotten back home to New Bedford sometime during the last few days of August, 1857. *The New Bedford Daily Mercury* announced on September 3: "We understand that Mr. Albert Bierstadt, who has been pursuing his studies in Europe, has returned to this city." A short railroad ride down from Boston or from New York by rail or by a ship of the Fall River Line would have brought him home soon after he landed. There would have been no reason for him to dawdle in the city, and this loving son and brother was eager to see his family after four years away.

He found a town oppressed by hard times. The previous year, in a country torn by dissent over the problems of Secession and Compromise, the Democrats had nominated James Buchanan and the Republicans the glamorous John C. Frémont, who was later to become a friend and neighbor of Bierstadt. Frémont was firmly rejected, the Civil War was avoided for another four years, and the country was at "the flood tide of prosperity."[1] But the economic health of New Bedford, then as now, did not reflect the general prosperity. Whaling, upon which the finances of the town rested, was in a decline. The artist's own father depended upon the health of the whaling business—the less whale oil the less cooperage—and family prospects were grim. Furthermore, few New Bedford citizens considered art one of life's necessities.

There were a number of the artist's paintings already in New Bedford houses: the Hathaways and Blacklers, at least, owned Bierstadts. But his reputation was still only private. When he first opened his studio to the public, soon after he returned, his work seemed to take New Bedford by surprise. They had had no idea how good he was. He had brought back with him a great many studies and sketches to be worked up into finished pictures, and he immediately began to work with an energy that did not fail him for the next forty years.

Within a month he had presented four major European landscapes. He also put out a feeler for an oil-painting class. His pictures and his evidently excellent relationship with his fellow townsmen—not to mention the prospect for advertising—elicited a paean of praise from *The New Bedford Daily Mercury:*

> We may be in error, as there is great latitude of opinion in matters of taste, but we cannot remember any landscape painter in the country

who produces better pictures than our townsman. There are four new landscapes, a morning in Switzerland, very attractive with its rock and mountain scenery, distant peaks and cataract showering its spray down the steep precipice; this wild scenery contrasted with the homelike Swiss cottage, in the foreground. Another, a scene on the Roman campagna, is a work of rare merit, both from its accuracy as to scenery and the beauty of the spot chosen, a bridge in shadow with a picturesque group of Italian peasants passing over; a most agreeable foreground with water, and a tower in shade with distant mountains. The aerial effect of this picture is striking, the dark clouds and their deep shadows contrasted with the Italian charm of figures and building. The Landscape of the "Upper Glazier of Rosenloai, on the Wetterhorn," is a novel and admirably faithful work, and the "Spearing Fish by torchlight, Lake Lucerne," deserves high commendation. Everyone who enjoys the sight of fine works of art, should visit these pictures.

After an absence of three years [*sic*] in Europe, spent chiefly at the celebrated school of painting, at Düsseldorf, on the Rhine, Mr. Bierstadt has returned to his native city, a fit representative of the later students at Düsseldorf, who have added to the rather cold and hard style of the older masters in this school, more of the modern English and French manner. Nature is the foundation of their style, and Mr. Bierstadt has been a most industrious student of out-door life and brings home a collection of invaluable studies. Mr. Bierstadt has resolved to form a class for instruction in oil-painting, in compliance with the request of many of our citizens. His rooms are at No. 15, Pierian Hall building.[2]

Upper Glazier of Rosenlaoi and *Spearing Fish by Torchlight, Lake Lucerne* soon came into the possession of Bierstadt's friend and patron John Hopkins. *Spearing Fish,* incidentally, may have come down to us as the scene now at the Los Angeles Athletic Club (Fig. 27). What "a morning in Switzerland" and "a scene on the Roman campagna" were, is another matter. Perhaps the Swiss view was the *Lake Lucerne* that the artist chose for his first official exhibition picture, at the National Academy of Design the following spring. And perhaps the Roman Campagna was the "serene and mellow"[3] *Paestum* exhibited the following July in

28. *Martha Simon.* 1857.
Oil on cardboard, 19 × 13″
(48.2 × 33 cm.).
The Millicent Library Collection,
Fairhaven, Massachusetts

29. *The Old Mill.* 1858.
Oil on canvas, 44 × 37″
(111.7 × 94 cm.).
Private collection,
Oyster Bay, New York

the first art exhibition New Bedford ever had—although Paestum is scarcely in the Roman Campagna.

Pupils were harder to come by than paintings. The feeler for a class—"in compliance with the request of many of our citizens," an old dodge—aroused wide public apathy. It was another six weeks before the artist took a chance with an outright advertisement:

INSTRUCTION IN OIL PAINTING

Mr. A. Bierstadt having taken a Studio at No. 15 Pierian Hall Building, in compliance with the request of numerous citizens, is prepared to form a class in Oil Painting. Those wishing to join will make application soon, as only a limited number can be accommodated.[4]

A year and a half later, by the time Bierstadt took his first trip to the West, he had accumulated four pupils.

Bierstadt's impact on the town was also reinforced by the hanging of three landscapes on the walls of the newly opened public library. These were the ones that his friends had sold early in the previous year to help the artist with his expenses abroad. "We are happy to see that the Trustees of the City Library do not neglect the patronage of the Fine arts," *The Mercury* commented. And *The Standard* reported, "There are now in the public library . . . three . . . landscape views by Mr. A. Bierstadt of this city."[5] The paper's opinion of the artist's work remained exalted, and New Bedford's citizens were urged to buy:

> We make no profession of being connoisseurs in painting, and can only say that we have been very much pleased with these pictures, without claiming the ability to canvass their merits or defects with critical acumen. As an artist who has faithfully studied his favorite art, and has settled among us to prosecute it, Mr. Bierstadt is worthy of the patronage of our citizens and we hope will meet with liberal encouragement.[6]

Before the year was out, Bierstadt visited Martha Simon, an old Nemasket Indian living in a hut on Sconticut Neck across the harbor, and painted her portrait, one of the few in his career (Fig. 28). He called her a Narragansett, but that was incorrect.

The artist's enormous energy waxed with the cold weather and waned not through the winter. Besides continuing to turn out major works, he became involved in the establishment of a local art association. This may have been stimulated by an invitation issued in February, 1858, by the Washington, D.C., Art Association to sundry local organizations to meet in Washington to discuss "the adornment of the national Capitol and its grounds."[7] An art commission to consult with the government was to be formed, and the working artists of America were invited to help choose it. Delegates from Boston, New York, Philadelphia, Baltimore, Washington, Richmond, Charleston, and other places met at the Smithsonian Institution on March 20–23, 1858. Bierstadt was not an official delegate, and he may not have even attended. But his name was set down as one of the forty-nine "memorialists," and there is little question that the formation of the New Bedford Art Association was connected with the national movement.

But government art matters, as involved as he was to become in them later in his life, mattered little to the artist compared with what now filled his mind—his first official American exhibition. For this his attention naturally turned to New York and the upcoming Annual of the National Academy of Design. For the Annual he chose a view of Lake Lucerne. "The large picture by our gifted fellow-citizen, Mr. Bierstadt," *The Mercury* reported, "is now in the

30. The Portico of Octavia, photographed c.1870?
From Margaret R. Scherer,
Marvels of Ancient Rome, 1955

31. *The Portico of Octavia, Rome.* 1858. Oil on canvas, 28½ × 37″
(72.4 × 94 cm.). Museum of Fine Arts, Boston.
Deposited by the Boston Athenaeum. Formerly known as *Roman Fish Market*
or *The Arch of Octavius*

32. *The Portico of Octavia, Rome* (detail) ▶

great annual exhibition at New York, in company with 635 other paintings."[8] The editor also quoted *The Crayon*'s "fastidious discernment":

> The *Crayon,* a high-toned monthly magazine of Art, very brief and fastidious in all its notices of pictures—so much so that an ounce of its positive adjectives is worth a pound of superlatives from other art-critics—is the best authority on the subject in this country. The editor thus remarks: "Bierstadt's *Lake Lucerne* invites study; the foreground is indicative of great command of landscape elements. The trees are admirably drawn, and the road and grass finely painted. The same ability on a smaller scale would be more roundly appreciated.[9]

What was to become a hue and cry from the critics was now expressed for the first time: Why must all your pictures be so *big,* Mr. Bierstadt? *The New York Post* pointed out that *Lake Lucerne* was the largest among all the 636 paintings in the exhibition. Why this young German-American chose to make his debut canvas so unconventionally large, and thus inevitably fix an impression of his style, is conjectural. It is significant that the large size, though remarked upon, did not strongly offend the viewers. They wondered why—and wondered also if it was a good idea—but it did not disturb them to the point where it prevented them from seeing the painter's artistic qualities. This must have been because it did not strike them as pretentious, but simply as Bierstadt's way of painting. This way later became standard, and was the cause of much harsher criticism than the artist now received.

The *Crayon*'s adjectives were, as a matter of fact, rather more positive than those of *The New York Post* or *The Tribune. The Post* contented itself mostly with a scenario of the picture and with only a word or two of safe praise—"a grand and solemn landscape," "effective contrasts," "harmony of design"[10]—while *The Tribune* called *Lake Lucerne* "in some respects a successful picture" with "fine feeling."[11] *The Herald* swept most of the exhibit away:

> We have rarely seen assembled such an aggregation of crude effects and commonplace conceptions. Most . . . would disgrace the *atelier* of a sign painter. . . . In this mass of rubbish, however, it is consolatory to find that there are a few pictures which go far to redeem American art from the stigma which such a description conveys.[12]

Then the critic published a short list of exceptions from his strictures. Presumably, however, since his name was not on this list, Bierstadt's *Lake Lucerne* was part of the Annual's "mass of rubbish."

With the Annual and its reviews comfortably behind him, Bierstadt moved his big painting back to New Bedford and gave the town its first art exhibition. He leagued forces with John Hopkins, who owned several of his works, and announced an "Exhibition of Painting."[13] With great energy he had set about borrowing pictures, and on July 1 the doors of Hopkins's rooms in the Ricketson Block were thrown open on 150 pictures. The public was charged twenty-five cents for a single admission, and they could go back as often as they liked for a dollar.

The exhibition was not a financial success—"the balance of profit and loss . . . is inconveniently on the wrong side of the leger," *The Mercury* reported.[14] But its artistic success was resounding. Well-known American names made the exhibition as representative of the best in American art as any that had recently been organized: William Beard, Thomas Birch, William Bradford, J. W. Casilear, Frederick E. Church, Thomas Cole, J. F. Cropsey, Asher Durand, Alvin Fisher, Sanford Gifford, William Hart, G. P. A. Healey, George Inness, J. F. Kensett, George Lambdin, Emanuel Leutze, W. T. Richards, Thomas Sully, and William Wall. Such foreign names as Achenbach, Landseer, and Calamé gave a continental tang to the show.[15]

There were fourteen Bierstadts, more than any other single artist's work. The titles, as listed in the catalogue, were: *Paestum, Bay of Naples, Bay of Gaeta, Roman Fish Market, Moonlight, View near Düsseldorf after Sunset, Bay of Salerno, On the Weser, Upper Glacier of Rosenlaui [sic], Blue Grotto (Capri), Fishing by Torchlight (Lake Lucerne), Lake Lucerne, Storm Among the Alps,* and *Old Mill (Westphalia). The Old Mill* was evidently bought by the Hathaway family, and it has been with a branch of that family ever since (Fig. 29).

By now the local papers felt they had said about all there was to be said in praise of their local artistic hero. "They are all so well known here that it needs only to mention [them,]" *The Standard* commented.[16] But *The Mercury* pointed out a significant new picture, one that became the most celebrated of Bierstadt's early career. It was also the first to be bought by an American museum. This was *Roman Fish Market,* later to be known as *The Arch of Octavius,* and *The Portico of*

33. *Indian Summer, New Hampshire.* 1858.
Oil on cardboard, 7¼ × 10¼″
(18.4 × 26 cm.).
Kennedy Galleries, New York City

34. Inscription on back of *Indian Summer, New Hampshire*

Octavia, Rome, which was sold to the Boston Athenaeum the following December for four hundred dollars (Figs. 31 and 32).[17] "We recognize a portrait in the foreground," *The Mercury* said, "beside the sleeping Lazarone."[18] This must have referred to the dog—Bierstadt's?

In September *Lake Lucerne* was shown in Boston at the Athenaeum, and its enthusiastic reception by Bostonians may have helped persuade that institution to buy *Roman Fish Market.* Meanwhile, the artist and his friend William Bradford, later to become famous as a painter of the Arctic, went to Newport for several weeks and brought back numerous studies.

For all his artistic and financial success, the artist remained throughout his life a craftsman who wanted those who had his paintings to *like* them and who tried to do what he could to see that they did. In December he wrote to a New York buyer: "Should the subject not please you, I will paint you another, do not hesitate to speak your mind, for it would give me more pleasure to hear that you was well pleased than indifferently."[19] At Christmas, seeking to please New Bedford citizens, he painted a number of "beautiful little pictures . . . especially for the holidays."[20]

At Christmastime also, he painted, for Thomas Nye, Jr., a local worthy, his first known historical painting, *Gosnold at Cuttyhunk, 1602,* depicting an episode in New Bedford's founding days (Fig. 35). "The picture is very faithful," *The Standard* commented, "and abounds in artistic merit, reflecting high credit upon the genius of its painter."[21] This work, showing Bartholomew Gosnold, the interloper from civilization, as the ravager of the American wilderness, is an early intimation of Bierstadt's central aesthetic motivation. The call of the wild—in this case the American West—the artist heard again on the fourth day of the new year, 1859, when Bayard Taylor, famous traveler, lecturer, and author of *Eldorado,* came to town and talked of his travels in the American West.

58

35. *Gosnold at Cuttyhunk, 1602.* 1858. Oil on canvas, 28 × 49″ (71.1 × 124.5 cm.).
The Whaling Museum, New Bedford, Massachusetts. Gift of Miss Emma B. Hathaway

Notes: 1   David Saville Muzzey, *History of the American People* (New York: Ginn, 1934), p. 340.

2   *The New Bedford Daily Mercury*, October 2, 1857.

3   *The New Bedford Daily Standard*, July 8, 1858.

4   *The New Bedford Daily Mercury*, November 20, 1857.

5   *The New Bedford Daily Standard*, November 25, 1857.

6   *Ibid.*

7   "Proceedings of the National Convention of Artists," Washington, D.C., 1858, Henry Francis du Pont Winterthur Museum, Winterthur, Delaware.

8   *The New Bedford Daily Mercury*, May 5, 1858.

9   *Ibid.*

10   *The New York Evening Post*, May 1, 1858.

11   *The New York Tribune*, May 4, 1858.

12   *The New York Herald*, April 23, 1858.

13   *The New Bedford Daily Mercury*, June 22, 1858.

14   *Ibid.*, August 8, 1858.

15   *Catalogue of the New-Bedford Art Exhibition, commencing July 1st, and closing August 7th, 1858*, The Whaling Museum, New Bedford, Massachusetts.

16   *The New Bedford Daily Standard*, July 7, 1858.

17   Now called *Portico of Octavia, Rome* thanks to the excellent work of Margaret Scherer, *Marvels of Ancient Rome* (New York: Phaidon, 1955), figs. 47, 48. I am grateful to Miss Scherer for help with this section. A nineteenth-century photograph shows almost the same view Bierstadt saw (Fig. 30). *Roman Fish Market* was bought by the Boston Athenaeum on December 11, 1858, "with the liberty of exchanging for a Landscape that will be acceptable to the Comm. at some future day" (Athenaeum accession records). In 1877 it was deposited at the Boston Museum of Fine Arts, where it has remained to this day. Near the end of his life, in 1901, Bierstadt wanted to trade the painting for another. But the Boston Museum and Athenaeum authorities demurred: "He asks for it because he has never of late done work equal . . . an exchange [is] inadvisable as Bierstadt's late work [is] not as good as this" (Athenaeum accession records).

18   *The New Bedford Daily Mercury*, July 16, 1858.

19   Bierstadt to unidentified correspondent, December 7, 1858, Archives of American Art, New York City.

20   *The New Bedford Daily Mercury*, December 15, 1858.

21   *The New Bedford Daily Standard*, January 1, 1859.

Four

The First Trip West

1859

36. *Surveyor's Wagon in the Rockies.* 1859? Oil on paper mounted on canvas,
7¾ × 12⅞″ (19.7 × 32.7 cm.). Saint Louis Art Museum. Gift of J. Lionberger Davis.
(Incorrect title; see CL-140.)

IN SEPTEMBER, 1857, the same month that Bierstadt returned to New Bedford from four years' study in Europe, across the continent, in a high meadow near Cedar City, Utah, a group of Mormons leagued with Indians set upon and massacred 128 Arkansas emigrants. The emigrants had sworn, it was reported, to "kill every God Damn Mormon in Utah" and to make slaves of their women and children. The facts are still in dispute, but both the Mormons and their apologists agreed that the Mountain Meadows Massacre was a tragic mistake, both for the natives and the interlopers; although Brigham Young pronounced later at the site of the tragedy, "Vengeance is mine; I have repaid saith the Lord"—and, it is reported, grinned as he said it.

Whether Young or his Mormons were happy or sad over the event, the westward emigrants were dismayed. Their immediate reaction was to reroute the Overland Trail to the north, and thus escape the depredations of the Saints. This unsettled the Indians along the earlier trail, who had carried on a considerable trade with the travelers. Colonel Frederick West Lander, then Chief Engineer of that division of the Overland Trail, was sent upon an annual trip to survey an alternative route and placate the Indians concerned (Fig. 51). In the spring of 1859, Lander was ready to go again, this time to improve the "Cut-Off" he had laid out and to advise on a further trail to California.

Bierstadt, chafing at the narrowness of his New England bailiwick and learning of the expedition from the newspapers, resolved to go with Lander and see for himself what the West looked like. *The New Bedford Daily Mercury* announced his plans on January 17, long before the artist knew how he was going to get there, and even before Lander's plans for the new season were made:

> MR. BIERSTADT.—It is understood that the New Bedford artist is about to start for the Rocky Mountains, to study the scenery of that wild region, and the picturesque facts of Indian life, with reference to a series of large pictures. He expects to remain more than one year, and has engaged companions, among them a photographer. We wish him all success and a safe return.[1]

Bierstadt's "companions" turned out to be only one: F. S. Frost, a Boston artist, who evidently volunteered to help Bierstadt with the photography.

New Bedford citizens were advised to buy a Bierstadt while the buying was

37. Bierstadt at about twenty-nine. c.1859.
The Whaling Museum, New Bedford,
Massachusetts

good. "Life," *The Mercury* warned, "especially in the wilderness, is uncertain, and we advise our citizens to honor our city by securing at once a good specimen of the work of one of the best of living artists. . . . If the horrors in gilt-frames on many parlor walls were apparent to their owners, we fear they would be desperately moved to take down the daubs and hang themselves on the nails."[2] Whatever fate awaited Bierstadt in the Wild West, he certainly had the home folks rooting for him.

Leaving eight recent oils, including the Boston Athenaeum's *Roman Fish Market,* to languish on the walls of the forthcoming National Academy Annual,[3] he secured an introduction (he never lacked connections) from John B. Lloyd, President Buchanan's Secretary of War, and was on his way:

> The bearer of this note, Mr. A. Bierstadt, who proposes to accompany Colonel Lander's wagon road party, has been introduced to me as an *artist* and a gentleman of character, and as such I commend him to the courtesy and kind attention of the commanders of such military posts as he may visit.[4]

Bierstadt's journey with Lander would have been only incidentally helped by a War Department recommendation, since Lander's work was with the Department of the Interior. But it served him in good stead at Forts Kearney and Laramie, which he was soon to visit.

By the fifteenth of April, Bierstadt and Frost had set out.[5] By the twenty-seventh, they had settled down in Saint Joseph, Missouri, to collect supplies for the long trip overland. On that day the artist, realizing how excited they would be to get a letter from the last outpost of civilization, wrote his four New Bedford pupils a long, kind letter:

> My Dear Friends.
>
>   I find quite a change here, from my comfortable studio in New Bedford, with your very agreeable company, but I see in my trip here some future pictures, picturesque figures are very common here and were it not a rainy day, it would have been a little later before I had written you, but you my pupils, as you choose to term yourselves, have been so kind and so attentive to your studies, that I cannot forbear any longer going without writing, as that is next best to

seeing you myself. How *hugely* I should have liked to have taken you all with me, but I am afraid you would not have enjoyed it so well as I shall, for I see enough to keep me busy already, and I could not furnish you with such comfortable chairs . . . every day brings up the pleasant recollections of the past, and makes me think of the short summer which will pass away, and I will be with you again, with my curious collection of studies and costumes. I could stay here a month and make studies of frontier men, one who told me yesterday of having a "right smart sickness," lately. I shall try and paint, the town is full of men bound for the gold regions, and the Hotels are so full that we had to camp out in one of the rooms, the same as we shall do on the prairies. We liked it quite well except the paying of two dollars a day for such accommodations, and the meat so tough that you want a row of Pike's Peaks to eat it with. . . .

Col Lander has from 50 to 100 applications a day for men wanting to go with his train; he is very popular, and the party now numbers 50 men . . . several hundred go from here every day, and a good many with hand carts and hand barrows . . . in a few days [we] shall go into camp, where corn bread and beef from Buffalo, together with a little bacon, will constitute my food. I think in about six months I shall feel like painting pictures again, and particularly to see my pupils again, and see what progress I have made for them. . . .

I send this enclosed to my brother who will deliver it to you, and now I will give you my address, which is quite long:

Independence Post Office. Mo.
    Salt Lake way Mail
Lander Wagon road exhibition [*sic*]
    of Gilbert's Station, south pass.

This I am told is all necessary and I shall expect something from you. Now My Dear Friends good bye till next time

Truly Yours,
A Bierstadt[6]

The gold rushers that Bierstadt wrote about were men in the endless to-and-fro trek to the Pikes Peak gold fields. There had been a flood of guide

38. *Pikes Peak Emigrants, Saint Joseph, Missouri.* 1859. Stereograph, probably by Bierstadt. Kansas State Historical Society, Topeka

39. *Indian Pony, Kansas.* 1859. Stereograph, probably by Bierstadt. Kansas State Historical Society, Topeka

40. *Bellemont.* 1859. Stereograph, probably by Bierstadt. Kansas State Historical Society, Topeka

41. *Wolf River Ford, Kansas.* 1859. Stereograph, probably by Bierstadt. Kansas State Historical Society, Topeka

42. *Ogalillah Sioux, Horse Creek, Nebraska.* 1859. Stereograph, probably by Bierstadt. The New-York Historical Society, New York City

43. *Shoshone Children.* 1859. Stereograph, probably by Bierstadt. The New-York Historical Society, New York City

44. *Shoshone Warrior, Nebraska.* 1859. Stereograph, probably by Bierstadt. Kansas State Historical Society, Topeka

books the past year, and these sounded as though all that was needed for a fortune was a basket big enough to hold the nuggets that could be picked out of Colorado streams. Most were disappointed, and by the time the Lander train got to the Crossing of the Platte, many were trying to get back home.

There are no studies that can be positively identified with these days in Saint Joseph, but Bierstadt or Frost—or both—took a number of stereographs. The next year the artist's brothers, Charles and Edward, set themselves up in the photographic business and issued a catalogue of stereo views. Fifty-one of these had been shot on Albert's trip west, and five or more during the stay in Saint Joseph.[7] Only seven of these have been found (Figs. 38–44). None of the fifty-one western stereographs shows Lander himself, which is curious, since there was evidently a strong mutual respect between the men. This respect is clear in a note Lander wrote to Bierstadt during the Saint Joseph stay, introducing a Dr. Bernhisel (a Mormon who later horrified the artist and his friend Fitz Hugh Ludlow with his "blatant" freedom about sexual matters): "I take pleasure in introducing to your valuable acquaintance, regard, and esteem. . . . If not objectionable to you . . . he would like to join your mess. Please introduce him to the members of it."[8]

On May 4, a farewell dinner was given by the townspeople to Lander, and it is safe to say that Bierstadt and Frost were among the guests. It was an occasion "long to be remembered," the local paper reported, and one of "jollity and good humor."[9] The reporter decided not to report it in detail, since "such feasts, though generally enjoyed at the time by those who participate in them are extremely dull and insipid to the public when spread out in the newspapers afterwards."[10]

Since the May fourth supper was a farewell, and since we know that Lander was gone three days later, the train may well have left Saint Joseph on May 5. A short distance across the dry prairie at Troy, Kansas, Lander found that the mules he had wintered there, and which he had been counting on for this trip, were unfit for travel. So the party was further delayed.

But they were soon off again, across the plains to the Little Blue and the Platte at Fort Kearney. About ten days out of Troy they reached the Crossing of the Platte. They had come up the south bank of the river, and at the point where the river branched into its North and South forks they had to cross the South Fork to continue their journey up the North. Here they met a new concentration

CROSSING THE PLAINS.

A PIKE'S PEAKER.

CROSSING THE PLATTE.

45, 46, 47. Woodcuts after Bierstadt, from *Harper's Weekly*, August 13, 1859

of Pikes Peakers, with the Sioux sitting about watching the excitement and smoking the peace pipe with Lander and his staff. A *Harper's Magazine* correspondent was along, and an account of the proceedings appeared the following August 13 in his magazine. It is particularly interesting because it was accompanied by three excellent woodcuts based on sketches by Bierstadt (Figs. 45–47).

Many photographs and many studies later, on June 24, the train reached South Pass, near Gilbert's Station—where the artist had asked his pupils to write him. They were now in the southern skirt of the fabled Wind River Mountains, which entranced Bierstadt (Figs. 52 and 53). Here the artist and his companion, together with a muleteer, left the Lander train, loitered about the area for a few weeks, and started home. He wrote of visiting the headwaters of the Colorado, but there are so many branches of the river there that it is impossible to say exactly what spots he saw. His canvases are of little help. On one occasion, at least, he got his geography mixed up and described a view sketched on July 1 as being "northwest" from the Wind River Mountains looking toward the Wasatch Range, whereas the latter is southwest from any possible point in the Wind Rivers (Fig. 53).

While still in this magnificent country, but beginning to feel that he should start home before the rains, the artist, on July 10, wrote his often quoted letter to

The Crayon. It was published in that magazine in September of the same year:

Rocky Mountains, July 10, 1859.

Dear Crayon:

If you can form any idea of the scenery of the Rocky Mountains and of our life in this region, from what I have to write, I shall be very glad; there is indeed enough to write about—a *writing* lover of nature and Art could not wish for a better subject. I am delighted with the scenery. The mountains are very fine; as seen from the plains, they resemble very much the Bernese Alps, one of the finest ranges of mountains in Europe, if not in the world. They are of granite formation, the same as the Swiss mountains and their jagged summits, covered with snow and mingling with the clouds, present a scene which every lover of landscape would gaze upon with unqualified delight. As you approach them, the lower hills present themselves more or less clothed with a great variety of trees, among which may be found the cotton-wood, lining the river banks, the aspen, and several species of the fir and the pine, some of them being very beautiful. And such charming grouping of rocks, so fine in color—more so than any I ever saw. Artists would be delighted with them—were it not for the tormenting swarms of mosquitoes. In the valleys, silvery streams abound, with mossy rocks and an abundance of that finny tribe that we all delight so much to catch, the trout. We see many spots in the scenery that remind us of our New Hampshire and Catskill hills, but when we look up and measure the mighty perpendicular cliffs that rise hundreds of feet aloft, all capped with snow, we then realize that we are among a different class of mountains; and especially when we see the antelope stop to look at us, and still more the Indian, his pursuer, who often stands dismayed to see a white man sketching alone in the midst of his hunting grounds. We often meet Indians, and they have always been kindly disposed to us and we to them; but it is a little *risky*, because being very superstitious and naturally distrustful, their friendship may turn to hate at any moment. We do not venture a great distance from the camp alone, although tempted to do so by distant objects, which, of course, appear more charming than those near by; also by the figures of the Indians so

48. *On the Platte River, Nebraska.* Undated. Oil on pasteboard, 8 × 10″ (20.3 × 25.4 cm.). Thomas Gilcrease Institute, Tulsa

49. *Nooning on the Platte* [correct title?]. 1859?
Oil on paper mounted on canvas, 6¾ × 12⅞″ (17.2 × 32.7 cm.).
Saint Louis Art Museum. Gift of J. Lionberger Davis

50. *Ox.* Undated. Oil on cardboard,
11½ × 18¼″ (29.2 × 46.3 cm.).
The Oakland Museum, California

enticing, travelling about with their long poles trailing on the ground, and their picturesque dress, that renders them such appropriate adjuncts to the scenery. For a figure-painter, there is an abundance of fine subjects. The manners and customs of the Indians are still as they were hundreds of years ago, and now is the time to paint them, for they are rapidly passing away; and soon will be known only in history. I think that the artist ought to tell his portion of their history as well as the writer; a combination of both will assuredly render it more complete.

We have taken many stereoscopic views, but not so many of the mountain scenery as I could wish, owing to various obstacles attached to the process, but still a goodly number. We have a great many Indian subjects [Figs. 42–44]. We were quite fortunate in getting them, the natives not being very willing to have the brass tube of the camera pointed at them. Of course they were astonished when we showed them pictures they did not sit for; and the best we have taken have been obtained without the knowledge of the parties, which is, in fact, the best way to take any portrait. When I am making studies in color, the Indians seem much pleased to look on and see me work; they have an idea that I am some strange medicine-man. They behave very well, never crowding upon me or standing in my way, for many of them do not like to be painted, and fancy that if they stand before me their likenesses will be secured.

I have told you a little of the Wind River chain of mountains, as it is called. Some seventy miles west from them, across a rolling prairie covered with wild sage, the soap-plant (?) and different kinds of shrubs, we come to the Wasatch, a range resembling the White Mountains. At a distance you imagine you see cleared land and the assurances of civilization, but you soon find that nature has done all the clearing. The streams are lined with willows, and across them at short intervals they are intersected by the beaver dams; we have not yet, however, seen any of their constructors. The mountains here are much higher than those at home, snow remaining on portions of them the whole season. The color of the mountains and of the plains, and, indeed, that of the entire country, reminds one of the color of Italy; in fact, we have here the Italy of America in a primitive condition.

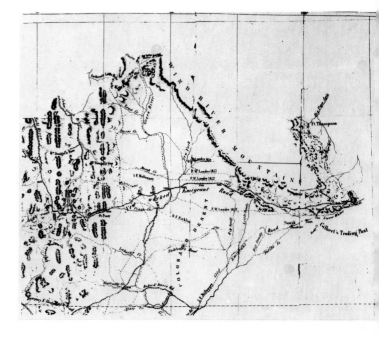

51. Area of Bierstadt's Wind River Mountains visit in 1859. Detail of map by W. H. Wagner, published for the Department of the Interior, probably in 1858

52. *Wind River Country.* 1859.
Oil on paper, 14½ × 23½"
(36.8 × 59.7 cm.).
Collection Jo Ann and
Julian Ganz, Jr., Los Angeles

53. *View from the Wind River Mountains,
Wyoming.* 1860. Oil on canvas,
30¼ × 48½" (76.8 × 123.2 cm.).
Museum of Fine Arts, Boston.
M. and M. Karolik Collection

54. *Horse in the Wilderness.* 1859–60? Oil on board, 14 × 20″ (35.6 × 50.8 cm.). Private collection, Washington, D.C.

55. *Big Sandy River,
Wind River Mountains.* 1860.
Oil on academy board,
16½ × 24″ (41.4 × 60.9 cm.).
Collection Dr. and Mrs. David Kruger,
Alexandria, Virginia

We came up here with Col. F. W. Lander, who commands a wagon-road expedition through the mountains. At present, however, our party numbers only three persons: Mr. F_____, myself, and a man to take charge of our animals. We have a spring-wagon and six mules, and we go where fancy leads us. I spend most of my time making journeys in the saddle or on the bare back of an Indian pony. We have plenty of game to eat, such as antelope, mountain grouse, rabbit, sage-hens, wild-ducks, and the like. We have also tea, coffee, dried fruits, beans, a few other luxuries, and a good appetite—we ask for nothing better. This living out of doors, night and day, I find of great benefit. I never felt better in my life. I do not know what some of your Eastern folks would say, who call night air injurious, if they could see us wake up in the morning with the dew on our faces!

We are about to turn our faces homeward again, the season being a short one here, and to avoid the fall deluge on the plains, which renders the roads almost impassable.

Yours,

B.[11]

Bierstadt spoke of obstacles to stereographs of mountain scenery, and these

56. *Thunderstorm in the Rocky Mountains.* 1859. Oil on canvas, 19 × 29″ (48.2 × 73.7 cm.). Museum of Fine Arts, Boston.
Given in memory of Elias T. Milliken by his daughters, Mrs. Edward Hall and Mrs. John Carroll Perkins

57. *Thunderstorm in the Rocky Mountains* (detail) ▶

59. *Indians near Fort Laramie.* 1859? Oil on paper on cardboard, 13½ × 19½" (34.3 × 49.5 cm.). Museum of Fine Arts, Boston. M. and M. Karolik Collection

58. *Chimney Rock.* 1859.
Oil on paper, 4 × 9"
(10.2 × 22.9 cm.).
Northern Natural Gas Company
Collection, Joslyn Art Museum, Omaha

surely had to do with the awkward wet collodion process; besides, stereos did not show up scenery well. Of the fifty-one offered by his brothers the following year, only four, judging from their titles, were of pure scenery. Bierstadt's "goodly number" must have included several that were so poor that they were not offered for sale. Evidently neither Bierstadt nor Frost was much of a technician.

The artist would not have been far wrong if he had said that the Salt River Range—and not the Wasatch—was seventy miles west of where he was on July 10. He was, of course, speaking in a pedagogical, rhetorical fashion when he said "some seventy miles west . . . we come to the Wasatch." Evidently the three men did not get very much farther than the vicinity of South Pass, and perhaps a few miles west and north along the way that Lander took on his Cut-Off (Fig. 51). Bierstadt's account, recorded eight years later by the art historian Henry T. Tuckerman, is incorrect, either as a result of the artist's faulty memory or Tuckerman's bravura:

> . . . he left Lander's party while it was still . . . in the Wasatch range . . . and set out on his return to the States, through a dense wilderness and mountainous region, occupied by a savage people, and with only two men as attendants. For a great part of their journey they were obliged to depend entirely upon the game they could obtain, and in several instances were days without water. The party reached Fort Laramie in safety, after a journey of many days, through a country perilous even for a body of armed troops.[12]

Recollected among the Victorian splendors of Bierstadt's great house on the

80

60. *Scout* [*Jim Bridger?*]. 1859. Oil on board,
13¼ × 9½″ (33.7 × 24.2 cm.).
Northern Natural Gas Company Collection,
Joslyn Art Museum, Omaha

62. *Trapper.* 1859? Oil on paper, 19 × 13″ (48.2 × 33 cm.).
Thomas Gilcrease Institute, Tulsa

61. *Scout* [*Jim Bridger?*]. 1859.
Oil on composition board, 10 × 7″ (25.4 × 17.8 cm.).
The National Cowboy Hall of Fame and Western
Heritage Center, Oklahoma City

63. *The Wolf River,*
Kansas. 1859?
Oil on canvas,
48¼ × 38¼"
(122.5 × 97.1 cm.).
The Detroit Institute
of Arts.
The Dexter M. Ferry
Jr. Fund

64. *Indian Encampment,
Shoshone Village.* 1860.
Oil on canvas mounted
on board, 24 × 19″
(60.9 × 48.2 cm.).
The New-York Historical
Society, New York City

65. *Indian Encampment,
Shoshone Village* (detail) ▶

66. *Morning in the Rocky Mountains.* 1862. Oil on paper mounted on canvas, 8½ × 11½″ (21.6 × 29.2 cm.). The R. W. Norton Art Gallery, Shreveport, Louisiana (see Fig. 75)

67. *Moose.* 1859?
Oil on board, 12¾ × 18⅜″
(32.4 × 46.7 cm.).
Collection Andrew Wyeth

Hudson, the Wind River excursion may indeed have seemed arduous. But when he was there, the artist was clearly having the time of his life.

A letter of September 3, written from Wolf River, Kansas, is almost exhilarated. He had to live on bread and water, but the scenery was so delightful that he did not mind:

> . . . before we reached Laramie, we found ourselves suddenly out of provisions, and for several days were obliged to subsist on bread and water; the scenery being of so delightful a character, we found no time to hunt. I assure you, however, that it amply repaid us for the temporary deprivation in the sketches which we were enabled to add to our portfolios.[13]

At Fort Laramie they made many new friends and found among them "many lovers of art." These friends persuaded local Indians to sit for portraits (Fig. 59)—not an easy procedure, for the Indians thought it would shorten their lives. "One old chief," Bierstadt wrote, "declared to the officers that I had killed more of the Sioux tribe than any man who had ever been among them."[14] Perhaps here, at Fort Laramie, Bierstadt also made a profile and a full-face sketch of a man who appears to be the famous scout Jim Bridger (Figs. 60 and 61).

The artist's route lay along the Platte, on which he and his companion depended for wood and water. By this time he had come around to thinking that, Bernese Alps or not, the American West was the best landscape in the world for artists:

> For the most part, the weather has been delightful, and such beautiful cloud formations, such fine effects of light and shade, and play of cloud shadows across the hills, such golden sunsets, I have never before seen. Our own country has the best material for the artist in the world. On the opposite side of the river, for hundreds of miles, the prairie was on fire, making a dense smoke, but presenting a fine appearance in the night.[15]

One day Bierstadt saw a buffalo approaching, and although he hid himself behind a bluff, rifle in hand to shoot the animal, he was so fascinated by its wild beauty that he let it go. Mosquitoes were so bad, he wrote, that they had to cover up their faces to escape them.

86

The party arrived in Buttonwood Springs on August 21 and were glad to find a clear, cool spring from which to drink after the muddy water of the Platte. They also found three ranches that had not been there on their way out. They crossed the Big Blue on August 31; then to Maryville, Capionia, and Hiawatha, arriving in Wolf River, Kansas, on September 3. Here the artist wrote his long letter home. They planned to stay two weeks and looked forward to much sketching:

> The trees are really fine, and such beautiful trailing vines, growing in such profusion, forming such graceful arches, across the river, the wildness and abandon of nature here is very attractive to an artistic eye, and every day nature seems to grow more lovely and beautiful.[16]

The arches over the river are evident in a stereograph the men took during their Wolf River sojourn (Fig. 41), and the general charm of the place is expressed in the artist's versions of an Indian village (Figs. 63–65). They were now only a short distance from Saint Joseph and the railhead, and soon the artist would exchange his "stubborn mule for the iron horse which will bear us swiftly to our eastern homes."[17]

Soon he was back in the bosom of his family with "much material in sketches, photographs and stereoscopic views."[18] Whether or not he took any photographs other than stereos is uncertain. In any case the facts are somewhat leaner than Lander made them:

> A. Bierstadt, esq., a distinguished artist of New York, and S. F. Frost [sic], of Boston, accompanied the expedition with a full corps of artists, bearing their own expenses. They have taken sketches of the most remarkable of the views along the route, and a set of stereoscopic views of emigrant trains, camp scenes, &c., which are highly valuable and would be interesting to the country. I have no authority by which they can be purchased or made a part of this report.[19]

Lander had been given only $25,000 to spend for the whole trip, so it is easy to understand why he did not have the money for such frills as photographs. If he had, perhaps we would have a better idea of just what the artist saw on his 1859 trip into the Rocky Mountains wilderness. The exaggerated programs of his canvases, elegant and inspiring as they are, are sadly lacking in distinguishing

68. *Grizzly Bears (American Black Bears).* 1859?
Oil on paper mounted on canvas, 14 × 16″ (35.6 × 45.7 cm.). Milwaukee Art Center. Layton Art Gallery Collection

69. *Antelope.* Undated. Oil on pasteboard, 9 × 15″ (22.8 × 38.1 cm.). Thomas Gilcrease Institute, Tulsa

topographical or geographical specifics. Tuckerman wrote that "an eminent American officer,"[20] possibly John C. Frémont, had identified every feature of *The Rocky Mountains*, Bierstadt's most celebrated depiction of the Wind River Range. If so, Frémont could do what present-day specialists cannot.

NOTES: 1   *The New Bedford Daily Mercury*, January 17, 1859.

2   *Ibid.*

3   These were: *View near Newport; View near Minden, Westphalia; The Bernese Alps, as Seen near Kusnach; The Temple of Paestum; Mt. Washington from Shelburne, N.H. St. Peters and the Castle of St. Angeleo—Sunset* [sic]; *The Arch of Octavius;* and *Capri, Bay of Naples. Roman Fish Market,* cleansed by a few months in the Boston Athenaeum, had become *The Arch of Octavius.*

4   Text from a photograph of the letter kindly supplied by Beaumont Newhall.

5   *The Crayon*, April 15, 1859, p. 161.

6   Bierstadt to C. B. H. Fessenden, E. Merrill, E. C. Leonard, and S. (?) Hopkins, April 27, 1859, Haverford College Library, Haverford, Pennsylvania.

7   The 1860 catalogue is in a private collection and unavailable, but the 1859 western group of stereographs was published in *The Kansas Historical Society Quarterly*, Vol. XXIV, no. 1 (Spring 1958), pp. 4–5. It shows only five Saint Joseph stereographs.

8   Lander to Bierstadt, May 4, 1859, Henry Francis du Pont Winterthur Museum, Winterthur, Delaware.

9   *Weekly West* (Saint Joseph, Missouri), May 8, 1859.

10   *Ibid.*

11   *The Crayon*, September 1859, p. 287.

12   Henry T. Tuckerman, *Book of the Artists* (New York: G. P. Putnam, 1867), p. 390.

13   *The New Bedford Daily Mercury*, September 14, 1859.

14   *Ibid.*

15   *Ibid.*

16   *Ibid.*

17   *Ibid.*

18   *The Crayon*, November 1859, p. 349.

19   U.S. Congress, House Executive Document 64, 36th Congress, 2nd session.

20   Henry T. Tuckerman, *loc. cit.*

Five

First Great Successes

1859-1863

70. *Platte River, Nebraska.* 1863. Oil on canvas, 36 × 57½″ (91.4 × 146 cm.)
On loan from the Jones Library, Amherst, Massachusetts, to the Mead Art Building, Amherst College

BIERSTADT MUST HAVE DECIDED to move to New York before he left for the West, for by the end of 1859 he was settled in his home on West Tenth Street, in the famous new Studio Building at Number 15 (Fig. 71). But before he left New Bedford, always mindful of family and friends, he helped his older brothers Charles and Edward get started in the photographic business. They had been in the "plain and Fancy turning and sawing business,"[1] but about the time brother Albert had been wending his way through the wilds of Nebraska, they had been burned out. "A cartload of rare and valuable lumber, comprising more than a hundred varieties of wood"[2] was lost.

The local newspaper announced the Bierstadt brothers' new business on November 29, 1859. The following summer they issued a catalogue combining Albert's western stereographs with other photographs taken in and around New Bedford and in the White Mountains. Both became well-known photographers, Charles moving to Niagara Falls in 1867 as an independent, and Edward moving to New York, where he became celebrated in the photoreproducing business. Edward must have joined Albert on the Civil War battlefields around Washington late in 1861, for both were there, and an 1865 catalogue issued by Edward and Charles lists nineteen stereographs of Washington and the Northern troops. Edward evidently took a celebrated photograph of Lincoln when he was there (Fig. 72).[3]

A separate book could (and should) be written about the delightful place into which Bierstadt moved late in 1859. From the time it was built in 1857—by the architect William Morris Hunt at the instance of James Boorman Johnson—until 1867 its address was Number 15 on West Tenth Street; from 1867 until its destruction in 1955 it was 51. The later number was the better known, and has led many to think that "15" was an error, a reversal of the correct figure.

The New Bedford artist found distinguished names in American art already ensconced—at $200 a year—in the building's twenty-five studios, all with efficient coal stoves and all with "light, air, privacy and convenience in a measure far beyond the tenants' wildest dreams."[4] John La Farge and Frederick E. Church were already there, and William Page moved in at the same time. Sooner or later others were established: Worthington Whittredge, William H. Beard, J. G. Brown, Seymour Guy, Henry T. Tuckerman, Thomas Buchanan Read, Sanford Gifford, William Merritt Chase (who took over Bierstadt's studio and enlarged

71. Tenth Street Studio Building, New York City, as it was in 1876. New York Public Library, New York City

93

it), Regis Gignoux, John Casilear, John Kensett, John F. Weir, Eastman Johnson, Augustus Saint-Gaudens, and even Winslow Homer.

Bierstadt lived at the Tenth Street Studio until 1866, when his house in Irvington was finished. He kept it as a New York pied-à-terre until 1881, when he moved his studio into the magnificent Rensselaer Building at 1271 Broadway. Meanwhile, befitting his wealth and position, the studio was only his studio and not his living quarters: these were at the Brevoort Hotel, two-and-a-half blocks away. In 1879, Bierstadt held a luncheon at his studio for a hundred guests in honor of Lord Dunraven and D'Arcy Osborne, son of the duke of Leeds (see Chapter 10). Delmonico's did the catering, and Bierstadt may have borrowed the big exhibition gallery that took up most of the first floor of the Studio Building. There can be no doubt that by this time the artist had taken over considerably more than the fifteen-by-twenty-foot space of his first, 1859, studio.

Bierstadt brought back from his Lander trip, besides numerous sketches, a number of Indian artifacts, which he may have left in New York on his way back to New Bedford. These were a peculiar part of the Bierstadt public image for the rest of his life, and some have survived to this day. "In Bierstadt's room," *The New York Tribune* reported, "were a good many evidences of his Indian and other prairie studies, in the drape of buffalo skins and other articles of border life."[5] These accouterments were immediately utilized in the production of his first big western painting, variously known as *The Base of the Rocky Mountains, Laramie Peak; Laramie Peak;* or simply *The Rocky Mountains,* generating the first big case of confusion in identifying the artist's western works. (*The Rocky Mountains* is also the title commonly attached to one of Bierstadt's most famous canvases, now in the Metropolitan Museum, Fig. 108.)

The enthusiastic reviews of *Lake Lucerne* in the National Academy of Design 1858 exhibition had become faint echoes in the public ear. And the eight paintings he had shown at the 1859 Annual caused little comment in New York, whatever enthusiasm one of them, *Roman Fish Market,* or *The Arch of Octavius,* stimulated in Boston. *The Base of the Rocky Mountains, Laramie Peak* likewise caused little reaction when it was shown at the Academy Annual in April, 1860, and though offered for sale, found no purchaser. It established its creator, however, as the artistic spokesman of the American Far West and prepared his public for the great success of the following years.

Perhaps in happier days the artist's work would have been snapped up, but

72. Abraham Lincoln. 1861.
Photograph, possibly by Edward Bierstadt, from Charles Hamilton and Lloyd Ostendorf, *Lincoln in Photographs: An Album of Every Known Pose.* Copyright 1963 by the University of Oklahoma Press

the nation was rushing toward Civil War. Within the next year, twelve states, led by South Carolina, seceded from the Union.

Three days before the bombardment of Fort Sumter, *The New York Evening Post* agreed that things were in a bad way for artists:

> The political troubles have affected the artists' profession . . . but our artists need not despair, let them avail themselves of the present lull to give more time to the detail and finish of the works upon their easels, and they will find they are not losers in the end from this temporary inactivity in the "picture market."[6]

All artists lamented "the unprofitable state of Art in these warlike days, but are taking a sensible view of the matter, and laying in a stock of work which will in turn remunerate them for present trial and disappointment."[7]

The Base of the Rocky Mountains, Laramie Peak had an interesting—if dismaying—subsequent career. When the Buffalo, New York, Fine Arts Academy was organized late in 1862, Bierstadt presented it with a scene of Capri (Fig. 73). "May I ask you to accept whatever is good in it," the artist wrote, "as a sincere expression of my best wishes for the true and abundant success of the Academy, and a small payment on account of the large debt which every artist owes to his profession."[8] Today this picture hangs in an honored place on the walls of the Albright-Knox Art Gallery in Buffalo, the direct descendant of the Fine Arts Academy. But the other Bierstadt painting, *The Base of the Rocky Mountains, Laramie Peak,* which was bought by the Academy shortly after it had been given *The "Marina Grande" in Capri,* has been lost. In 1922 it was loaned to a Buffalo high school and by 1933 had disappeared without a trace—not even a photograph.

For a future explorer in Buffalo basements or attics, a contemporary newspaper account of this four-and-a-half-by-nine-foot canvas may help identification, although its description of this Bierstadt work (of a quality comparable to *Wind River Country,* Fig. 76, painted at the same time) adds to our frustration:

> The picture of Laramie Peak, Rocky Mountains, cannot but be much admired by all that share a love for the beautiful. In the back-ground of this picture is the lofty range of the Rocky Mountains with Laramie

95

73. *The "Marina Grande" in Capri with the Faraglioni Rocks in the Background.* 1859. Oil on canvas, 42 × 72″ (106.7 × 182.9 cm.). Albright-Knox Art Gallery, Buffalo, New York

Peak towering to the skies, whose summet [sic] almost lost in the clouds, is covered with a mantle of perpetual snow, while at its base vegetation indigenous to the climate and country lends enchantment to the scene. In the fore ground, is a broad, beautiful and almost boundless prairie through which courses in its winding way the silvery waters of a river bordered by bluffs and table lands, and covered in many places by trees of cotton wood, willow and Aspen, while on the bluffs and over the broad prairie are enormous herds of Bison, roaming with all the freedom of the natives of the forest and prairie, the combined effect of which, as given in the picture is most pleasing, and will earn for the artist a fame not "unknown, unhonored and unsung."[9]

Wind River Country, now in a private collection, has been so-named by the modern gallery that sold it to its present owner. But the artist himself identified the locale, and at the same time, fixed himself on the horns of his own dilemma by identifying the peak as Frémont's, whereas three years later, in another painting, he called the same peak Lander's. The far mountain range in *Wind River Country* is itself a melodramatic version of what the southern profile of the Wind River Mountains actually looks like. This can be seen in a recently discovered sketch (Fig. 107). And the rocky outcroppings in the middle distance of *Wind River Country* appear to have their originals in another privately owned study (Fig. 52). Bierstadt sold *Wind River Country* to a man in Boston, and his covering letter is now in the Massachusetts Historical Society:

> I have at last completed your picture, and in a few days shall send it to you. I have taken the liberty of having a frame made for it, and hope it will please you. The scene I have chosen for the picture is among the Rocky Mountains. In the distance is seen a part of the Mountains called the Wind River Chain, prominent among which rises Fremonts Peak. This range is covered with snow the entire season. The low hills are covered with pine forrests, and along the River, Sweetwater its name, we find the Willow, Aspen, Cottonwood, and Spruce. A very picturesque variety of pine, found only among the Rocky Mountains, I have introduced into the foreground, and also a Grizzly bear, feeding on an Antelope. . . . Should this picture not prove satisfactory, I will try again. Should you come to New York at any time I shall be most happy to see you, at the Studio Building, 15 Tenth Street.[10]

The summer of 1860 may have been at least partly spent with brothers Charles and Edward in the White Mountains, with the painter making sketches and choosing points-of-view for his brothers' photographs. "We would call the

74. *The Brothers' Burial*
(or *The Brother's Burial*). 1861.
Oil on canvas, 18 × 32½″ (45.7 × 82.6 cm.).
George Walter Vincent Smith Art Museum,
Springfield, Massachusetts

75. *Wasatch Mountains, Wind River Country, Wyoming.* 1861. Oil on canvas, 26½ × 40½″ (67.3 × 102.9 cm.).
The New Britain Museum of American Art, New Britain, Connecticut (see Fig. 66)

76. *Wind River Country*. 1860. Oil on canvas, 30 × 42½″ (76.2 × 108 cm.). Collection Britt Brown, Wichita, Kansas

attention of admirers of photographs to [these]," *The Crayon* announced. "The artistic taste of Mr. Albert Bierstadt, who selected the points of view is apparent in them."[11] In the autumn the artist was involved in a plan for a "Rotary" exhibition at the Pennsylvania Academy of the Fine Arts.

The artist's western views still did not make much of a furor. Two more, titled *Emigrants Camping* and *Platte River Indians Encamped*,[12] were shown at the National Academy of Design 1861 Annual but gained little critical attention. A European painting, *Recollections of Capri*, evidently painted from studies made when the artist was in Capri with Gifford in 1857, excited more comment. "It is a very clever picture," *Leslie's* said, and "a rich and effective bit of coloring."[13]

In the fall of 1861, restless in the confines of the city and eager to become involved in the action of the war, Bierstadt and his old friend from Düsseldorf days, Emanuel Leutze, got a five-day pass from General Winfield Scott's aide-de-camp and, like the artist's brother Edward, visited the country around Washington in search of material. *Guerrilla Warfare* (Fig. 77) and *The Ambush*—possibly a dealer's title for a painting now in Boston's Museum of Fine Arts, Fig. 78—may have come from this visit. Another Civil War subject, the great *Bombardment of Fort Sumter* (Fig. 79), was made entirely from imagination: no one, least of all an artist, could have gotten into Charleston at the time this painting was evidently done. In April, 1863, two years after the fact, the New York newspapers were full of eye-witness accounts of the bombardment, and it seems likely that Bierstadt produced the Fort Sumter painting at this time, shortly before he left on his second trip west. It is a work full of light and space and may have actually profited from a lack of studies taken on the site, which often forced the artist's work into congealed agglomerations, the like of which existed nowhere on heaven or earth.

In New York, Bierstadt was an active participant in the social life of a number of the city's artistic lights. The Thomas Bailey Aldriches, the Charles Henry Stoddards, the Edmund Clarence Stedmans, the Bayard Taylors, Parke Godwin, the Edwin Booths, the Fitz Hugh Ludlows, in addition to the artists of the Tenth Street Studio and their wives, all were a part of the social whirl that Bierstadt always seemed to enjoy. Mrs. Aldrich, in an insufferably coy autobiography, recalls that she and her husband-to-be were invited to a soiree that Bierstadt, "probably the most talked-of artist in New York," gave in honor of the Booths.[14]

100

77. *Guerrilla Warfare.* 1862.
Oil on panel, 14¾ × 17½″
(37.5 × 44.5 cm.).
Century Association, New York City

78. *The Ambush.* 1876?
Oil on canvas, 30 × 50½″ (76.2 × 128.3 cm.).
Museum of Fine Arts, Boston.
M. and M. Karolik Collection

79. *The Bombardment of Fort Sumter.* 1863? Oil on canvas, 26 × 68″ (66 × 172.8 cm.).
The Union League of Philadelphia

Sometime late in 1861, after returning from his short trip to Civil War sites, Bierstadt dug up the study he had made of the church door in Cassel in 1855, added architectural details and a woman and baby to it, called it *Sunshine and Shadow* (Fig. 81), and submitted it to the forthcoming Academy exhibition. He had offered it to James T. Fields, the publisher and editor of *The Atlantic Monthly*, but Fields, with the times "sadly out of joint," felt that he must "deny myself the great pleasure of owning your charming church."[15]

Fields's "charming church" became the artist's first big critical success in New York. When it appeared at the Academy Annual in April, 1862, *The Post* heaped superlatives upon it:

> No. 34, simply entitled "Sunshine and Shadow," is probably the most perfectly satisfactory painting the artist has ever produced. The spectator is before the front of an old continental church, through whose portal is seen the bright stained glass of the interior window . . . and on these old statues, on the church porch, on the balustrades and on the tessallated pavement before the porch, the sunlight falls, broken in checquered patches by the foliage of an old oak. . . . The only figure is that of an old woman seated on the step of the church, with a sleeping child on her lap, and the whole work is one of the happiest delineations of noonday repose which we have ever seen.[16]

Sunshine and Shadow still survives, along with the original study.

Although he wanted to go to Colorado and other parts in the summer of 1862, the artist had to content himself with a stay at the Glen House in the White Mountains. While there he met the artist and writer Charles Lanman, who wanted to buy a picture for one hundred dollars, "before you begin to command fabulous prices," and who wrote that Bierstadt was "bound to lead the brotherhood of American Landscape Painters."[17]

The plans for the visit to the West had been laid in March, and Bierstadt went to Washington to elicit the aid of no less a person than the distinguished senator from Massachusetts, Charles Sumner, in the project. He persuaded Sumner to write a letter for him to the secretary of war, whose recommendation would be needed if the artist and his companions were to have a welcome at U.S. Army forts:

80. *Emigrants Resting at Sunset.* 1861? Oil on canvas, 37 × 58″ (94 × 147.3 cm.).
The R. W. Norton Art Gallery, Shreveport, Louisiana

82. *The Trappers' Camp.* 1861. Oil on millboard, 13 × 19″ (33 × 48.3 cm.).
Yale University Art Gallery, New Haven, Connecticut. The Whitney Collections of Sporting Art

◀ 81. *Sunshine and Shadow.* 1862. Oil on canvas, 39 × 33½″ (99.1 × 85.1 cm.).
Argosy Gallery, New York City

My dear Sir,
I believe that our country will gain in honor, if you can give Mr. Bierstadt any opportunities or advantages at the Rocky Mountains. His expedition will benefit us all, & I am anxious that Govt. should do every thing possible to promote it.

Faithfully yours,
Charles Sumner[18]

Considering Sumner's immense, almost hysterical preoccupation with the war, his letter is as much as could fairly be expected. Yet when Bierstadt did not get the desired letter from the secretary of war, his reaction was petulant. He wrote Alpheus Hyatt,[19] the Harvard paleontologist, as soon as he got back from Washington, apparently not appreciating the fact that the secretary of war might have something more important to do than concern himself with a joy ride into the mountains:

My Dear Hyatt:
I have just come back to New York, did not get the letter I wished from the Sec. of War, he was inclined to look on us as imposters almost. I think if Sumner had taken a little more interest in the matter in the outset we should have got all we wanted, but he seems to be so much absorbed in the Paleontology of the *nigger* that he forgets there are fossils in other parts of the U.S. and since my return to New York I have seen the contractor who takes the mails to California and he tells me the stations beyond Ft. Laramie have been destroyed by the Indians, the horses and mules run off and some of the keepers murdered, several regiments have been ordered out there. I fear we shall have to give up our trip this year. I regret it very much. The Indians you see will be driven into the mountains just when we want to go, and if they meet us there all of Spaulding's glue will not keep our scalps on. Now the question is will you and your companions run the risk; employ another man besides Spaulding to prepare glue for us, and start off. If we go we must go to Denver City first for that is the only place where we could get any mules. A mule cannot be bought on the frontier. The government has taken them all. I think if we give this up this summer I shall go up

the Missouri river in a steamer and spend a few weeks at Ft. Pierce. It would cost about $100 a month to go there. Please write me if you think you would like to go. The Steamers start in three weeks. I think I told you I had a letter from the Sec. of the Interior introducing us to the Indian agents. Remember me to Agassiz and tell him how difficult it is and next summer the government may give us $10000 to do what we please with. Let us hope to live a summer yet, in the far west.

Truly Yours in haste
A Bierstadt[20]

They all missed the steamer in May, and Bierstadt went to the White Mountains again instead. But the next summer he finally got to his beloved mountains, and garnered enough inspiration and studies to last for years.

NOTES: 1 According to New Bedford directories.

2 *The New Bedford Daily Standard*, August 25, 1859.

3 This photograph, a *carte de visite*, was published as an enlargement in Charles Hamilton and Lloyd Ostendorf, *Lincoln in Photographs* (Norman, Okla.: University of Oklahoma Press, 1963), p. 90. Although the text does not say so, the *carte* was imprinted "Bierstadt Brothers / Photographers / New Bedford, Mass." on its reverse (*The New Bedford Standard-Times*, February 12, 1958). Edward is said to have set up his base of operations in a tavern seven miles above Georgetown (*ibid.*). I think we cannot rule out the possibility that Albert Bierstadt had a hand in the production of the Lincoln photograph.

4 Mary Sayre Haverstock, "The Tenth Street Studio," *Art in America*, September–October 1966, p. 49.

5 *The New York Tribune*, January 20, 1860. The same newspaper, on March 27, 1861, also referred to the artist's "Indian trophies."

6 *The New York Evening Post*, April 9, 1861.

7 *Ibid.*, June 19, 1861.

8 *The Buffalo Daily Courier*, February 6, 1863.

9 *Buffalo Morning Express*, January 20, 1863.

10 Bierstadt to Gardner Brewer, February 10, 1860, Massachusetts Historical Society, Boston.

11 *The Crayon*, January 1861, p. 22.

109

12 Possibly paintings with similar titles in the R. W. Norton Art Gallery in Shreveport, Louisiana (Fig. 80), and in a private collection in Washington, D.C., respectively.

13 *Frank Leslie's Illustrated Newspaper*, April 20, 1861.

14 Mrs. Thomas Bailey Aldrich, *Crowding Memories* (Boston: Houghton Mifflin, 1920), pp. 21–23. See also Marie Hansen Taylor [Mrs. Bayard Taylor], *On Two Continents* (New York: Doubleday, 1905), p. 77.

15 Fields to Bierstadt, January 29, 1862, Henry Francis du Pont Winterthur Museum, Winterthur, Delaware.

16 *The New York Evening Post*, April 22, 1862.

17 Lanman to Bierstadt, August 4, 1862, Henry Francis du Pont Winterthur Museum, Winterthur, Delaware.

18 Sumner to [presumably] Edwin M. Stanton [Lincoln's secretary of war], March 31, 1862, Henry Francis du Pont Winterthur Museum, Winterthur, Delaware.

19 Alpheus Hyatt (1838–1902) was about to graduate from Harvard's Lawrence Scientific School as a specialist in paleontology. He was a protégé of Louis Agassiz. After his graduation he enlisted in the army, and this, if nothing else, must have kept him from joining Bierstadt's expedition to the West in 1863. For the rest of his life he was in charge of fossils at the Cambridge Museum of Comparative Zoology, was a founder of the Peabody Academy of Sciences, *The American Naturalist* (the first American periodical concerned with biology), and the marine biology laboratory at Woods Hole. He taught for many years at M.I.T., Boston University, and the Boston Society of Natural History, and contributed many notable writings to his field.

20 Bierstadt to Hyatt, April 27, 1862, Metropolitan Museum of Art Library, New York City.

Six

The Second Trip West
1863

83. Bierstadt at thirty-one.
1861. Trick double photograph
by Charles Bierstadt.
Collection Albert Morton
Turner, Orono, Maine

THE *Post* CRITIC WHO HAD so delighted in *Sunshine and Shadow* was a man who was to play an important role in Bierstadt's personal life. Fitz Hugh Ludlow, six years younger than the artist, and his attractive young wife, later to become Bierstadt's wife, had been a scintillating part of the New York literary scene since their marriage in 1859 (Figs. 85 and 86). The son of the abolitionist minister of the Presbyterian Church of Poughkeepsie, Ludlow had experimented with the newly introduced hasheesh[1] in a local pharmacy and was at once hooked by it. For Ludlow, the drug turned his Union College pasture into a field filled with Tartar warriors, and a tiny creek flowing into the Hudson into "the Nile! the Nile! the eternal Nile!"[2] Shortly after leaving college he wrote a book describing his experiences with the drug, *The Hasheesh Eater.* It became a best seller, and Ludlow in 1857 "held the town in his slender right hand."[3]

Now, six years later, at the beginning of 1863, and although the Union victories at Vicksburg and Gettysburg were still to come, the North was recovering from its economic doldrums. The year 1862, in spite of the Battle of Shiloh, weighed in favor of the North, and strong trade ties with England—from which Bierstadt was to benefit particularly—were helping to restore confidence in business. With this new strength the art market became brighter, and New York was the scene of many auctions, exhibitions, and artists' receptions.

Many of these were held in the Studio Building on West Tenth Street. They were gala affairs, with each artist standing at the door of his studio, and the city's most brilliant society passing from one to the other and through the great central exhibition hall. Other receptions were held elsewhere, and one of the favorite places was Dodworth's, at 806 Broadway, just a few blocks away. Both Ludlow and Bierstadt were lionized, and at Dodworth's reception on March 18, 1863, both were conspicuous: Bierstadt, "the acknowledged Prince of mountain regions,"[4] stands by his new *Rocky Mountains, Lander's Peak* (Fig.108), listening to praise from Nathaniel Parker Willis, a prominent writer; "that tall, large man in spectacles, with the retreating forehead and brown, almond-shaped eyes, is Bayard Taylor"; and "not far distant, with his beautiful wife at his side, [is] Fitz Hugh Ludlow, the author of 'The Hasheesh Eater,' a work of unrivaled eloquence and genius; his dark eyes have a somewhat remote and dreamy expression as if he were still haunted by the remembrance of its perilous glooms and glories."

Since marrying Rosalie Osborne four years previously, Ludlow's fortunes,

84. Bierstadt at about thirty. c.1860. Author's collection

113

85. Fitz Hugh Ludlow at about twenty-five. c.1861. Collection Mrs. Orville DeForest Edwards, Dobbs Ferry, New York

86. Thomas Buchanan Read. *Rosalie Osborne Ludlow.* c.1863. Oil on canvas, 30 × 24 1/16″ (76.2 × 61.1 cm.). Collection Mrs. Orville DeForest Edwards, Dobbs Ferry, New York. Rosalie, who later married Bierstadt, was in her twenties when this portrait was painted

evidently thanks to his drug addiction, were mercurial, with more downs than ups. The bride's mother had been anxious from the first, surely knowing about her prospective son-in-law's habits through his celebrated book. She wrote Eliphalet Nott, the eighty-five-year-old president of Ludlow's alma mater, Union College, about her daughter's fiancé and was assured by Nott that everything was all right:

> I have had little personal intercourse with [Ludlow] since he left the Institution. . . . Feeling however a deep interest in his welfare I have frequently inquired after him and been gratified to learn, that the stand taken by him in New York was such as to justify . . . the hope that he was destined to make a distinguished professional or literary man. In that hope I myself have sympathized and most cordially wish him and your daughter, should their destinies be united, every blessing.[5]

Nott is said to have been a self-preoccupied teacher famous for his class in Lord Kames's *Elements of Criticism:* more Nott than Kames it was said. Incredible as it may seem, Ludlow's best-selling *The Hasheesh Eater* must have escaped his attention.

Rosalie's troubles began at once. Her prospective father-in-law's congratulatory letter was far from reassuring. What was she getting into?

114

We cherish pleasing hopes that the union will be a mutual blessing. Our dear Rosa will I know with most conscientious economy and prudence conform to providential circumstances and keep you my son within the limits of your income. . . . Your *happiness* will depend upon the most rigid economy—the most punctilious payment of what you owe *when* you owe. With the Divine blessing upon your labors my son—and her prudence, I calculate you will have a happy life.[6]

That fall, a few months after the marriage in the new Mrs. Ludlow's home town of Waterville, New York, the groom's father wrote again:

Come then dear Rosa, to hearts large enough to lodge you and warm enough to make you truly at home in them. I do not ask you to forget the lovd ones at W[aterville] or to love us better or even as well as them—but come with the heart of a loving child and Sister—and give us next to them your love.[7]

Rosalie Ludlow was ill-prepared for what awaited her. Only eighteen at the time of her marriage to Ludlow, she was youthful, inexperienced, evidently spoiled by her family and others who admired her beauty. For one who had always been taken care of, taking care of someone else was a difficult task. Soon it became impossible. Ludlow, always harassed for money, tried everything to get it—even, according to Osborne family tradition, selling his wife's jewels. Two years after his marriage he wrote to Union College, pleading for an instructorship:

I should have been very glad if Union had ever appeared to care for my connection with it as much as I did. Without having the least reason to claim such thing as a right, I have sometimes wondered why among the offers made to other men of a place on her faculty my name has not been thought of.[8]

Rosalie herself tried to get her husband a job. When Edmund Clarence Stedman offered him a place as correspondent for a newspaper, she wrote: "It was so kind and brotherly of you. . . . There's something about you, Stedman, that one doesn't find in every man—something that I like and respect amazingly."[9] There is something coy enough about this letter to suggest that

87. Bierstadt's westward journeys of 1859 and 1863, from *The Art Bulletin*, September 1964. The route between Troy and the Platte, and between Salt Lake City and Virginia City, is uncertain

Ludlow's cousin Carrie's later accusation might have some foundation: "Flo Clark . . . rather raves over Rosa, her beauty &c&c, but I think she has acted rather absurd for a married lady this winter from all accounts. I have but little respect for a married *flirt*."[10] But life as the wife of a man such as Ludlow could become intolerable for most, let alone such a girl as Rosalie.

Now, in the spring of 1863, with Bierstadt planning a trip to the Far West, and his friend Ludlow ailing, it was decided that the two should join forces and make the trip together. Ludlow would take "copious notes,"[11] and Bierstadt would make copious sketches of the scenery. The idea that it would give Rosalie a rest must also have been in their minds. After sending *The Rocky Mountains, Lander's Peak* off to Boston for exhibition—it had been seen by the New York cognoscenti in both the artist's studio and, evidently, at the Dodworths' reception—the two set out, accompanied by two other friends from Providence and New Bedford. Bierstadt had asked Louis Agassiz to recommend some young man to go along, but the great Harvard naturalist was "sorry to say that those of my young friends whom I could fairly recommend as desirable companions on your journey are not in a position for going & those who could go I would not recommend."[12]

Before the two left New York, Ludlow made a speech at the press preview of the new National Academy of Design opening on April 11, and later gave Bierstadt another rave in his paper:

116

Bierstadt's "Mountain Brook" (6) is a *chef d'oeuvre* of the same kind and nearly the same degree of excellence as his marvellous Light and Shadow. . . . In both his mastery over broken lights seems well-nigh absolute. In the present picture he has provided his main effect by throwing the shadow of an inclined birch across the sunny face of a forest water-fall in such a fashion that it seems barred like some exquisite damask tissue—as though threads of shadow were woven into its quivering gold rather than a band of darkness superimposed upon it. The look of the cool, slippery channel-stones seen through the transparent black water of a deep wood-rivulet finds inspired delineation at Bierstadt's hands, and never better than here. . . . The "North Fork of the Platte, Nebraska" (35), is a picture of broader lights and distances. Its breadth of light . . . is indeed admirable. Great tubular masses of limestone, upended and broken into successive ledges . . . are more picturesque than any remains of British abbeys . . . pure to the last degree. . . . [Both paintings] afford an excellent register of his fine range of capacity, from the delicate tints and subtlest lights to the broadest fields of illumination and color.[13]

Shortly after the National Academy opening Bierstadt, Ludlow, and their two companions set off. They traveled in style to their Kansas jumping-off place, Atchison. Railroad presidents, beginning with Scott of the Pennsylvania and ending with Sturgeon of the Northern Railroad of Missouri, gave the whole party free passage. "There can scarcely be a better indication," Ludlow wrote, "for the future of Science, Art, and Literature in our country, than the cordiality which such a course as that of these gentlemen shows existing between those professions and Commerce."[14] These contacts must have been made by Bierstadt: throughout his life he showed a remarkable sensitivity to the importance of knowing the "right people." He was also remarkably successful in being able to get to know them.

Ludlow's paper announced the western trip a month after it had begun:

Bierstadt, the artist, has departed on his journey to the "far West." He is accompanied by Fitz Hugh Ludlow, who, it is understood, will make copious notes of the tour, which, on his return, will be published in book form. Mr. William W. Hill, of Providence, and Horatio W. Durfee, of New Bedford, also accompany the artist. The party go directly from here to San Francisco, stopping only for brief periods here and there, on their route, to make sketches and notes of the scenery and the people. While in the Yo Semite Valley they will be joined by two artist friends of Bierstadt—Messrs. Perry and Williams, of San Francisco—and after a sojourn in the valley of two or three weeks, the entire party will proceed to the latter-named city. . . . They propose to be absent from six to eight months, so that it will probably be Christmas before they get back to New York.[15]

But *The Post* left out the most interesting part. Although Ludlow does not mention it in his account of the movements of "our party" from New York to Atchison, he was met in Saint Louis by his wife, who had come to that city with her cousins. They both wrote long letters to Ludlow's father; Rosalie then got aboard the *Denver* for a trip up the Missouri River to Omaha, and Ludlow continued with his friends on the overland journey. Rosalie got back to Saint Louis on June 2, hoping for a letter from Fitz, but was disappointed. She was beginning to think about him "as one forever lost."[16] In spite of her desolation, however, she managed to lose herself in pleasant musings about her shipboard companions:

My Dear Father and Sister
I should have advised you long ere this of Fitz's movements after leaving St. Louis but I myself was in suspense until just before I came on board this boat en route for Omaha with a pleasant party of St. Josephians. . . . I am taking the first opportunity I have had since hearing from Fitz. . . . How I do wish you could have been with us on this trip. The steamboat of the Western Waters is as different from its Sister of the East as a brunette from a blonde. . . . Our party numbers thirteen; Cousin William, his wife and two daughters and their guest, a lady from Washington and myself; five gentlemen, one of whom carries my waterproof for me and sees that I don't get starved, three grass widows and two belles—Somehow or other this don't number up right but I can't stop to correct it. We have had superb weather, the best staterooms in the boat, the best seats at table and the preference everywhere. Brig. Gen. Sully came on board with us and in his company

and that of his staff we spent—or at least I did—some very pleasant hours. Then amongst ourselves we have had plenty of pleasure dancing at night in the cabin when we did not prefer moonlight-promenades on deck; innocent fortune telling by a witch of a pretty girl; chess and card playing, conversation and last but not least an hourly attendance upon the scales to see if we gained flesh as well as spirits with our trip. . . . Omaha is one of the loveliest spots I was ever in. The view from the Capitol hill is like a dream from which you awake refreshed. We arrived there at night; the next morning the Captain gave us two hours to visit the city and we all sent for carriages and improved the time. . . . Well, I hope I shall hear from Fitz and you soon. . . . But good-bye until I feel better.

Your aff. daughter & sister
R.[17]

Meanwhile, in the bustling town of Atchison, where Bierstadt's party stayed at the "very creditable" Massasoit House (and saw a lynching), they gathered supplies and otherwise prepared themselves for their arduous journey. They left Atchison on the Overland Trail some days before May 29, laden with necessaries and dressed to kill, according to Ludlow's account:

. . . our commissary stores in boxes under our feet, where they might be easy of access in any of those frequent cases of semi-starvation which occur at the stations between the Missouri and the Pacific. Our guns hung in their cases by the straps of the wagon-top; our blankets were folded under us to supplement the cushions. To guard against any emergency, we were dressed exactly as we should want to be, if need occurred to camp out all night. We wore broad slouch hats of the softest felt, which made capital night-caps for an out-door bed; blue flannel shirts with breast-pockets, the only garment, as far as material goes, which in all weathers or climates is equally serviceable, healthful, and comfortable; stout pantaloons of gray Cheviot, tucked into knee-boots; revolvers and cartouche-boxes on belts of broad leather about our waists; and light, loose linen sacks over all.[18]

Across the Big Blue into Nebraska, they soon arrived at Comstock's Ranch

88. *Comstock's Ranch.* 1863.
Woodcut after Bierstadt,
from Fitz Hugh Ludlow,
The Heart of the Continent, 1870

89. *Jean Baptiste Moncrévié.* 1863.
Woodcut after Bierstadt,
from Fitz Hugh Ludlow,
The Heart of the Continent, 1870

on the Little Blue (Fig. 88). At Comstock's they met Jean Baptiste Moncrévié (Fig. 89), who had come west with Audubon, and saw their first buffalo. Here they lingered a while, riding into the field, with Ludlow observing and Bierstadt making sketches. At this point in Ludlow's account he makes his first direct reference to Bierstadt: "After dinner the artist opened his color-box, and began making a study of the antelope head, which had been left entire for his purpose."[19]

But the principal and most intimate account of the way the artist improved his time and his art is the passage on the dying buffalo:

> Our artist, though a good shot, and capable of going to market for himself whenever there was any game, as well as most people, had seen enough buffalo-hunting on other expeditions to care little for it now, compared with the artistic opportunities which our battue afforded him for portraits of fine old bulls. He accordingly put his color-box, camp-stool, and sketching umbrella into the buggy, hitched a team of the wagon-horses to it, and, taking one of our own party in with him, declared his intention of visiting the battlefield as "our special artist."[20]

Soon he came upon a wounded buffalo:

> [Munger] had ridden upon as big a bull as ever ran the Plains, stopped him with a series of shots from a Colt's army revolver, and was holding him at bay in a grassy basin, for our artist's especial behoof. He, on his part, did not need three words to show him his opportunity. He leapt from the buggy; out came the materials of success following him, and in a trifle over three minutes from his first halt, the big blue umbrella was pointed and pitched, and he sat under it on his camp-stool, with his color-box on his knees, his brush and palette in hand, and a clean board pinned in the cover of his color-box. Munger's old giant glowered and flashed fire from two great wells of angry brown and red, burning up like a pair of lighted naphtha-springs, through a foot-deep environ-ment of shaggy hair. The old fellow had been shot in half a dozen places. He was wounded in the haunch, through the lower ribs, through the lungs, and elsewhere. Still he stood his ground like a Spartacus. He was too much distressed to run with the herd; at every plunge he was

120

easily headed off by a turn of Munger's bridle; he had trampled a circle of twenty feet diameter, in his sallies to get away, yet he would not lie down. From both his nostrils the blood was flowing, mixed with glare and foam. His breath was like a blacksmith's bellows. His great sides heaved laboriously, as if he were breathing with his whole body. I never could be enough of a hunter not to regard this as a distressing sight. . . . Munger, Thompson, and I rode slowly round the bull, attracting his attention by feigned assaults, that our artist might see him in action. As each of us came to a point where the artist saw him sideways, the rider advanced his horse, and menaced the bull with his weapon. The old giant lowered his head till his great beard swept the dust; out of his immense fell of hair his eyes glared fiercer and redder; he drew in his breath with a hollow roar and a painful hiss, and charged madly at the aggressor. A mere twist of the rein threw the splendidly trained horse out of harm's way, and the bull almost went headlong with his unspent impetus. For nearly fifteen minutes, this process was continued, while the artist's hand and eye followed each other at the double-quick over the board. The signs of exhaustion increased with every charge of the bull; the blood streamed faster from wounds and nostrils; yet he showed no signs of surrender, and an almost human devil of impotent revenge looked out of his fiery, unblinking eyeballs.

But our Parrhasius was merciful. As soon as he had transferred the splendid action of the buffalo to his study, he called on us to put an end to the distress, which, for aught else than art's sake, was terrible to see. All of us who had weapons drew up in line, while the artist attracted the bull's attention by a final feigned assault. We aimed right for the heart, and fired. A hat might have covered the chasm which poured blood from his side when our smoke blew away. All the balls had sped home; but the unconquerable would not fall with his side to the foe. He turned himself painfully around on his quivering legs; he stiffened his tail in one last fury; he shook his mighty head, and then, lowering it to the ground, concentrated all the life that lasted in him for a mad onset. He rushed forward at his persecutors with all the *elan* of his first charges; but strength failed him half way. Ten feet from where we stood, he tumbled to his knees, made heroic efforts to rise again, and came up on

90. Sketches of dogs. 1863?
Pencil on paper, 5 × 8″ (12.7 × 20.3 cm.).
Collection John P. Kelly, Connecticut

91. *A Rest on the Ride.* 1863–64. Oil on canvas, 30 × 50″ (76.2 × 127 cm.).
Private collection, Annapolis, Maryland

one leg; but the death-tremor possessed the other, and with a great panting groan, in which all of brute power and beauty went forth at once, he fell prone on the trampled turf, and a glaze hid the anger of his eyes. Even in death those eyes were wide open on the foe, as he lay grand, like Caesar before Pompey's statue, at the feet of his assassins.[21]

This buffalo may well have found immortality in a painting in the Thomas Gilcrease Institute in Tulsa (Fig. 92).

When Bierstadt and Ludlow left Comstock's at 11 P.M. on May 30, they traveled without their two friends, who were going to meet them in Denver. Traveling "at the average Overland stage rate of a little over one hundred miles in twenty-four hours,"[22] and catching their first glimpse of the mountains outside Fort Kearney, they passed a wagon train of Germans going to Oregon. This event has been immortalized in two nearly identical paintings by Bierstadt (Figs. 93 and 94), and in the following words by Ludlow, who, Rosalie or not, had quite an eye for the ladies:

About two o'clock, we passed a very picturesque party of Germans going to Oregon. They had a large herd of cattle and fifty wagons, mostly drawn by oxen, though some of the more prosperous "outfits" were attached to horses or mules. The people themselves represented the better class of Prussian or North German peasantry. A number of strapping teamsters, in gay costumes, appeared like Westphalians. Some of them wore canary shirts and blue pantaloons; with these were intermingled blouses of claret, rich warm brown, and the most vivid red. All the women and children had some positive color about them, if it only amounted to a knot of ribbons, or the glimpse of a petticoat. I never saw so many bright and comely faces in an emigrant train. One real little beauty, who showed the typical German blonde through all her tan, peered out of one great canvas wagon cover, like a baby under the bonnet of the Shaker giantess, and coqueted for a moment with us from a pair of wicked-innocent blue eyes, drawing back, when the driver stared at her, in nicely simulated confusion. . . . Every wagon was a gem of an interior such as no Fleming ever put on canvas, and every group a *genre* piece for Boughton. The whole picture of the train was such a delight in form, color, and spirit that I could have lingered near it all the way to Kearney.[23]

123

92. *Buffalo Chase.* Undated.
Oil on canvas, 20 × 28″ (50.8 × 71.1 cm.).
Thomas Gilcrease Institute, Tulsa

The party followed the Platte nearly to Denver, which they apparently reached on June 4. While in Denver, and under the aegis of Evans, the territorial governor, they made side trips. One of these was to the Garden of the Gods, where their hosts were disappointed because Bierstadt was not inspired and did not paint a big picture of the local pride and joy. On another excursion Bierstadt was taken by a guide, William Newton Byers, to the country near Idaho Springs. Here he made studies for what later became *Storm in the Rocky Mountains,* a canvas that is now lost. Byers's account gives interesting sidelights into the artist's working methods as well as his way with trout:

The locality of the present charming little city of Idaho Springs was visited in 1863 by Albert Bierstadt, the greatest of American landscape painters. . . . I was ahead to show the way, the pack animals followed, with Bierstadt behind to prod them up. There was no chance to talk, but plenty of time to think. I knew that at a certain point the trail emerged from the timber, and all the beauty, the grandeur, the sublimity, and whatever else there might be in sight at the time. . . . Bierstadt emerged leisurely. His enthusiasm was badly dampened, but the moment he caught the view fatigue and hunger were forgotten. He

93. *Emigrants Crossing the Plains.*
1867. Oil on canvas, 60 × 96″
(152.4 × 243.8 cm.).
The National Cowboy Hall of Fame
and Western Heritage Center,
Oklahoma City

94. *The Oregon Trail.* 1869.
Oil on canvas, 31 × 49″
(78.7 × 124.5 cm.).
The Butler Institute of
American Art, Youngstown, Ohio

said nothing, but his face was a picture of intense life and excitement. Taking in the view for a moment, he slid off his mule, glanced quickly to see where the jack was that carried his paint outfit, walked sideways to it and began fumbling at the lash-ropes, all the time keeping his eyes on the scene up the valley. I told him I would get out his things, and proceeded to do so. As he went to work he said, "I must get a study in colors; it will take me fifteen minutes!" He said nothing more. . . . Nothing was said by either of us. At length the sketch was finished to his satisfaction. The glorious scene was fading as he packed up his traps. He asked: "There, was I more than fifteen minutes?" I answered: "Yes, you were at work forty-five minutes by the watch!" We resumed the march and soon reached the foot of the lake. Bierstadt wanted to cross over the valley and make a sketch from a certain point that he indicated, so I took charge of all the animals and passed up along the north side of the lake to its head and made camp. After getting things in shape I started fishing. I could see plenty of them, but failed to catch any except one small specimen. . . . I walked over to Bierstadt and told him that I had failed to catch any trout and we would have to eat sardines. As we walked across the meadow I showed him the trout in the outlet. He looked at them a little while and admired them of course. Then he said, "I'll see if I can catch some." I laughed at him, and here comes in the fish story at which the reader will laugh, but it is the truest fish story you ever heard or read:

Bierstadt took from his pocket a combination table fork and knife, made for camp use; he detached them, and, taking the fork (which was five or six inches long when opened) in his right hand, dropped down beside the stream on his knee and began fishing. He would put his hand in the water near a fish and move it along gently until he touched the fish, when with a sudden motion he would pin it to the bottom or bank with the fork. It was so easy and certain that after a few captures he put the fork in his pocket and caught them with his naked hand. Sometimes he would touch the fish with the ends of his fingers and rub it back and forth very gently for quite a little time before seizing it. The fish appeared to enjoy the sensation and would lean up against his fingers. I called it "tickling them out of the water." In this way he caught, in a few

95. *Wagon Train.* Undated. Oil on paper, 13½ × 18⅞″ (34.3 × 47.9 cm.).
Buffalo Bill Historical Center, The Whitney Gallery of Western Art, Cody, Wyoming

96. *The Great Salt Lake.* 1863?/1881?
Oil on paper mounted on board,
14 × 19½″ (35.6 × 49 cm.).
Charles and Emma Frye Art Museum,
Seattle, Washington

minutes, I think, eighteen. . . . Mr. Bierstadt worked industriously during our stay, making many sketches in pencil and studies in oil—these latter in order to get the colors and shade. I caught easily all the fish we could eat, and there was no object in taking more. We climbed to the upper lake, and eventually to the crest of the rim of the upper basin and to Summit Lake, and beyond that to the summit of the highest snowy peak in the group, which Bierstadt named "Mount Rosa," after one of the loftiest summits of the Alps. The return journey to Idaho Springs and thence to Denver was uneventful. Mr. Bierstadt soon went home to New York, and in a little over two years had finished his great picture of "A Storm in the Rocky Mountains."[24]

Byers was wrong about "Mount Rosa." Bierstadt had called it "Rosalie" after Ludlow's wife. Who knows what sly thoughts he was having?

On June 23, artist and writer left Denver for Salt Lake City, where they arrived late in the evening of the twenty-eighth. They found the city getting ready for the Fourth of July, a celebration they hardly expected to encounter among Brigham Young's followers, who had seceded from the United States. They had breakfast with Young's son-in-law in their hotel and took a swim in

Great Salt Lake, where they lay on their backs *on*, rather than *in*, the water (Fig. 96). Mormon habits constantly shocked them. They met Bierstadt's friend of the Lander trip, Dr. Bernhisel, and Ludlow, at least, was moved nearly to violence:

> No more overwhelming proof can be offered for Mormonism's degradation of the marriage tie and its extinction of man's chivalric feelings of respect and protection toward woman, than the fact that men of refined, gentlemanly, and scholarly antecedents like Dr. Bernhisel, for instance, can hear one of their own sex talk in public to their sisters, mothers, daughters, and wives, upon the most private subjects in the most blatant way, and not tear him in pieces where he stands.[25]

They left Salt Lake City and on the first day out entered "a terrible defile . . . great, black, barren rocks."[26] There were ten rifles in the party, and they were glad to have them: in the middle of the canyon the overland station had been burned and six men murdered. They could still smell the roasting flesh of horses. The Goshoot Indians were responsible for this, Ludlow wrote. By the time they got to Washoe (*i.e.*, Carson City) their "very marrows [had been] almost burned out by sleeplessness." But at "the brink of the glorious Lake Tahoe" their "feet pressed the borders of the Golden State," and they felt "translated into heaven."[27] Continuously along the route Bierstadt had made studies. Upon these, and upon others made in later trips, he drew for the rest of his life.

The two arrived in San Francisco on July 17, where they put up at the Occidental Hotel. They had never seen anything like it "for elegance of appointments, attentiveness of servants or excellence of *cuisine*."[28] Here they were joined for their trip to the Yosemite Valley by Virgil Williams, whom Bierstadt knew in Rome, and Enoch Wood Perry, with whom he had studied in Düsseldorf. Both of their new companions were well-known local artists. Williams was to paint an interesting account of this trip, showing Bierstadt himself. They also were accompanied by a Dr. John Hewston, "a highly scientific metallurgist and physicist generally."[29] By August 1, they were on their way, and the Stockton newspaper predicted that they would have "a jolly time of it."[30]

Before entering the valley they stopped at Mariposa, where they met Galen Clark, the Yosemite pioneer, whom Bierstadt painted at the base of one of the

97. *Western Landscape—Mount Rainier, Mount Saint Helens.* 1863. Oil on canvas, 13¼ × 18¾" (33.6 × 47.6 cm.). Whereabouts unknown

great trees (Fig. 98). Clark gave them "the nicest poached eggs and rashers of bacon, home-made bread and wild-strawberry sweetmeats"[31] in the state.

Nothing quite equaled for Ludlow his first sight of the Yosemite from Inspiration Point:

> That name had appeared pedantic, but we found it only the spontaneous expression of our own feelings on the spot. We did not so much seem to be seeing from that crag of vision a new scene on the old familiar globe as a new heaven and a new earth into which the creative spirit had just been breathed. I hesitate now, as I did then, at the attempt to give my vision utterance. Never were words so beggared for an abridged translation of any Scripture of Nature.[32]

Down in the valley, in a meadow on the Merced River, they pitched their camp, and named it Camp Rosalie, "after a dear absent friend of mine and Bierstadt's."[33] It has been said that the two may have made the journey to help them settle in their own minds which one was to have Rosalie, but it was too early in the drama for such a scene—the Ludlows had not yet given up on each other.

It has also been suggested that Bierstadt may have gone to California to escape the draft. As a matter of fact, during the time he was in Yosemite his name was among 794 drawn in his New York City ward from among 5,680

98. *California Redwoods*. 1875?
Oil on canvas, 117 × 50″ (297.2 × 127 cm.).
Private collection, New Hampshire.
This is the tree known as "Giant Grizzly," in the
Mariposa Grove. The Yosemite pioneer Galen Clark
stands at its base

eligible. This was reported by *The San Francisco Evening Bulletin* on September 15, while he was still in the valley. However, National Archives records indicate that he had paid his $300 exemption and was therefore excused.

During their stay in Yosemite, Ludlow wrote, "most" of them got up at dawn and took a bath in the ice-cold Merced. Then they breakfasted on flapjacks and coffee—and sometimes game:

> Then the artists with their camp-stools and color-boxes, the sages with their goggles, nets, botany-boxes, and bug-holders, the gentlemen of elegant leisure with their naked eyes and a fish-rod or a gun, all rode away whither they listed, firing back Parthian shots of injunction about the dumpling in the grouse-fricassee.
>
> Sitting in their divine workshop, by a little after sunrise our artists began labor in that only method which can ever make a true painter or a living landscape, color-studies on the spot; and though I am not here to speak of their results, I will assert that during their seven weeks' camp in the Valley they learned more and gained greater material for future triumphs than they had gotten in all their lives before at the feet of the greatest masters. . . . At evening, when the artists returned, half an hour was passed in a "private view" of their day's studies; then came another dinner, called a supper; then the tea-kettle was emptied into a pan, and brush-washing with talk and pipes led the rest of the genial way to bed-time.[34]

Soon the camp was moved five miles up the valley to the base of the Yosemite Falls, or "Cho-looke" as it was then called. Here Bierstadt made studies for one of his finest paintings of the valley, one which is still with us (Fig. 1). Near one camp on August 21, the artist wrote his name on Register Rock. His name, however, along with many others of interest, was carefully sand-blasted off near the turn of the century by a zealous U.S. Army officer who thought the place needed cleaning up.

After leaving the valley and returning to San Francisco, Ludlow and Bierstadt stayed for "more than a fort-night," making various excursions in the Bay area. But this "lotus-eating life soon palled." They "burned to see the giant Shasta, and grew thirsty for the eternal snows of the Cascade Peaks still farther north."[35] Accordingly, they set out again "one glorious September day," the twenty-fourth, and boarded the boat for Sacramento. Up the river they went, beyond the capital city to Bluffs and the base of Shasta, where they had a delightful visit with a settler from Illinois named Sisson in his two-story ranch in Strawberry Valley. Here they passed "the pleasantest, as distinct from grandest" week of their California stay:

> No family whom we encountered lived in such wholesome and homelike luxury as Sisson's. . . . Bless [Mrs. Sisson]! how she could broil things! No man who has not built up his system during a long expedition with brick after brick of pork fried hard in its own ooze . . . can imagine what a blissful bay in the ironbound coast of bad-living Sisson's seemed to us both in fruition and retrospection . . . the great stand-by of our table was venison, roast, broiled, made into pasties, treated with every variety of preparation save an oil-soak in the pagan frying-pan of the country. As for chickens and eggs, it "snewe in Sisson's house" of that sort of "mete and drinke." . . . Cream flowed in upon us like a river; potatoes were stewed in it; it was the base of chicken-sauce; the sirupy baked pears, whose secret Mrs. Sisson had inherited from some dim religious ancestor in the New England past, were drowned in it; and we took a glass of it with magical shiny rusk for nine-o'clock supper, just to oil our joints before we relaxed them in innocent repose. Our rooms were ample, our beds luxurious, our surroundings the grandest within Nature's bestowal.[36]

Onward through northern California to Oregon they plunged, then Ludlow got pneumonia, and Bierstadt, "the best friend I ever travelled with,"[37] nursed him with wet compresses. They paid sixty dollars for five days' board, as much as they had paid at the Occidental in San Francisco, and received the explanation that it was because the lady of the house had felt for Ludlow "like a mother." Ludlow observed that "maternal tenderness" in Oregon "was a highly estimated virtue." Twenty miles south of Salem they saw "one of the most magnificent views in all earthly scenery." Seven snow-clad peaks were before them in one vista: the Three Sisters, Mount Jefferson, Mount Hood, Mount Adams, and Mount Saint Helens. There was also a dim suggestion of an eighth "colossal mass which might have been Rainier." "No man of enthusiasm," Ludlow wrote, "will

133

wonder that my friend and I clasped each other's hands before it, and thanked God we had lived to this day."

Down the Willamette River to Portland, they put up at the Dennison House, where they were as comfortable as they had been since they left Strawberry Valley. They went up the Willamette to the Columbia as guests of the owners of the steamship line and stayed overnight at Fort Vancouver, where they had a family dinner with General Benjamin Alvord, the commandant. The next morning at seven they boarded the *Wilson G. Hunt* for the trip up the Columbia to The Dalles "and went immediately to breakfast."[38] They steamed up the Columbia, took the six-mile railroad portage at the Columbia Falls to The Dalles, where the accommodations of the Umatilla House waited them, and Ludlow indulged in flirtations of his own in the hotel parlor. The next morning Bierstadt made sketches of Mount Hood from a point of view several miles out of town. Ludlow thought the resulting studio painting better even than *The Rocky Mountains, Lander's Peak,* whose glories they had seen off to Boston just before they left home.

That afternoon they visited a town called Celilo, and from there they went back down the Columbia to Portland to catch the San Francisco steamer, which was scheduled to arrive in Portland in a day or two. But their haste did them little good: when they got back to Portland they were confined in their hotel for a week by drenching rains. They were back in San Francisco by November 14, and spent a busy, happy fortnight there. They were seen off on the Pacific Mail Steamship Company's *Constitution* on November 23 by no less a personage than Thomas Starr King, California's great preacher.[39] (Also on board, incidentally, was Haraszthy de Mokcsa, the California wine pioneer.) They arrived in Panama on December 5, crossed the Isthmus the same day, and were in New York on December 17, 1863.

NOTES: 1 Although described as early as 2727 B.C., hasheesh (modern "hashish") was largely unknown in the West until 1839, when a British physician serving in India (where it had been used for a thousand years) described his own use of the drug. Ludlow was thus introduced to the drug early in its career in America.

2 Fitz Hugh Ludlow, *The Hasheesh Eater* (New York: Harper, 1857), p. 93.

134

3   Quoted by Morris Bishop in *Union Worthies*, no. 8 (Schenectady, N.Y.: Union College, 1953), p. 14.

4   This and the following quotations are from an unidentified clipping of March 26, 1863, in a private collection.

5   Nott to Mrs. Amos Osborne, January 3, 1859, private collection. The family sometimes spelled "Osborne" with an "e" and sometimes without. For consistency I have used "Osborne."

6   Henry Ludlow to Fitz Hugh Ludlow, April 19, 1859, Ludlow Papers, New York State Historical Association Library, Cooperstown.

7   Henry Ludlow to Rosalie and Fitz Hugh Ludlow, September 22, 1859, *ibid.*

8   Ludlow to unknown addressee [on an *Evening Post* letterhead], October 8, 1861, Union College archives, Schenectady, New York.

9   Quoted by Laura Stedman and George M. Gould, eds., in *Life and Letters of Edmund Clarence Stedman* (New York: Moffat, Yard, 1910), Vol. I, p. 253.

10   Carrie Ludlow to her mother, January 24, 1864, Ludlow Papers, New York State Historical Association Library, Cooperstown.

11   *The New York Evening Post,* May 12, 1863.

12   Agassiz to Bierstadt, April 28, 1863, Henry Francis du Pont Winterthur Museum, Winterthur, Delaware.

13   *The New York Evening Post,* May 22, 1863. Although this account did not appear until May 22, its style and content suggest that Ludlow wrote it before he left.

14   Fitz Hugh Ludlow, *The Heart of the Continent* (New York: Hurd and Houghton, 1870), pp. 1–2. Four sections of this account of the trip, containing additional material, were published in *The Atlantic Monthly:* "Among the Mormons," April 1864; "Seven Weeks in the Great Yo-Semite," June 1864; "On Horseback into Oregon," July 1864; and "On the Columbia River," December 1864. The book was illustrated with many wood engravings from Bierstadt sketches.

15   *The New York Evening Post,* May 12, 1863.

16   Rosalie Ludlow to Henry and Helen Ludlow, May 31, 1863, Ludlow Papers, New York State Historical Society Library, Cooperstown.

17   *Ibid.,* June 2, 1863.

18   Fitz Hugh Ludlow, *The Heart of the Continent* (New York: Hurd and Houghton, 1870), p. 9.

19   *Ibid.,* p. 50.

20   *Ibid.,* p. 62.

21   *Ibid.,* pp. 67–69.

22   *Ibid.,* p. 107.

23   *Ibid.,* pp. 110–12.

24   William Newton Byers, "Bierstadt's Visit to Colorado," *Magazine of Western History,* Vol. XI, no. 3 (January 1890), p. 237ff.

25   Fitz Hugh Ludlow, *The Heart of the Continent* (New York: Hurd and Houghton, 1870), p. 509.

26   Fitz Hugh Ludlow, "Among the Mormons," *The Atlantic Monthly,* April 1864, p. 493.

27   *Ibid.,* p. 495.

28   Fitz Hugh Ludlow, *The Heart of the Continent* (New York: Hard and Houghton, 1870), p. 410.

29   *Ibid.,* p. 419.

30   Quoted by *The San Francisco Alta,* August 1, 1863.

31   Fitz Hugh Ludlow, *The Heart of the Continent* (New York: Hurd and Houghton, 1870), p. 421.

32   *Ibid.,* p. 426.

33   Fitz Hugh Ludlow, "Seven Weeks in the Great Yo-Semite," *The Atlantic Monthly,* June 1864, p. 749.

34   Fitz Hugh Ludlow, *The Heart of the Continent* (New York: Hurd and Houghton, 1870), p. 436.

35   *Ibid.,* p. 445.

36   *Ibid.,* p. 464.

37   Fitz Hugh Ludlow, "On the Columbia River," *The Atlantic Monthly,* December 1864, p. 703.

38   Fitz Hugh Ludlow, *The Heart of the Continent* (New York: Hurd and Houghton, 1870), p. 480.

39   Thomas Starr King (1824–1864) enjoyed a kind and degree of prestige in San Francisco at this time that is perhaps without parallel today. He was more than merely famous, though he was one of the city's best-known citizens. Beginning in 1846 he held a series of Universalist and Unitarian pastorates in Charleston, Massachusetts, and Boston, and became one of the most popular lecturers in the country. At some personal sacrifice he accepted a call to the struggling San Francisco Unitarian parish and soon rid the church of its $20,000 debt and helped build a new $90,000 church. His eloquence is credited with being a powerful force in keeping California in the Union during the Civil War and with raising a large part of the money necessary to support the U.S. Sanitary Commission. When he died of pneumonia the year after Bierstadt and Ludlow were in San Francisco, the state legislature adjourned for three days. The following fall Bierstadt saw Mrs. King and her children in New York.

Seven

Critical Acclaim

1863-1867

99. *Valley of the Yosemite*. 1864.
Oil on prepared millboard, 11¾ × 19¼″ (29.8 × 49.5 cm.).
Museum of Fine Arts, Boston. M. and M. Karolik Collection

IT WAS IN 1864 THAT BIERSTADT came up to, equaled, and, some said, surpassed Frederick E. Church as America's most celebrated landscapist. Church's *The Heart of the Andes* (Fig. 100) had been having a popular and critical success that was unprecedented in the history of American art. It had been presented to the public in Church's studio in the Tenth Street building the very year Bierstadt moved in and, combined with the critical success of Church's *Niagara* two years earlier, induced a celebrity that raised its creator's reputation above all his compatriots'. "On this American more than any other," London's *Art Journal* commented, "does the mantle of our greatest painter appear to have fallen."[1] He had become the successor of Turner—and that was the most any Englishman could say.

Bierstadt's debut painting, *Lake Lucerne,* had had middling reviews, and his subsequent western works—*The Base of the Rocky Mountains, Laramie Peak,* chiefly—elicited what might be called a pleasant reaction from the critics and their public. But there was no great success until *Sunshine and Shadow* called forth superlatives at the 1862 Academy Annual. Many in New York had already seen the new painting that was to be the chef d'oeuvre of Bierstadt's early career, *The Rocky Mountains, Lander's Peak* (Fig. 108, hereafter called *The Rocky Mountains*), but they had seen it only in the artist's studio just before he went West. After that, it had been sent to the relative obscurity of Boston. Church's *Cotopaxi* was then the rage in New York, and it is not beyond credibility that Bierstadt did not want to compete with Church just yet.

By the time he was back in New York the painting had returned, too, and the artist immediately set about making a small copy for the engraver James Smillie. In spite of a curious statement to the contrary—which reported in March, 1864, that the engraver's drawing was "now nearly or quite finished"[2]—the print from this engraving did not appear until early in 1867. For many years afterward, when the artist wished to pay his friends a particular compliment, he gave an autographed copy of this reproduction of his most famous work.

Besides laying plans for the exhibition of *The Rocky Mountains*, the artist evidently painted a small picture of the Yosemite, possibly his first representation of the valley and one of his best. This work survives in the Boston Museum (Fig. 99). Thinking also that he should have something respectable for the National Academy's forthcoming Annual—he did not want to waste his big *Rocky*

140

100. Frederick E. Church.
The Heart of the Andes. 1859.
Oil on canvas, 66⅛ × 119¼"
(168 × 302.9 cm.).
The Metropolitan Museum of Art,
New York City.
Bequest of Mrs. David Dows, 1909

Mountains on that exhibition—he brought forth another scene from the Wind River Mountains. *The Herald,* reviewing the Annual, said that it was painted with "great breadth and brilliancy."[3] It is possible that this work may be the one the artist painted in 1861, now called *Sunset Light* and in the public library of his native New Bedford (Fig. 101).

But it was to the great American public that Bierstadt most wanted to speak. Now, he thought, they were ready to be convinced that Frederick Church had found his match. His first step in this noble enterprise was to put his big *Rocky Mountains* in a New York gallery, that of Seitz and Noelle, at 625 Broadway. He knew that it would be there only a short time and that soon it would be one of the sights at the Sanitary Fair now about to be opened.[4] But before that, he wanted to start some talk.

And start it he did. "Mr. Bierstadt's picture deserves to take rank among the highest existing productions of American landscape art,"[5] wrote one critic, and that put its creator squarely in Church's league. By the end of the year the famous art critic James Jackson Jarves had also applied his imprimatur, conceding that the artist was now Church's rival. To his accolade, however, Jarves added a strong dissent:

But a competitor [of Church] for the popular favor in the same

141

101. *Sunset Light, Wind River Range of the Rocky Mountains.* 1861.
Oil on canvas, 39 × 60″ (99.1 × 152.4 cm.). Free Public Library, New Bedford, Massachusetts

102. *Yosemite Valley.* Undated. Oil on canvas, 35½ × 58″ (90.2 × 147.3 cm.).
Pioneer Museum and Haggin Galleries, Stockton, California. Haggin Collection

direction has appeared in Bierstadt. He has selected the Rocky Mountains and Western prairies for his artistic field. Both these men are as laborious as they are ambitious, regarding neither personal exposure nor expense in their distant fields of study. Each composes his pictures from actual sketches, with the desire to render the general truths and spirit of the localities of their landscapes, though often departing from the literal features of the view. With singular inconsistency of mind they idealize in composition and materialize in execution, so that, though the details of the scenery are substantially correct, the scene as a whole often is false. Neither manifests any grand conception of nature, nor appreciation of its poetry. Graphic beauty of composition and illustration are their chief points. Bierstadt uses the landscape also to illustrate Indian life. His figures are picturesquely grouped, prosaically true to actual life, giving additional interest to most observers, though rendering his great work, the Rocky Mountains, confused, and detracting from its principal features, beside making it liable to the artistic objection of two pictures in one, from different points of view. We form our estimate of him from this picture. It is to be welcomed, because it recalls one from the delusive enchantments of the Church style to a more strictly scientific expression of nature. . . . In many respects Bierstadt has been very successful. If he has no liking for the broad, imaginative treatment of Titian, neither has he any more for the conventional lifelessness of the mechanical Düsseldorf school. He seeks to depict the absolute qualities and forms of things. The botanist and geologist can find work in his rocks and vegetation. He seizes upon natural phenomena with naturalistic eyes. In the quality of American light, clear, transparent, and sharp in outlines, he is unsurpassed. Cloud-shadows flit and play over sunlit hills and distant snow-peaks, rising clear and cold against the lofty horizon, with truthful effect. But his light is pitched on too high a key, which leaves his color cold and glaring, and produces overmuch transparency of atmosphere, whereby distances are in some degree confused and deceptive. As a colorist, Bierstadt appears to better advantage in his Sunshine and Shadow, a reminiscence of the Rhine. On the whole, however, he has well depicted the silvery clearness and translucency of

103. *Sunset in the Yosemite Valley.* 1868. Oil on canvas, 35½ × 51½″ (90.2 × 130.8 cm.).
Pioneer Museum and Haggin Galleries, Stockton, California. Haggin Collection

104. *The Yosemite Valley* [incorrect title]. 1867.
Oil on canvas, 35⅜ × 49⅝″ (89.8 × 126 cm.). Wadsworth Atheneum, Hartford

the mountain-air of the West, and managed to avoid the prominent defects of the school in general. At the same time, we must confess that our taste has but transient sympathy with its hard-featured rationalism, no matter to what degree it compels admiration of its executive qualities.[6]

But the caterwauling of art historians such as Jarves—as opposed to those who wrote for the newspapers and magazines and who set the direction of taste—was irrelevant in March, 1864, when *The Rocky Mountains* graced the walls of the Seitz and Noelle Gallery. So much good was said of it that when it arrived at the Sanitary Fair's Art Gallery in time for the opening on the first of April, more comment would have been anticlimax. The artist never had a more complimentary review:

> Even dismissing the question of inspiration, and looking at "Lander's Peak" from a purely technical point of view, we are compelled to accord the picture a rank with the foremost achievements in form and color. There are certain passages of it which indicate an acquaintance with artistic means unsurpassed in any painting of our age and country . . . the handling of these particulars is of a perfection which would entitle Bierstadt to the name of a great workman, did he not deserve that of a great artist more justly still.
>
> We have studied the picture under all circumstances of external light, in dark and in bright weather, in bad and in good positions. It needs advantages as little as any picture we ever saw. Its sunlight seems self-supporting. It illumines a twilight room . . . these facts are decisive of the artist's place in the very first rank of American genius. . . . Human skill and patience, audacity and tireless enterprise of knowledge, have pioneered their way, all these thousands of dangerous slow miles into the very vestibule of virgin Nature. But the Holiest of Holies locks its door against them. The inmost, topmost spirit of things closes the gates of sight behind it and retires into the silent bosom of the Heavens. Skill cannot fly nor patience climb to the opalescent cradle of that glacier-stream. The King of the World is denied his subject's grandest confidence, and stands dwarfed in the valley, mutely, hopelessly gazing whither Nature is closeted alone with God![7]

105. *Valley of the Yosemite*. Undated. Oil on canvas, 14 × 19″ (35.6 × 48.3 cm.).
Joslyn Art Museum, Omaha. Gift of Mrs. C. N. Dietz

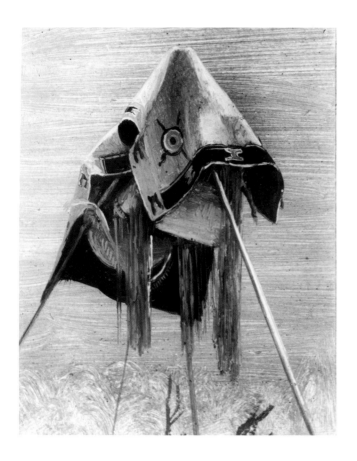

The artist had taken the mountain range of his *Wind River Country*, exaggerated it, dramatized it, added glaciers, a waterfall, and an Indian camp—all in a juxtaposition quite unknown to those who know the Wind River Range—and created his masterpiece.

At the Sanitary Fair (Fig. III), *The Rocky Mountains* directly faced Church's *The Heart of the Andes,* across the room—as it did until recently in the Metropolitan Museum. Bierstadt also installed a number of his Indian artifacts and arranged for a visit from a group of Indians. "Beside the nineteen Indians," *The Herald* reported, there were "a few hundred curiosities, including a large wigwam, in which the Red men of the forest live."[8] There were about six hundred other works of art in the gallery, including, at the end of the room, Leutze's *George Washington Crossing the Delaware.* At night this flowering of American art was lighted by 490 gas jets. All this confusion led *The Times* to comment that perhaps the Bierstadt and Church paintings would "retain their reputation better if they had not intruded into the presence of so much splendid art as everywhere surrounds them."[9] *The Tribune* commented that although the Düsseldorf School had infected Bierstadt, "he is recovering from the disease."[10]

Besides a review by George Bancroft, the famous historian and friend of Bierstadt—who began to negotiate for a painting in March, 1864, and fourteen months later was still negotiating[11]—little could be added to what had already

(*left*) 106. *Indian Amulet.* 1859.
Oil on paper, 5 × 4⅜″ (12.7 × 11.1 cm.).
Author's collection.
This was used as a study for
The Rocky Mountains (Fig. 108)

107. Study for *The Rocky Mountains.* 1862?
Oil on canvas, 7¼ × 10″ (18.4 × 25.4 cm.).
Collection Fred A. Rosenstock, Denver

149

108. *The Rocky Mountains*. 1863.
Oil on canvas, 73½ × 120¾″ (186.7 × 306.7 cm.).
The Metropolitan Museum of Art, New York City.
Rogers Fund, 1907

109, 110.
The Rocky Mountains
◀ (details) ▶

111. The Art Gallery at the New York
Sanitary Fair, 1864, showing
The Rocky Mountains.
The New-York Historical Society,
New York City

been said. Only Sally Popcorn from Pumpkinville, New York, found anything more to say. "Sally Popcorn" was the pseudonym of the author of a regular column, written in heavy-handed nineteenth-century-style country humor for the fair's official publication, *Spirit of the Fair.* Her reaction to the Church and Bierstadt paintings came late, on April 23, when the fair was about to close:

There's two big pictures, one on each side of the room. The biggest one they call the "Heart of the Andes," and it's a very stony heart it seems . . . splashes of water shinin' and comin' down to see what's goin' on in the village, this side of the mountain. But the stream don't stop there long, it comes wanderin' along, sometimes tumblin' down and bilin' into steam, till it gits right up close to you, and if Nephew Jebial could see what a splendid spot there is fur catfish in the corner, he wouldn't do any thing, but dig worms for a week. . . . After I look at this awhile, I went to see whose heart the other one was, but it didn't 'pear to belong to anybody—like an old maid's. There was a big mountain in the back part, and some nice pasture lots and a tolerable wood lot, but the wood's been cut off, I guess to make a road for the Ingins to travel on to. Ingins and horses and tents and dogs and trappers and camp-fires and old bones bleached white in the grass, are scattered all around the medder in front, but they must be shiftless folks to let their fences git down altogether.[12]

There was also an auction for the benefit of the fair, and Bierstadt's little *Valley of the Yosemite* (Fig. 99) sold for $1,600. *The Rocky Mountains* itself, after having been exhibited the next year in Chicago's Sanitary Fair, was sold to James McHenry, an American living in London, for a reported $25,000.[13] This was perhaps the largest price that had ever been paid for an American painting. After returning from Chicago, the painting was exhibited for a while at the place of its public debut, the Seitz and Noelle Gallery. Then it went to Europe, where it received an award at the Paris Universal Exposition, to the Haymarket, and finally to McHenry's great house, Oak Lodge, set on ten acres in the heart of London. The artist bought it back in 1898 and gave it or sold it to his brother Edward. In 1907, after Edward's death, his daughter Mary Adeline sold it to the Metropolitan Museum, where it remains.

Meanwhile, during its New York exhibitions the painting was "going

154

through the ceremonies of exhibition and puffery preparatory to being engraved."[14] Although the job took three years, it was one with which the artist was very concerned: an income from a comfortable sale of engravings represented to him, as it did to other artists of the time, a respectable part of the financial reward for work. *Sunshine and Shadow* had already been chromolithographed—by Storch & Kramer—and a copy of that was soon to hang in far-off Utah, in the office of no less a personage than Brigham Young himself. *The New Path*, a New York magazine, gives a colorful account of the public relations process attendant upon such projects:

> . . . the upholsterer has done his work, and ten lorgnettes and the magnifying glass have been duly provided, the puff-disinterested has been written, printed on the sheet of letter paper that etiquette prescribes, and distributed, and the gentleman-in-waiting stands ready, at all hours, to enter in his subscription book the names of those who desire to add this combined result of Mr. Bierstadt's genius and Mr. Smillie's talent, to their plethoric portfolios.[15]

The "puff-disinterested," or flyer, that Bierstadt published, incorrectly gave the year of the Lander expedition, and that error has been multiplied.

Leaving Mr. Smillie to his arduous work, Bierstadt turned to other projects with a vengeance. Soon he was at work on a large painting of Mount Hood, taken from his studies at The Dalles the previous November. "[It] will prove," *The Post* reported, "to be his finest work."[16] Besides his *Mount Hood*, which is lost, the artist worked hard well into the summer. Even in June, with the days the longest in the year, he worked into the night by gaslight. While working on the Mount Hood painting, he did two others—*Camping in the Yosemite* (Fig. 1) and a Yosemite moonlight scene, apparently the one now in the Yosemite National Park Museum (Fig. 114). *The Post* promised its readers that both, along with *Mount Hood,* would be among the artist's best works.[17]

During these busy June days, with the kindness and generosity the artist showed during his entire life, he took off time to write his young nephew Oscar Albert, Edward's son, a note of congratulation:

My Dear Oscar Albert.
I have noticed with much pleasure your admission into the high school.

112. R. C. Holdredge. *Indian Village in the Sierra.* 1884? Oil on canvas, 28⅜ × 50″ (72.1 × 127 cm.). E. B. Crocker Art Gallery, Sacramento, California. An obvious imitation of Bierstadt's work by a respected California painter

113. *Mountain Lake.* Undated. Oil on panel, 14 × 20″ (35.6 × 50.8 cm.).
Northern Natural Gas Company Collection, Joslyn Art Museum, Omaha

115. *The Golden Gate: San Francisco.* 1865.
41½ × 65½″ (105.4 × 165.1 cm.).
Photograph taken from a Kende Galleries, Inc.,
auction catalogue,
May 4, 1945, New York City. This painting,
evidently formerly belonging to John C. Frémont,
is now unlocated

114. *Night at Valley View.* 1884.
Oil on canvas, 34 × 27⅛″ (86.4 × 69 cm.).
Yosemite National Park Museum, Yosemite, California.
Formerly *Moonlight on the Merced*

I congratulate you. I sincerely hope you will retain your position as a scholar, and a good boy. I was very proud to see your name at the head of the list and I know it must be gratifying to all the family. Set a good example to other boys. Do not use bad language, always do what is right. God will bless you then and above all things, do not forget to pray to him for he is our dearest and best friend. Conduct yourself in all things in such a manner that we all shall be proud of you, and write to me sometimes and tell me how you are doing. Give my love to Mother, Father, sisters and brother.

From your dear Uncle
Albert Bierstadt[18]

On October 21, 1864, Bierstadt's mother Christina died at her home in New Bedford, and her artist son, visiting his family there, donated one of his pictures to the local National Sailors' Fair.

Early the next year, in a meeting of the Travelers' Club in Bayard Taylor's rooms, Bierstadt may have met Herman Melville. Here he also met General Orlando Bolivar Willcox, to whom he later gave an autographed print of *The Rocky Mountains*. Willcox was near Petersburg when the Civil War ended and invited Bierstadt to visit him there during a visit the artist planned—but evidently did not make—to Richmond. Melville was also invited (we do not know if he went) to the National Academy's Annual which opened in April. A Yosemite picture graced the walls of this exhibition, as well as the now lost *Golden Gate* (Fig. 115), which had been sold to General John C. Frémont for $4,000.[19] The Yosemite picture was called *Looking Down Yo Semite Valley,* and had mixed—though generally favorable—reviews. *The New York Times* sat in the middle, as did *Watson's Weekly Art Journal:* "The picture is full of a fine enthusiasm, of a free exultation in the grander forms of nature. . . . There is, perhaps, a little hardness, a certain dryness in the work, notwithstanding the magnificence."[20]

The Rocky Mountains had barely left Seitz and Noelle's before the artist announced another painting. This was his *Storm in the Rocky Mountains,* under way, according to *Watson's,* eight months before it was finished (Figs. 116 and 117). It first saw public light at a benefit for the Nursery and Children's Hospital early

116. Sketch for *Storm in the Rocky Mountains.* 1863? Pencil on paper, 5 × 8″ (12.7 × 20,3 cm.). Collection John P. Kelly, Connecticut. Possibly Bierstadt's earliest conception of the painting

117. Chromolithograph after *Storm in the Rocky Mountains.* 18⅜ × 32⅜″ (46.7 × 82.2 cm.). Author's collection. The original of this work is now lost

118. W. C. Sharon. *Western Landscape.* Undated. Oil on canvas, 20 × 33″ (50.8 × 83.8 cm.). The M. H. de Young Memorial Museum, San Francisco. Gift of Edgar William and Bernice Chrysler Garbisch. Copy by an amateur artist after Fig. 117

in February, 1866, and by the time it had been removed on February 24, had earned $2,200 for this charity.

Now Bierstadt's dissenters were growing. Jarves's "hard-featured rationalism" and *Watson's* "dryness" and "hardness" were only foretastes of the invectives that greeted the new picture. It is not difficult to agree with a criticism of the artist's understanding of the "laws of gravitation":

> The truth is, we fear, Mr. Bierstadt has undertaken a subject much beyond his powers. . . . To suggest God's nature on canvas required a depth of feeling which not every artist possesses, and a severity of study which few artists care to bestow. . . . This depth of feeling Mr. Bierstadt does not seem to evince . . . [his] cold, brilliant talent . . . produces work which may impose upon the sense, but does not affect the heart, which may astound but does not elevate, for God's reality enters into it in a very slight measure. . . . The whole science of geology cries out against him. . . . The law of gravitation leagues itself with geological law against the artist. Away up, above the clouds, near the top of the picture, the observer will perceive two pyramidal shapes. By further consultation of the index-sheet, the observer will ascertain that these things are the two "spurs" of Mount Rosalie. Now, let him work out a problem in arithmetic: The hills over which he looks, as we are told, are three thousand feet high; right over the hills tower huge masses of cloud which certainly carry the eye up to ten or twelve thousand feet higher; above these . . . the two "spurs;" what is the height of Mount Rosalie? Answer: approximately, ten thousand miles or so. Impossible.[21]

Such strictures, however, were still not the rule. Another critic, for example, said the painting "surpassed, both in tenderness and *grandeur* of expression, either *The Rocky Mountains* or *Mount Hood*. To this 'Storm in the Rocky Mountains' may aptly be applied the epithet sublime."[22] Grand it may be—but tender? And surely neither Byers—the artist's guide to Idaho Springs, where studies for the painting were made—nor anyone else, then or now, would or could identify the locale with anything in Colorado, the Rocky Mountains, or, indeed, anywhere on earth.

One of the artist's large Yosemite paintings was offered in 1866 as second prize in the Crosby Opera House lottery. The opera house itself, in Chicago, was first prize; Bierstadt's painting, second; and a large Cropsey, third. The winning numbers were drawn on January 21, 1867, but the holders were not immediately known. The next day, however, their names were revealed. About thirty thousand tickets were unsold and remained in the hands of Crosby himself. "By a singular chance," *The Rocky Mountain News* reported, "numbers included in Crosby's group drew the second, third and ninth prizes."[23] There was a furor, but nothing was done.

Late in 1866, the first of Bierstadt's numerous government projects loomed. It is possible that a meeting he had with Schuyler Colfax, later Grant's notorious vice-president, early in the year, was related to this project. In any case, by the end of the year it was already before the House of Representatives' Committee on the Library, and Bierstadt wrote of his plans. He would do his best to paint something "that would be if possible an ornament to the Capitol and an honor to himself."[24] The panels were to be for the chamber of the House, and the artist thought one should be of the Rocky Mountains and the other of Yosemite. "Strictly American," though, and for the job he would like $40,000 but would not refuse $30,000 cash. Some of the committee thought that perhaps an important event in American history might be depicted. *The Rocky Mountain News* reported on February 13 that the deal was sealed, but a month later the bottom fell out. The committee decided:

> That the Librarian be instructed to inform Mr. Bierstadt that no appropriation having been made to carry out the purpose of the House resolution respecting the panels in their Hall the Committee deemed it inexpedient in the present state of our finances to recommend an appropriation for the object in question.[25]

Undaunted by the reservations about *Storm in the Rocky Mountains,* Bierstadt must have gone immediately to work on a bigger, though more realistic western painting. *The Domes of the Yosemite* (Fig. 122) was the result, and it was nine-and-a-half feet high by fifteen feet long—the second largest canvas the artist ever painted. It was done on commission for a reputed $25,000 for Legrand Lockwood, who was building a magnificent mansion in Norwalk, Connecticut, and wanted a painting of this size for the rotunda (Fig. 119).

119. *The Domes of the Yosemite* (left) in the rotunda of the Lockwood Mansion, Norwalk, Connecticut. 19th-century photograph

120. *The Domes of the Yosemite* in the Saint Johnsbury Athenaeum, Saint Johnsbury, Vermont. 19th-century photograph. Collection Mrs. Orville DeForest Edwards, Dobbs Ferry, New York

161

121. Chromolithograph after *The Domes of the Yosemite*. c.1868.
21 × 32″ (53.3 × 81.3 cm.). Amon Carter Museum of Western Art,
Fort Worth, Texas

122. *The Domes of the Yosemite*. 1867.
Oil on canvas, 116 × 180″ (294.6 × 502.9 cm.).
Saint Johnsbury Athenaeum, Saint Johnsbury, Vermont

Lockwood's mansion, incidentally, saved from demolition by devoted local efforts, still stands.

In the midst of this, Frederick Church, about to send his *Niagara* to the Paris Universal Exposition, wanted the opinion of a man he thought knew more about it than anyone else. He wrote to Bierstadt:

> I am coming coming—I propose to go to New York about Wednesday next week and stay a day or two—and with your permission will use the big easel for one day to put the last touches on my Niagara . . . I want a criticism or two . . . so brush up your intellect and be ready to find all the fault you can. I am anxious to see it before I send it abroad in a new light, and under different circumstances.[26]

The Domes of the Yosemite went on exhibition in the Studio Building on West Tenth Street on April 26, 1867, for the benefit of the Ladies Southern Relief Association, for thirty cents a view. *The Tribune* thought it dreadful, "destitute of grandeur, commonplace" and the artist "under the delusion that the bigger the picture the finer it is."[27] *The Times* straddled the fence, finding the picture "attractive," and "the largest and most splendid" of the artist's western pictures. It inveighed, however, against the Düsseldorf method which Bierstadt could neither "unlearn" nor "forget." All his pictures—and this one was no exception—were superficial, "beautiful" but "destitute of sentiment."[28] *The Albion* had a somewhat parallel reaction, being impressed by the painting's grandeur but not taken with its depth of feeling. Again Düsseldorf comes in for blame:

> On first glancing at this picture, the observer is held by the absolute grandeur of the scene depicted, and it is only after repeated visits that the judgment can shake itself free from the bias naturally conveyed to it by this, and view the subject candidly in its bearings as an artistic composition. . . . We cannot aver that there is much of idealization, or what is called the poetry of nature, in this remarkable picture—for that it certainly is. The hard truth is given here, though, with wonderful skill—only it has too much of the hardness of the school in which the painter once studied.[29]

Some critics had warned the artist against his Düsseldorf influence for some time. As early as March, 1860, in a review of *The Base of the Rocky Mountains, Laramie Peak, The Crayon* had told its readers, "we should like to see less of the stereotyped Düsseldorf system of coloring." Other voices in 1867, however, were rhapsodic. A Philadelphia paper called *The Domes* "the best landscape ever painted in this country,"[30] and a New York paper predicted that the artist, now ascending the throne, would soon seat himself "as the monarch of landscape painters."[31]

The Domes of the Yosemite went later to Boston and then returned to Norwalk, where it was ensconced in a magnificent monogrammed frame in Lockwood's new house. Lockwood failed in the Panic of 1869, and after he died his widow sold his collection at auction in April, 1872. *The Domes* finally went to Saint Johnsbury, Vermont, to a museum presented to the town by Horace Fairbanks, the scales manufacturer. It is virtually true that the building was designed in large part for Bierstadt's painting (Fig. 120). The present-day visitor to the museum, the Saint Johnsbury Athenaeum, would do well to have his first glimpse of the painting at ten-thirty or eleven o'clock in the morning, when it is at its best. Such a visitor will find little of the Düsseldorf hardness lamented by the early critics.

This period of creativity was paralleled by a number of major events in the artist's personal life. In July, 1866, the artist lost his father, but in November of the same year, he gained a wife. Rosalie Osborne Ludlow, having at last divorced her first husband, married Bierstadt in Grace Episcopal Church, Waterville, New York, on November 21, 1866.

What young woman, caught in a difficult marriage to a disturbed and wayward husband such as Fitz Hugh Ludlow, could have resisted the prospect of a future with such a famous, wealthy man as Bierstadt? And with the whole town talking about *Storm in the Rocky Mountains*, whose central feature was "her" Mount Rosalie? It is also true that for all his secondary advantages, Bierstadt was a kind, generous, dignified, considerate, sensitive—and handsome—man.

Ludlow, on the other hand, had gone from bad to worse after he and Bierstadt returned from the West. In January, 1864, a cousin wrote that Ludlow was in "a very bad way, suffering from neuralgia."[32] A year later he "had sunk too low to be worth any consideration any more"[33] and was "an everlasting liar."[34] Soon he had put himself quite beyond the power of anyone but his

165

123. *Lawn at Malkasten* [correct title?]. Undated. Oil on paper, 12⅞ × 17½″ (32.8 × 44.4 cm.).
Wildenstein & Co., New York City

devoted sister Helen to tolerate him. He decamped for Saint Joseph, Missouri, with "his new lady, a Mrs. Ives," returned to New York and left his "affinity" in Kansas—all this at the expense of the lady's mother. "What the next scene in the drama will be needs no ghost to tell. There will be a new wedding sometime & somewhere, & you will have no invitation to it. . . . He occasionally writes to his father . . . pouring curses upon the head of poor Rose."[35] "He is a pretty fellow," his cousin Carrie wrote, "to be cursing poor Rose . . . if he had done as he should she never would have been so fond of the attentions of other men. I don't entirely excuse her, but I will stand up for her against him. I have no patience with him."[36] Then Ludlow went back to Kansas, summoned by his "affinity," brought her back East, then to Oswego where his father was pastor of a church. The family hoped Rosalie would not come up, for Fitz's immoralities would surely disgrace her. He stayed in Oswego, nursed by his sister. "What the miserable wicked F. would do no one could tell."[37] Ludlow's family's strictures even included his work. "Liquor & hasheesh & he are still intimate," his uncle wrote. "He sits up frequently all night writing his hack."[38]

In the fall of 1865 Ludlow went down to New York to take a water cure, first in Brooklyn and then in New York. These failed, and except for bare facts, we know little of his subsequent career. In December, 1867, he married a Maine widow. In June, 1870, he went to Switzerland for his health but died there in September. Today his mortal, tormented remains lie quietly on a hillside in the Rural Cemetery of Poughkeepsie, New York.

Perhaps it was the desire to establish Rosalie in a splendid setting—or the prospect of another summer's work in his hot, dark studio on Tenth Street—that convinced Bierstadt that he should build a home of his own. *Watson's Weekly Art Journal* gave the first report of these plans—and added a sarcastic comment about *Storm in the Rocky Mountains:* "The title of his next picture will be 'All Outdoors.'"[39]

The Home Journal, with characteristic floridness, described the artist's selection of the site near Sunnyside, Washington Irving's house, in Irvington on Hudson:

On a pleasant summer day . . . an artist, with sketch book in hand, was rambling among the hills that overlook the Hudson River, in the neighborhood of Tarrytown. Occasionally he would stop to survey the scene before him, and sometimes, with rapid pencil, would transfer the view to his note-book. . . . It was quite evident, judging from the careful scrutiny he bestowed, not only upon the distant landscape, but on his immediate surroundings, that something more than the simple desire to sketch the scenery about him had brought him among the hills of Westchester county that beautiful summer day.

In good sooth, he had a more important object in view than the making of a study for a picture. He was, in miner's parlance, prospecting for an eligible site on which to erect a house wherein to set up his Lares and Penates, as he sat gazing upon the scene before him, and listening to the caroling of the birds . . . a sudden hush fell upon the singers; and looking up to discover if possible the cause, he saw, wheeling in wide circles, high up in the air, a single hawk. Nearer and nearer it drew toward the earth, and, finally, settled upon the naked limb of a lightning-scathed pine tree, a few rods above him on the hillside. The artist watched him for some time, while the bird plumed his feathers, and gazed sharply about him. . . . With a single stroke of his strong wings, that sent him a hundred feet into the heavens, he soared away and soon was a mere speck in the blue azure. After watching him until he disappeared the artist turned to gaze on the scene before him, and as he realized its magnificence, we can imagine he thought, if he did not utter it, the exclamation of Archimedes of old: Eureka—I have found it![40]

The house Bierstadt built on the spot was one of the most "commanding and noticeable" on the Hudson, *The Home Journal* went on. It was of granite and wood, three stories high, with a tower rising another story (Figs. 124 and 125). The studio was seventy feet long, thirty feet wide, and thirty feet high—reduced from forty because of heating problems. These dimensions are *The Home Journal*'s: a later account in *The Art Journal* said that the seventy-foot length was achieved by throwing the studio and library together (Figs. 127–129). The doors between were hung with portieres of "Algerian stuff."[41] It was built on the side of a hill, and a visitor could step onto ground from every story. A billiard room, dining room, kitchen, butler's pantry, and laundry were on the first floor, and library, bedrooms, and baths filled the remainder of the house. Bierstadt's

124. Malkasten, Bierstadt's home in Irvington on Hudson, New York. 19th-century engraving. Collection Mrs. Orville DeForest Edwards, Dobbs Ferry, New York

125. Malkasten, Bierstadt's home in Irvington on Hudson, New York, with the artist at work on the lawn. Engraving from Martha Lamb, *Homes of America*, 1879

126. *Malkasten Lawn with Figures.* c.1866? Oil on canvas, 13¼ × 18″ (33.7 × 45.7 cm.). Collection Mrs. Peter McBean, Hillsborough, California. A view of the Hudson River from Malkasten

127, 128, 129. Interiors of Malkasten. 1866–71?
Stereographs by Charles Bierstadt.
Collection Mrs. Orville DeForest Edwards,
Dobbs Ferry, New York

130. *Sunset Glow.* Undated. Oil on canvas, 26 × 36" (66 × 91.4 cm.).
Philbrook Art Center, Tulsa. Possibly a view of the Hudson River

bedroom was over the library and had a sliding door leading to the gallery over the studio, "admitting the occupant, with true Venetian stillness, into the splendours of the room below."[42] Mrs. Bierstadt's room was also on this floor, "exquisitely furnished," filled with furbelows, bric-a-brac, and objets d'art from top to bottom and side to side. In short, all that "one would expect the wife of a fine artist to possess and appreciate."[43] Off the mistress of the house's room was a gallery five or six feet wide and thirty feet long, called, according to the "fair maiden" who showed it to the Home Journal reporter, "Flirtation Gallery." This "fair maiden" may have been Mrs. Bierstadt's sister Esther. Let us hope it was not Mrs. Bierstadt, for though "a small white hand" was present, the writer "did not attempt to take it. Had he been younger and less married than he was, there is no telling what he might have sought to do."[44]

Outside were verandas, piazzas, stables, carriage houses, an icehouse, everything set among trees, bushes, gardens, and lawn. It was only a mile to the railroad station at Irvington, down a private road with an easy grade, built in cooperation with the artist's neighbors. From the drawing room windows, it was said, one could see West Point on one side and New York itself on the other. (If this latter was ever possible, it is not today—even without smog.) Bierstadt painted a number of small sketches showing the environs of the house (Figs. 123 and 126), but only one that I have found, possibly a view across the Hudson, can be ranked as a "fully realized" painting (Fig. 130). Another such view, smaller in size, was shown at the Soldiers and Sailors benefit exhibition in New York late in 1870; it was a view, the artist wrote to a neighbor, "across the Hudson from your hill or mine."[45] The site is a little way up the hill and south from the Gould mansion, Lyndhurst. It is so overgrown with vegetation today that one can scarcely see the Hudson—let alone anything across it. Although the house was called Hawksrest when the Home Journal reporter visited it, it soon became known as Malkasten, after the artists' club of the old Düsseldorf days.

Bierstadt was ecstatic over his new life with Rosalie: "My only regret is," he wrote a month after their wedding, "that I did not know my wife when I was twelve years old, and could have married her then. I am the happiest man living."[46] Besides a new house, Rosalie got a princely wedding trip. In June of 1867 the couple sailed on a two-year trip to Europe.

NOTES: 1 *The Art Journal* (London), October 1859.

2 Undated, but obviously March 1864, clipping, collection Mrs. Orville DeForest Edwards, Dobbs Ferry, New York.

3 *The New York Herald*, April 15, 1864.

4 At this time the United States Sanitary Commission was established. Under its sponsorship various Sanitary Fairs were held throughout the country. It was the purpose of these fairs to raise money to help take care of the Civil War wounded: little else could be done for them besides keeping them "sanitary."

5 Undated, but obviously March 1864, clipping, collection Mrs. Orville DeForest Edwards, Dobbs Ferry, New York.

6 James Jackson Jarves, *The Art Idea* (New York: Hurd and Houghton, 1864), p. 233ff.

7 Undated, but obviously March 1864, clipping, collection Mrs. Orville DeForest Edwards, Dobbs Ferry, New York.

8 *The New York Herald*, April 5, 1864.

9 *The New York Times*, April 6, 1864.

10 *The New York Tribune*, April 16, 1864.

11 Bancroft to Bierstadt, March 21, 1864, and May 9, 1865, Henry Francis du Pont Winterthur Museum, Winterthur, Delaware.

12 *Spirit of the Fair*, April 23, 1864, in the New York Public Library.

13 The price of this painting, as well as its buyer, has been misstated. A correspondent of the Utica, New York, *Morning Herald* wrote that a Mr. Russell had bought it (November 11, 1865). The same writer confirms that the price was $25,000. This is the sum *The Post* (October 11, 1865) and *Watson's Weekly Art Journal* (October 28, 1865) gave.

14 *The New Path*, April 1864.

15 *Ibid.*

16 *The New York Evening Post*, May 24, 1864.

17 *Ibid.*, June 6 and June 21, 1864.

18 Bierstadt to Oscar Albert Bierstadt, June 7, 1864, private collection.

19 Frémont to Bierstadt, April 8, 1865, Henry Francis du Pont Winterthur Museum, Winterthur, Delaware. Bierstadt's Golden Gate paintings are a complex study. Beneath the Emanuel Leutze painting in the Capitol in Washington, *Westward the Course of Empire Takes Its Way*, there is a long panorama called *The Golden Gate*. It has been said that it is Bierstadt's, at least in part, and that Leutze, not knowing how the Golden Gate looked, asked his friend Bierstadt to paint the sky. But the painting was acquired in 1862, before Bierstadt saw the Golden Gate, and

thus cannot be his. The *Golden Gate* that Frémont bought in 1865 for $4,000 (and later sold, when he got hard up, for the same price) was sold at a Kende Galleries auction in New York in 1945. It was 41 1/2 x 65 1/2″, and signed and dated 1865 at the lower right. It is now unlocated. In a later, patronizing—and inaccurate—account it was said that the artist's easel for this work was set up in front of the Frémont house in Oakland, and that it was "quite a sunset and the foreground is embellished with a Greek temple or two" (Ruth Gillette Hardy, "A Mountain Traveler," *Appalachia*, June 1950, p. 63ff). The easel was set up at Black Point, not in Oakland, and there are no temples of any sort, Greek or otherwise, in the painting. A second Bierstadt *Golden Gate* was painted in 1898. This was 38 x 61″ and was signed at lower right with the artist's customary "A Bierstadt," with the initials in monogram. This is the painting shown in Worcester in 1901 (see Chapter 12). It is also unlocated.

20 *Watson's Weekly Art Journal*, May 20, 1865.

21 *Ibid.*, March 3, 1866.

22 Undated clipping, collection Mrs. Orville DeForest Edwards, Dobbs Ferry, New York.

23 *The Rocky Mountain News*, January 31, 1867.

24 Bierstadt to "Adams," December 17, 1866, New York Public Library.

25 Charles E. Fairman, *Art and Artists of the Capitol of the United States of America* (Washington: U.S. Government Printing Office, 1927), p. 270.

26 Church to Bierstadt, March 1, 1867, Museum of Fine Arts, Boston.

27 *The New York Tribune*, May 11, 1867.

28 *The New York Times*, May 2, 1867.

29 *The Albion*, May 11, 1867.

30 1867 clipping, collection Mrs. Orville DeForest Edwards, Dobbs Ferry, New York.

31 *Ibid.* For a further discussion of Bierstadt's *Domes*—and his Irvington house—see Gordon Hendricks, "Bierstadt's *The Domes of the Yosemite*," *The American Art Journal*, Vol. III, no. 2 (Fall 1971), p. 23ff.

32 Unidentified cousin of Ludlow to her aunt, January 8, 1864, Ludlow Papers, New York State Historical Association Library, Cooperstown.

33 Carrie Ludlow to her mother, January 8, 1865, Ludlow Papers, *loc. cit.*

34 *Ibid.*

35 Ellen Ludlow to unidentified aunt, Ludlow Papers, *loc. cit.*

36 Carrie Ludlow to her mother, April 9, 1865, Ludlow Papers, *loc. cit.*

37 Samuel Ludlow to his sister, May 11, 1865, Ludlow Papers, *loc. cit.*

38 *Ibid.*, May 30, 1865, Ludlow Papers, *loc. cit.*

39   *Watson's Weekly Art Journal*, October 28, 1865.

40   "Hawksrest, The Residence of Albert Bierstadt" (a *Home Journal* article dated 1871 by the keeper of the clippings album in the collection of Mrs. Orville DeForest Edwards, Dobbs Ferry, New York) raises interesting problems in chronology. The writer, Barry Gray, based his material on a few days spent with the artist "in strawberry-time, not many months ago." He also described a painting then on the easel—"a landscape in California, near the line of the Pacific Railroad. The point of view is from near the summit of a mountain . . . Donner Lake . . . five or six thousand feet below." Assuming "strawberry-time" to be the summer of 1871, the artist's *Donner Lake from the Summit*, which is evidently described, was in progress then. But the very earliest date for a beginning on *Donner Lake* would have been the fall of 1871, after the artist had visited the site with C. P. Huntington, who commissioned the painting, and after he got back to Irvington, either for his visit in the fall of 1871 or at the end of 1873, when he returned to stay.

41   *The Art Journal*, 1876, p. 45.

42   *Ibid.*

43   Barry Gray, "Hawksrest, The Home of Albert Bierstadt," *The Home Journal*, 1871, *loc. cit.*

44   *Ibid.*

45   Bierstadt to unknown addressee, December 29, 1870, Historical Society of Pennsylvania, Philadelphia.

46   Bierstadt to "Adams," December 17, 1866, New York Public Library.

Eight

Europe
Critical Dissents   1867-1871

131. Bierstadt at about thirty-seven. c.1867.
Carte de visite by Napoleon Sarony, New York City.
The New York Public Library, New York City

132. Mrs. Albert Bierstadt in presentation gown.
Collection Mrs. Orville DeForest Edwards, Dobbs Ferry,
New York

WHEN THE BIERSTADTS SAILED on June 22, 1867, for two years' stay among the more luxurious of Europe's fleshpots, the dissent against the bigness and what was thought to be the pretentiousness of the artist's canvases had become general. "Bierstadt has gone to Europe," *Watson's* reported. "It is to be hoped that while there he will learn to reform his style, and be taught that merit consists in quality rather than quantity."[1] It is difficult to believe, however, that had any of his critics been painters themselves and faced with the demands with which Bierstadt was faced, they would have behaved any differently. His customers, who usually had great houses with great walls, wanted great paintings. And these they paid for with great prices. These prices had enabled the artist to live in a style to which few of his detractors were accustomed.

The Bierstadts' first stop was London, as it probably had been for the artist fourteen years before, on his way to Düsseldorf. This time, however, the residence was the Langham Hotel, one of the most luxurious in the city. During this visit, or later on the same trip, they visited the James McHenrys, who had bought *The Rocky Mountains*, and went to the theater with them to see Henry Irving. They were also house guests of Lord Campbell, a son of the duke of Argyll and brother-in-law of Princess Louise, daughter of Victoria. Before the year was out, they had met Victoria herself, and Bierstadt gave an autographed print of his *Rocky Mountains* to the chamberlain who had attended to the exquisite details. Two of his pictures had been sent down to the Isle of Wight for Her Majesty, *The Rocky Mountains* and *Storm in the Rocky Mountains*, where they were "admired immensely."[2] *Storm in the Rocky Mountains* was said to have been sold in Paris for $20,000 to Sir Morton Peto.[3] *The Rocky Mountain News* soon made this $40,000.[4] The artist and his wife were to remain friends of Princess Louise and her husband, first the marquis of Lorne and then, at his father's death, the duke of Argyll, for the rest of their lives (Figs. 133 and 134).

Visits to Paris, Rome, Munich, Dresden, Berlin, Vienna, Switzerland, followed the first London visit. Exactly when these took place is a mystery. Mrs. Bierstadt kept diaries, but these have been lost, and the historian must depend on the discursive letters of an elderly niece and a scrapbook containing hundreds of clippings—virtually innocent of dates.

In Rome they visited Liszt. Rosalie, with some literary pretentions—she was, for at least one issue, the New York correspondent of the Waterville *Times*—and considerable self-confidence and even pertness, took on "a certain English Lord"

179

133. Princess Louise, daughter of Queen Victoria

134. The marquis of Lorne, later the duke of Argyll, Princess Louise's husband

Figs. 133, 134: Collection Esther R. Bascom, Rosalie R. Rooks, Joyce R. Edwards, and Pauline R. Perry

who held that the Erard, a European piano, was the best in the world. Rosalie flung herself into the fray in defense of the American Chickering, "and you can fancy how delighted I was when Liszt, himself, came to my assistance, confirming all I had said by pointing to a magnificent Chickering Grand, standing invitingly at the end of his fine Salon."[5]

Of course the master played for them, and of course for only an intimate group of four, after the others had left—"Polish Counts and Countesses, Russian Nobles, German Barons without number, Italians of all ranks . . . Spanish artists and Ambassadors, English Lords, Americans and a French Marquis." It was twilight, "just the hour when music most enthralls." Liszt was "no longer man but the Master." Rosalie thought, even as he played, that he looked like George Washington.

He gave us first a little Caprice in Waltz time by his son-in-law Von Bulow; then something of his own. A composition illustrating certain phases in the life of St. Francis,—his hopes, his fears,—his mortal agony, his final release and transport,—a work requiring great feeling and great energy of execution; a favorite theme but one that he never renders, he told us, unless he feels he has sympathetic listeners. . . . This idea of putting the life of a Priest into the Chiarascuro of music,

180

reminds me of the experiences of Gottschalk. The latter averred that he perceived music through every sense.

(Mrs. Bierstadt had heard Gottschalk play when she was Mrs. Fitz Hugh Ludlow and had gone backstage for a tête-à-tête with the famous musician.)

After their visit to Liszt, the Bierstadts visited Hiram Powers's studio near Florence, and again, seeing the bust of Liszt, Rosalie thought the pianist looked like Washington. In Vienna they heard the three Strauss brothers in "an evening long to be remembered." In Switzerland, Bierstadt sketched the Jungfrau and made "almost fifty splendid studies."[6] All this—Rome, Florence, Munich, Dresden, Berlin, Vienna—was in 1867.

In Switzerland the two travelers attracted the attention of a correspondent of one of the undated newspapers in the clippings album kept by Mrs. Bierstadt's relatives:

I found myself sitting beside a charming young person at a table d'hôte at Grindelwald. So delicate, graceful and at once easy and natural, there was no mistaking her to be American though who she was or the happy man who sat on the other side of her, I knew no more than the man in the moon. "What could you be saying to that pretty woman at dinner to make her blush so?" asked, somewhat reproachfully, a female friend who sat opposite, in a tone as though I had done something to compromise myself or my good manners. "Ah! my dear madam," I replied "I have had the happiness to impart the purest gratification by the most unconscious praise, and find that I have just been telling Mrs. Bi-----dt, without being the least aware of it that the Rocky Mountains was the noblest portraiture of the sublimities of nature ever transferred to canvass and glory of the fine arts department of the greatest universal exposition the world has seen. It was even so; and just as I had finished my encomium, the lady to whom it was so appropriately, but wholly unconsciously addressed, had turned round and, blushing like a bride, had said simply: "The picture was painted by my husband," and presented me to Mr. Bi-----dt, who sat beside her. The great American artist, with indefatigable energy, has been covering yards of canvass with exquisite souvenirs of Swiss scenery travel and after ascending the Faulborn, the last time I heard of him, was seated, brush in hand, in

181

front of the Devil's Bridge on the St. Gothard. But everywhere in Switzerland this year the name and fame of America has been predominant.[7]

In 1867, Bierstadt was awarded the Legion of Honor, and a presentation at the court of Napoleon III was planned. But the presentation was put off because of the death of Maximilian on a hillside in far-off Querétaro, where he had been sent—and abandoned—by Napoleon. Later, in 1869, with Bierstadt's sister Eliza with them in Paris, the two ladies and the artist met the rulers of France. "The Emperor looks old and care worn but the Empress is very beautiful—and such perfect grace and elegance I never beheld in anyone. Her jewels consisting mostly of diamonds were in such profusion as to almost dazzle one."[8]

While in Rome in 1867, Bierstadt rented a studio and produced three or more pictures—a Sierra Nevada view and *A Storm in the Andes* among them. The first, *The Sierra Nevada in California*, was shown in Berlin at the Royal Academy's 46th exhibition, where it asserted "a noble presence among its compeers."[9] Either could have been a Yosemite or Rocky Mountain view: European ideas of American geography were vague. The Rome pictures then came to London, where they were shown at the artist's own Langham Hotel. They were on their way, a reporter "greatly feared," to New York.

In London, early in 1868, the artist painted a *Vesuvius*, of which only a study—or copy—is known, now in the Cleveland Museum where it is called *Mount Aetna* (Fig. 135). *Vesuvius* was shown at Putnam's Gallery in New York late in the year. It then traveled down to Philadelphia for a run at Earle's Gallery. *Arthur's Home Magazine* reported that the eruption depicted in the painting had occurred during the nights of January 4 and 5, 1868, when the artist was in London. Thus his work was from imagination, which may partly account for the fact that it is one of his less successful pictures.

The highlight of 1868 for the Bierstadts must have been the dinner they gave at the Langham on July 9 in honor of Henry Wadsworth Longfellow, who was in England to receive an honorary degree from Cambridge. The guests arrived at nine and did not leave until twelve. They were regaled with an elaborate menu of fish, game, veal, and chicken; artichokes and corn; and, as a compliment to the English guests, a George IV pudding. These guests included a number of members of Parliament, besides Robert Browning, Edwin

135. *Mount Aetna* [*Vesuvius*]. 1868. Oil on canvas, 17⅛ × 24″ (43.5 × 60.9 cm.).
The Cleveland Museum of Art. Gift of S. Livingstone Mather, Philip Richard Mather,
Katherine Hoyt (Mather) Cross, Katherine Mather McLean, and Constance Mather Bishop

San Francisco Dec 29th 1872.

Dear Mr Bordein.

I have just returned from the mountains and find an agreeable surprise awaiting me in the form of a letter from your Ambassador at Washington containing the announcement that His Majesty the Russian Emperor has conferred upon me the Order

136. Letterhead with Bierstadt's monogram "bee."
Henry Francis du Pont Winterthur Museum, Winterthur, Delaware.
Downs Manuscript Collection (No. 69 × 53a)

Landseer, the duke of Argyll, and Gladstone himself. Gladstone was persuaded to make a short speech, much to the distress of the guest of honor, who had asked that there be none. But the floodgates were opened, and there were speeches by Longfellow, the duke of Argyll (who proposed toasts to two American guests, who in turn gave speeches of thanks), and a clergyman, who proposed the health of Bierstadt. Bierstadt acknowledged the compliment "in one word . . . and the company immediately afterwards retired."[10] Notable Americans present were Cyrus Field, Admiral Farragut, Moran (the American chargé d'affaires who had arranged the Victoria interview), Charles Mackay, and Parke Godwin. During the evening there was music, Mrs. Bierstadt and other ladies presented themselves, and the guest of honor was given a small oil by Bierstadt, *Departure of Hiawatha.* At the top of the souvenir menu was Bierstadt's new monogram (Fig. 136).

Early the next year the artist was keeping a studio in Paris and made the acquaintance of William Riggs, brother of the American financier W. W. Corcoran's partner. He advised Riggs to sell any French gas stock he might have as "the present high price of Paris gas stock is unwarrantable, and . . . a few weeks will find it 3 to 400 francs less per share."[11]

In Paris he heard no less a distinguished critic than Théophile Gautier praise his *Storm in the Rocky Mountains:*

Albert Bierstadt is an American landscape painter who enjoys a high reputation in the New World, and one which he deserves, for he has much talent, as his "Storm in the Rocky Mountain" [sic] shows. The size of his canvas is decidedly beyond that which landscape painting generally employs, and we think that the artist has done well to adopt such large dimensions, having to express a nature so gigantic. Objects reduced to too small a scale lose their interest in their microscopic diminutiveness, and cannot be comprehended. . . . This picture, which initiates us into a new nature, besides the merit of representing scenery whose character is unknown to us, possesses that of being painted with great skill, and in a manner which recalls the handling of Calame, a painter who was not sufficiently appreciated in France, and who knew how to give Alpine scenes better than all others. Bierstadt may be proud of the resemblance.[12]

184

137. *Niagara Falls.* Undated. Oil on canvas, 19 × 27⅛″ (48.3 × 68.9 cm.).
The National Gallery of Canada, Ottawa

138. *Storm in the Mountains*. Undated.
Oil on canvas, 38 × 60″ (96.5 × 152.4 cm.).
Museum of Fine Arts, Boston. M. and M. Karolik Collection.
This has been called a scene of the Grosser Wachtman,
near Berchtesgaden

The artist was back in London by May 2, in time to hear Sir Francis Grant, President of the Royal Academy of Arts, praise the new Sierra Nevada picture as "one of the finest landscapes that adorn our walls."[13]

Before he returned to America, Bierstadt made a trip to Spain, arriving in Madrid on May 22. His party then traveled to Seville, Málaga, Granada, Valencia (where the artist bought black silk and peasant *mantos*), Barcelona, Gerona, over the Pyrenees to Perpignan, Toulouse, and back to Paris and London.

The previous year his eyesight began to fail him, but after a short rest it improved. Evidently, however, he still was not entirely well. Shortly before his return to America, he asked a friend to escort his wife and sister Eliza, who had joined them, to the London Zoo on a Sunday afternoon in July. "I am not very well and must remain quiet the Dr says."[14]

Back in the United States in 1869, the Bierstadts hurried off to Niagara Falls with Mrs. Bierstadt's sister Esther. There they visited brother Charles and sister Helen, who had married a New Bedford whaling master, Edwin P. Thompson. They were joined by Sir Morton Peto's son Herbert for a trip down the Saint Lawrence River to Montreal and thence to the White Mountains and the Glen House for a six weeks' stay. While in Niagara, Bierstadt may have produced a newly discovered view of the falls, which has a feeling of reality (Fig. 137). They were the last ones besides the staff to leave the Glen House. They then traveled to Boston, where they visited Alvin Adams of the Adams Express Company, who bought a painting for $25,000. In Boston they also visited the Thomas Bailey Aldriches, Longfellow, and Thomas Appleton, Longfellow's brother-in-law. Appleton had a beautiful house, Esther remembered, "and although a bachelor seemed very happy."[15]

While the artist and his relatives were cavorting about Canada and New Hampshire, one of his large pictures of the West—which one is still uncertain[16]—was burned in a fire at Earle's Gallery in Philadelphia. It was valued at $15,000, *The Philadelphia Press* reported, but "many would have valued it far beyond even that sum."[17] Another western picture, painted in Europe and called *Sunrise: Wind River Mountains,* was exhibited in the artist's studio in October. "Although not so large as some of the artist's former efforts," *The New York Evening Post* commented, "[it] is quite as commendable for its color and qualities."[18] *Vesuvius,* meanwhile, on its way to oblivion, was touring the country,

188

(*left*) 139. Painting misattributed to Bierstadt, after engraving of Thomas Moran's *The Upper Yellowstone Falls*

140. Engraving after Thomas Moran's *The Upper Yellowstone Falls*, from *Picturesque America*, 1873

and after a stay in Chicago was taken to Milwaukee. There it was shown "for the purpose of testing the appreciation of our community."[19] By now, also, *Storm in the Rocky Mountains* had been chromolithographed (Fig. 117).

Early in the new year the artist was asked to join the group that was organizing the Metropolitan Museum of Art. He declined the honor. The company was distinguished, so it may have been because he was too busy.

On February 7, 1870, the Leeds and Miner Galleries in New York auctioned the collection of the late Thomas Thompson, and Bierstadt was subjected to a public scandal. Thompson was an early patron of the artist, and *The Post* reported that there were forty-one Bierstadts in the group, including watercolors, monochromes, and crayon drawings. *The New York Sun* thought they were dreadful:

Among the forty-one contributed by Bierstadt there is not one which will repay a glance. They are not only among the worst, but they are the very worst of the collection. Nothing will tend to enrich the memory of Mr. Thompson so much as the constant kindness and patronage he showered upon this artist in the days of his obscurity. He must have been a penetrating observer to have discovered any talent in the artist, for no one, judging from the works exhibited, can discover one spark of

189

141. *The Coming Storm.* 1869. Oil on panel, 9½ × 13″ (24.2 × 33 cm.).
Addison Gallery of American Art, Phillips Academy, Andover, Massachusetts

142. *Black Hills, Colorado.* Undated. Oil on paper mounted on board, 14 × 19″ (35.6 × 48.2 cm.).
Thomas Gilcrease Institute, Tulsa

143. *The Storm.* 1870. Oil on canvas, 52½ × 82″ (133.4 × 208.3 cm.).
Collection Mr. and Mrs. Philip R. Herzig, New York City

capacity even of the most moderate kind. We would advise ambitious painters now struggling with obscurity to purchase one of these (they will sell for three or four dollars a piece) and to hang it up in the studio with the motto underneath, "Anch'io sono pittore." ["Even I am a painter."][20]

The Tribune had quoted Bierstadt as saying the collection would cost a half million if it had to be gotten together at the present time. Now, with many disparaging remarks being made about his work, the artist denied that he had said the collection was worth half a million and added that many of the works attributed by Thompson to himself were not actually Bierstadts. Many thought he disavowed the works because he thought his reputation might suffer unless he did. In a note to The Tribune he wrote:

> Not long since, a distinguished banker invited me to his home to inspect a picture bought at one of these auction sales, for one of mine. He had to have his doubts about it being genuine as it did not bear my signature—I need hardly say that I saw it for the first time on his walls.[21]

The Telegram felt "unfeigned regret" that so great an artist as Bierstadt should compromise himself in this way. "Anyone who had carefully read his letter . . . would have seen that he did not dare positively to deny them, although he endeavoured to make their authenticity questionable."[22] Bierstadt nevertheless withdrew a number of the paintings from the auction, which had not yet taken place. This brought forth the following damning comment from The Brooklyn Daily Eagle:

> That an artist can labor lovingly and patiently upon a canvas and strangely forget the work of his hands is, however, a proposition involving something more than modesty which becomingly adorns merit. It will seem passing strange . . . that [the dealers] have bills showing the precise sums charged by Bierstadt for the rejected paintings. . . . Artists who are subject to periods of absentmindedness would do well to mark their productions, like linen for the laundry, so that they may be identified beyond a doubt.[23]

144. *Buffalo.* 1870. Oil on canvas, 26 × 36″ (66.1 × 91.4 cm.). M. Knoedler & Co., New York City

145. *Sierra Nevada Morning*. 1870. Oil on canvas, 56 × 84″ (142.2 × 213.5 cm.). Thomas Gilcrease Institute, Tulsa

If what *The Eagle* said was true, then the best that can be said for the artist's action in disclaiming such works is that it was misguided; the worst, that it was dishonest. No artist need be ashamed of early, unsophisticated works. Bierstadt's action seems almost desperate, as though he had had enough of disparaging remarks from the critics and had decided to escape more.

Meanwhile, Bierstadt's brothers were busy with their own ventures. In the spring of 1870, Charles was in California and in the Yosemite; and Edward had embarked on the promotion of the albertype, a new photographic reproduction process. The albertype was not, as some have said, an invention of Edward's brother Albert, and thus named after him, but a European invention.[24] William Riggs, the Paris acquaintance, became interested in the process, and Albert tried to help his brother promote that venture. Letters late in the year and early in the next to an unidentified general urging his help in getting the process into use by various government departments are in the Manuscript Division of the Library of Congress. The artist went to Washington, selected sample maps from the Interior Department files, and took them back to New York for trial. A letter on April 5, 1871, from the Smithsonian suggests that the samples had not yet been returned, and that more than one government office was interested in using the process. Possibly the project was now turned over to brother Edward, for no more clearly relevant correspondence can be found.

The artist had hoped to make another trip to California in the summer of 1870; "although a pleasure [to stay in Irvington] I think I should enjoy much more the Yosemite."[25] He spent the time painting, either in Irvington or in a studio in the Tenth Street building which he shared, evidently for this year only, with William Page. A painting of a buffalo resulted (Fig. 144), but his principal work for this season was a canvas of the famous Emerald Pool in the White Mountains, one of his few paintings of eastern subjects (Fig. 147). It was produced from studies—two hundred, he was to tell the *San Francisco Alta* reporter—he had made the previous fall while at the Glen House and thereabouts. When it was finished, he sent it to Boston for exhibition, and at the beginning of the new year, to Earle's in Philadelphia. "I never had so difficult a picture to paint," he wrote a Boston friend, "as this White Mountains subject the Emerald pool," and added, "my artist friends think it my best picture and so do I"[26]—which sounds like whistling to keep up his courage.

146. *White Mountains, New Hampshire.* Undated. Oil on paper, 11 × 15″ (27.9 × 38.1 cm.). Thomas Gilcrease Institute, Tulsa

147. *The Emerald Pool.* 1870.
Oil on canvas, 76½ × 119¾″ (194.3 × 304.3 cm.).
Collection Huntington Hartford, New York City

More business in Washington, possibly having to do with the albertype promotion, and a stay in Waterville, helping his wife get ready for the long stay in California that was about to begin, occupied the artist's time until he was ready to step aboard the new overland flyer for San Francisco about July 14, 1871.

NOTES: 1   *Watson's Weekly Art Journal,* volume for 1867, p. 167.

2   Rosalie Osborne Mayer (Rosalie Bierstadt's niece) to Mrs. Ross Taggart, June 21, 1947, Museum of Fine Arts, Boston.

3   *Zeitschrift für Bildende Kunst,* 1870, p. 73.

4   *The Rocky Mountain News,* February 13, 1868.

5   This and the following are quotations from Rosalie's unlocated diaries or other writings preserved by Rosalie Osborne Mayer, collection Mrs. Orville DeForest Edwards, Dobbs Ferry, New York.

6   Rosalie Osborne Mayer to Mrs. Ross Taggart, June 21, 1947, Museum of Fine Arts, Boston.

7   Although unidentified, evidently from *The Newark Advertiser,* collection Mrs. Orville DeForest Edwards, Dobbs Ferry, New York.

8   Rosalie Osborne Mayer to Mrs. Ross Taggart, August 3, 1947, Museum of Fine Arts, Boston.

9   *The Art Journal* (London), August 1868.

10   Clipping of July 10, 1868, collection Mrs. Orville DeForest Edwards, Dobbs Ferry, New York.

11   Bierstadt to Riggs, March 8, 1869, Manuscript Division, Library of Congress, Washington, D.C.

12   *The San Francisco Alta,* August 8, 1869.

13   May 3, 1869, clipping, collection Mrs. Orville DeForest Edwards, Dobbs Ferry, New York.

14   Bierstadt to "My dear General," July 1869, Archives of American Art, New York City.

15   Handwritten reminiscences by Esther (this one was recalled in 1896), collection Mrs. Orville DeForest Edwards, Dobbs Ferry, New York. Herbert Peto and Esther were engaged for three weeks. He was a handsome man, Esther wrote, but "oh, so heavy and dull."

16   At first *The Rocky Mountain News* reported that the picture burned was a large Yosemite view; then, a few days later, it corrected itself and said it was *Storm in the Rocky Mountains.* The Philadelphia papers said it was a large Yosemite view but did not otherwise identify it.

17   *The Philadelphia Press,* September 2, 1869.

18   This item was quoted by *The Rocky Mountain News* on November 4, 1869, and was evidently the latest from New York.

19   *The Milwaukee Sentinel,* November 24, 1869.

20   *The New York Sun,* February 1, 1870.

21   *The New York Tribune,* January 29, 1870.

22   *The New York Telegram,* February 2, 1870.

23   *The Brooklyn Daily Eagle,* February 2, 1870.

24   The albertype was the first perfected collotype, and although based on the process of another, was named after Josef Albert (1825–1866), photographer to the Bavarian court. "Albertypes," it has been said, "show very fine half-tone" (Helmut and Alsion Gernshiem, *The History of Photography,* New York and London: Oxford University Press, 1955, p. 368). Very inexpensive prints, indistinguishable from photographs, could be obtained. Even at first, 200 prints could be made daily from one plate on a handprinting apparatus *(ibid.).* Bierstadt soon announced that 1,200 per hour could be made on his brother's new steam presses.

25   Bierstadt to "Russell," June 5, 1870, Manuscript Division, Library of Congress, Washington, D.C.

26   *Ibid.*

Nine

The Third Trip West

1871-1873

148. *The Overland Trail.* 1871? Oil on paper, 7 × 11″ (17.8 × 27.9 cm.). Collection Philip Anschutz, Denver

WHEN BIERSTADT AND LUDLOW had been in California eight years earlier, it took them several weeks of traveling to make the trip. Now, with the nation bound together coast-to-coast by the iron of the Central Pacific and Union Pacific railroads, the trip took six days. When travelers from the East arrived in Ogden, Utah, the telegraph announced their impending arrival to San Francisco, and *The San Francisco Alta* reported on July 20 that "Albert Burdstadt and Mrs. A. Burdstadt and servant" had passed through Ogden on the eighteenth. On July 21, the same paper reported their arrival at the Grand Hotel in San Francisco. "William A. Bierstadt, the great artist," was the way they spelled the name then.

With the artist, or arriving about the same time, came *The Emerald Pool* from Philadelphia. It was soon put on exhibition at the newly redecorated Snow and Roos Gallery on Kearney near Market Street. "The chief attraction, of course," *The Bulletin* reported, was Bierstadt's painting, which, "unlike some of Bierstadt's Pacific coast paintings . . . [was] not a composition from one or two hasty sketches, but an elaborately faithful transcript of an actual scene."[1] "We have seen no painting that came nearer our ideal of the best in landscape art, combining perfect truth with freedom, largeness and sentiment."[2]

The artist had scarcely arrived before he began to hurry about the state making sketches. By July 25, he was in the High Sierras east of Sacramento with C. P. Huntington, the crustiest of the Big Four who had built the Central Pacific from Sacramento to Utah. He was back in San Francisco four days later, after a visit to Lake Tahoe, and *The Alta* was "pleased to learn" that he planned to stay "for some weeks."[3] Little did they know that "some weeks" would be stretched to two years and three months.

From the beginning the artist, in his easy, friendly way, ingratiated himself with fellow workers as well as the local elite. He sketched a whale that had been beached at Fort Point for Charles Scammon, whose book on the marine mammals of the Northwest Coast was published in San Francisco the following year and soon became—and still is—the definitive work in its field. We do not know which or how many of the sketches of whales in Scammon's book are from Bierstadt's pencil, but we know that one or more are. The artist also quickly became involved with the affairs of the San Francisco Art Association. Many of his friends were members, and the membership included, as well, several art patrons. The artist was elected the Association's first honorary member on August 7, and was invited to contribute a picture or two to an exhibition. In his usual polite, uncondescending way, he expressed his regrets:

I have been hoping to make some arrangement by which your kind invitation could be accepted. Had I but known it earlier I should have been able to send my picture to your exhibition but I am afraid it is now too late. I have sent to the East however for a smaller work of mine which I hope will arrive in time to be placed there. I am sorry not to have seen you when you called, but shall do myself the honor of returning your visit soon.[4]

For some years, long after it was professionally important to do so, the artist loaned his paintings to the Association and as a result made many stout friendships among San Franciscans. One of them was William Alvord, who received a delightful little painting on August 15, which is still with us (Fig. 148).

On the same day he left for the mountains for more sketching. Back in the city to work up his sketches and savor San Francisco social life, he and his wife boarded a Central Pacific palace car in Oakland about September 17. *The Bulletin* announced his absence "for a few weeks" and at the same time told its readers that Leland Stanford had bought two paintings.[5]

He was going East to take care of a long-nourished project. Alexis, grand duke of Russia (Fig. 149), was planning a trip to America in October, and just before he left for California in July, Bierstadt had heard that Alexis wanted to see a buffalo hunt. What better person to know about such a wish than one of the most conspicuous Western specialists in the country? And what better person for Bierstadt to ask for help with the arrangements than General William Tecumseh Sherman, now commanding general of the army? The artist wrote Sherman:

I am off for the far west in a few days, and part of my object in writing you is to ask for the letters which you so kindly offered me, to the commanders of posts on the plains. You are doubtless aware that the Grand Duke Alexis of Russia is to be here in October, and I have learned that he is quite anxious of witnessing a *Buffalo Hunt*. As his visit partakes of a somewhat national character, would it not be well to give him one on a grand scale, with Indians included, as a rare piece of American hospitality?

206

If a large body of Indians could be brought together at that time, say the latter part of October, the performance of some of their dances and other ceremonials would be most interesting to our Russian guests. This would probably be the only way to give them a correct idea of *Red America*. Some of the best Indian hunters might go with the party on the buffalo hunt, to show the aboriginal style of "going for large game." The herd could be driven up at the proper time within reaching distance of the railroad.

It would add very much to the happiness and well being of our guests if you could find time to accompany them in person. In default of that it might accord with your views to delegate some officer of rank, as Sheridan for instance, in your place. This visit of the Grand Duke should be made a matter of no ordinary attention, as it has clearly a more important meaning than the mere pleasure trip of a Prince.

Very Sincerely Yours
Albert Bierstadt[6]

149. Grand Duke Alexis of Russia. 1871? Collection Esther R. Bascom, Rosalie R. Rooks, Joyce R. Edwards, and Pauline R. Perry

Taking no chances on Sherman, the artist wrote the secretary of war the same day about the same matter. The secretary replied that "there will be no difficulty in procuring for the Grand Duke all the amusement of that nature which can be desired."[7]

Back in New York, Bierstadt was involved in Alexis's visit in two ways. First, he kept the ball rolling for the buffalo hunt, and second, he was part of a committee that decorated the North River pier for Alexis's docking, and the "producer" for one of the two balls that feted the grand duke in New York. Bierstadt's ball was at the Academy of Music on November 29. Alexis's crossing began early in October and lasted forty days because of bad weather, and he did not arrive in New York until November 19. Bierstadt got back to New York by September 26 and immediately busied himself with such items as how much one hundred small Russian flags would cost, where to get mirrors for the walls of the banquet room, and printing menus and invitations (Fig. 150). His ball committee included such distinguished names as W. H. Aspinwall, E. W. Stoughton, James Taylor Johnston, and Henry Clews; his "Presentation Committee," with rooms in the Brevoort where the artist was staying, included C. P. Huntington (now back in New York), William Cullen Bryant, and John Jacob Astor.

150. Invitation to reception ball in honor of Grand Duke Alexis of Russia. 1871. Collection Mrs. Orville DeForest Edwards, Dobbs Ferry, New York

Bierstadt invited General Philip Sheridan, now Army commander in Chicago, but he could not come. However, Sheridan offered to cooperate in any way possible in the plans for the buffalo hunt. He had recently organized a hunt for James Gordon Bennett, the *New York Herald* publisher, and would be glad to make a repeat:

> If His Royal Highness desires the Buffalo hunt I will place myself at his service and can take him to large herds south of McPherson on the Union Pacific R Road, say from fifty to sixty or seventy miles. Spotted Tails band of Sioux Indians & Whistlers band are in the neighborhood & I can give them such inducements as will cause them to join us at least I think so.
>
> It will be cold probably but not half so cold as Russia.
>
> I cannot manage for more than twelve (12) persons in the suite of the Grand Duke & would like to have it a little less if possible.
>
> Should he desire to take this hunt, he can kill buffalo to his hearts content but must be willing to rough it a little . . . we ought to start for McPherson by the 10th of December at least.[8]

Buffalo Bill Cody, whom Sheridan had known of old, was hired, in exchange for a thousand pounds of tobacco, to see that the royal guest got his buffalo, and Cody arranged to have Chief Spotted Tail bring a thousand Indians into camp for local color. "Camp Alexis" was set up on Willow Creek south of North Platte, with many tents equipped with stoves, firewood, furniture, toilets, and flags waiting for the guests.

Alexis did not arrive in North Platte until January 12, and did not bring down his first buffalo until the fourteenth, his birthday. Bierstadt, having made the initial arrangements, did not stay for the hunt and left the slaughter to others. By January 6, he was back in San Francisco "to stay a long time."[9] A visit by Alexis to San Francisco, incidentally, was announced but did not come off.

On the sixteenth, the artist was at a reception for the Art Association, although pictures intended for the exhibition had not arrived from the East. Also at the reception was the celebrated photographer Eadweard Muybridge, later to be known as "the father of the motion picture." Muybridge was now about to do his first work for Leland Stanford and exhibited at the reception "some very effective views in the Russian River Valley."[10] Muybridge and

151. *Albert Bierstadt's "Studio."* 1872.
Stereograph by
Eadweard Muybridge.
The Bancroft Library,
University of California,
Berkeley. Taken at
the same time as Fig. 152

152. Bierstadt in
Mariposa. 1872.
Stereograph by
Eadweard Muybridge.
California Historical
Society, San Francisco

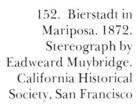

153. *Indians in Council, California.* 1872?
Oil on canvas, 16 × 20″ (40.6 × 50.8 cm.).
Collection Marvin J. Sonosky, Washington, D.C.

154. *Winter Scene, Yosemite.* 1872? Oil on canvas, 26 × 36″ (66 × 91.4 cm.).
Private collection, New York City

155. Sketch for *Winter Scene, Yosemite* and
Yosemite Winter Scene. 1863?
Pencil on paper, 5 × 8″ (12.7 × 20.3 cm.).
Collection John P. Kelly, Connecticut

156. *Yosemite Winter Scene.* 1872.
Oil on canvas, 32⅛ × 48⅛″ (81.6 × 122.2 cm.).
University of California Art Museum, Berkeley.
Gift of Henry D. Bacon

Bierstadt became friends, and were in the Yosemite together, where the photographer took pictures of the artist sketching Mariposa Indians (Figs. 151 and 152). Two of these have come down to us, showing Bierstadt sketching scenes that he later used in a painting (Fig. 153). Bierstadt later subscribed to a set of Muybridge's Yosemite pictures and endorsed them by saying, not quite grammatically, that the photographer showed "great skill in selecting the points of view, and the Artistic manner in which they are treated."[11]

By March, when a *Scribner's Magazine* article on the artist was published,[12] a number of sketches had been made for *Donner Lake from the Summit*, which had been commissioned by C. P. Huntington the previous year but which was not to see public light for another year (Fig. 169). By the last of February, Bierstadt had entered Yosemite in search of winter subjects. A number of these remain (Figs. 154 and 155); one, said to have been 45 1/2 x 20", was formerly in the Philadelphia Museum of Art but is now lost; another soon found its way into the collection of D. O. Mills, the San Francisco financier (Fig. 156). *The Bulletin* reported:

> As the spring advances and nature in California is putting on her most lovely garniture of verdure and flowers, the artists are preparing for sketching tours. Albert Bierstadt, who has taken up his residence in this State for some months, is first in the field. With characteristic enterprise, he has pushed into the Yosemite Valley this early—nearly three months in advance of ordinary tourists—to make sketches of the winter aspects of its unequalled scenery, when the peaks and cliffs are covered with snow, and the falls tumble amid icicles and ice sheeted rocks. He entered the valley ten days ago, by way of Haight's Cove and the canyon of the Merced River, and will spend considerable time there.[13]

Returning to San Francisco—probably via Sacramento—from a brief stay in Yosemite, the artist resumed his whirlwind activity. On the first of May he returned from the Farallon Islands and brought back studies (Fig. 158) that were to be the basis of many paintings. The Farallons were seven islands twenty miles off the Golden Gate; they were destitute of vegetation and human habitation except for a lighthouse keeper and his family and assistants. Bierstadt may have stayed for a time with the lighthouse keeper, as Carleton Watkins, the

157. *Seal Rocks, San Francisco.* c.1872.
Oil on canvas, 38½ × 58¼″ (97.8 × 148 cm.).
Collection Sandra and
Jacob Y. Terner, M.D., Beverly Hills,
California. Formerly in the collection
of A. T. Stewart, New York City

158. *Farallon Islands.* 1872.
Oil on cardboard mounted on canvas,
14 × 19″ (35.6 × 48.3 cm.).
California Palace of the Legion
of Honor, San Francisco.
Trustee Funds

159. *Seal Rocks, Farallon Islands.* 1873 or 1875. Oil on canvas, 30 × 45″ (76.2 × 114.3 cm.). The New Britain Museum of American Art, New Britain, Connecticut

160. *The Artist's Friends at the Milton S.
Latham House, Menlo Park, California.* c.1873.
Oil on canvas, 13 × 19″ (33 × 48.2 cm.).
Collection Jo Ann and Julian Ganz, Jr.,
Los Angeles. Previously titled *The Sewing Bee*

161. *Owens Valley, California.* 1872.
Oil on canvas, 14 × 19″ (35.6 × 48.3 cm.).
Whereabouts unknown

photographer, was to do two months later. During the breeding season thousands of sea lions cavorted about the rocks, and the year-round myriads of birds, chiefly gulls and murr (the eggs of which were sometimes gathered by San Francisco's Chinese for eating), flew about the place.

The evidence shows that Bierstadt produced four major, "finished" paintings of California seal rocks. Two were of the famous Sea Rocks immediately opposite the Cliff House in San Francisco: the painting bought by A. T. Stewart, the New York department store magnate, which is now in a private collection (Fig. 157); and another, a close parallel in both scenario and size, recently discovered and on the market in 1974. Two more were of seal rocks in the Farallons: one now in the New Britain Museum of American Art (Fig. 159), and the other sold at a Sotheby-Parke-Bernet auction in 1973.

With the regular flood of Yosemite visitors in May, the artist again took himself to his favorite haunt. He was evidently there alone, his wife having returned to Irvington for the summer. On May 24 he registered at the Yosemite Mountain House, California's answer to the Catskill Mountain House made famous decades earlier by the brushes of Hudson River artists. He had come to Yosemite from Owens Valley (Fig. 161), at the base of the newly discovered Mount Whitney, the highest peak in America, where he had gotten stuck in the snow. He then decided to pass the time pleasantly in Yosemite while waiting for the snow of Owens Valley to allow him to move about. While in Yosemite he climbed the new Glacier Point Trail and declared the view the best of all. From it he made studies for a Glacier Point picture, which has found its way into the Yale University Art Gallery (Fig. 162). Back in San Francisco, meanwhile, the Art Association exhibit was graced by a new *Mount Hood,* evidently the one now in the Portland Art Museum (Fig. 163), and D. O. Mills's *Yosemite Winter Scene* (Fig. 156).

By August 14, Bierstadt had joined the famous naturalist Clarence King in the country near Mount Whitney, and King was promised that he could use the artist's studies for his report. King had planned to use Watkins's photographs, but the difficulty in handling the photographic equipment persuaded him to abandon that project. Then Bierstadt returned briefly to San Francisco, took a look at the Art Association exhibition, and went back to Mount Whitney, "to further enrich his portfolio with sketches of the noble scenery of the region."[14] He and King were still in that part of the country in the middle of October,

217

162. *Yosemite Valley, Glacier Point Trail.* c.1872? Oil on canvas, 54 × 84¾″ (137.2 × 215.3 cm.).
Yale University Art Gallery, New Haven, Connecticut. Gift of Mrs. Vincenzo Ardenghi

163. *Mount Hood*. 1869. Oil on canvas, 36⅛ × 60¼″ (91.7 × 153 cm.). Portland Art Museum, Oregon

164. Study for *The Hetch-Hetchy Valley, California*. Undated. Oil on composition board, 16 × 24" (40.6 × 60.9 cm.). Collection Mr. and Mrs. E. E. White, Mamaroneck, New York

returning to San Francisco on the eighteenth. Much of the rest of 1872 was spent in the High Sierras east of Sacramento, making more studies for the Huntington picture and others. On December 13 his wife returned, bringing along her sister Esther and Minna Godwin, Parke Godwin's daughter and granddaughter of William Cullen Bryant.

The three ladies stayed for several months, throwing themselves into the San Francisco social melee. In the Occidental Hotel, where they all stayed, they found a vortex. Writing about their life forty years later, Esther garbled a number of particulars—including the year in which she was writing[15]—but provided a capricious, feminine account of the year's lighter side:

In January a party of 20 of us went down to Mr. Wm. Ralstons to spend two or three days. He asked Rose to invite her own party and she did so—three army and navy girls were asked . . . Minna Godwin, Rose, Mrs. Olmstead whose husband was in trade with China, Mr. Olmstead, Mr. Bierstadt . . . and several others whom I have forgotten. The driver changed horses several times. It took two char à bancs to take us, each holding ten people . . . their house had from thirty to forty bedchambers. We all made fine toilets. For dinner which was perfectly served by three or four liveried men servants. In the evening we went

165. *The Hetch-Hetchy Valley, California.* Undated. Oil on canvas, 37¼ × 58¼" (94.6 × 147.9 cm.). Wadsworth Atheneum, Hartford

into the music room and danced after the music of a musical piano which kept perfect time and played Strauss waltzes delightfully. . . . The Occidental Hotel was the headquarters of the Army and Navy—and General Neichler, Admiral Pennock and several other army and navy people were there. I remember several private balls. . . . I particularly remember a beautiful luncheon that Admiral and Mrs. Pennock gave on board the "California," a handsome, large American Man-of-war. Soon after Admiral and Mrs. Pennock sailed away in her to the Sandwich Islands. . . . A very warm friend of Rose's and Albert's was a Mr. [Samuel] Williams of "The San Francisco Bulletin." We saw a good deal of his wife and himself. . . . Albert had a little studio built on one of the high hills in San Francisco. He had his coachman Henry Campbell. . . . Saturday afternoons it was the fashion for the gay, fashionable world of San Francisco to drive and ride à cheval to the Cliff House where we danced, sat on the veranda, watched the seals on "Seal Rocks," drank lemonades, flirted, listened to the band, etc. Albert used to take us all every Saturday afternoon. He drove handsome horses and a light open carriage. "C" spring which was the style of carriage very much in vogue when we were there. When Albert was too busy painting, the coachman used to drive for Rose and me and we would

166. *Mountainous Landscape by Moonlight.* 1871.
Oil on canvas, 30 × 50″ (76.2 × 127 cm.).
The Corcoran Gallery of Art, Washington, D.C.

167. The Order of Saint Stanislaus, Second Class, of Russia, presented to Bierstadt in 1872. Collection Albert Morton Turner, Orono, Maine

often invite someone to go with us. . . . Mr. Thomas P. Madden who lived in the Occidental was a very warm friend of ours and kept Rose and me in bouquets. He was a sick old bachelor. We were invited to visit at Senator Stanford's in Sacramento. Mrs. Stanford was a very large woman—not particularly refined—and rather careless about her grammar but she wore magnificent jewels—such emeralds and diamonds! However, I think Mrs. A. T. Stewart of New York wore the finest emeralds that I ever saw. . . . In the early summer of 1872[16] Albert, Rose, Mr. Madden, Mr. Ver Miehr and I went to Yosemite Valley. We had to ride into the valley then on horseback. We stopped at Hutchings Hotel and spent six weeks in and about the valley then to the Hetch-Hetchy valley where we camped out [Figs. 164 and 165]. . . . When in California we saw a good deal of the Hall McAllisters. He was a brother of the famous Ward McAllister of New York society fame. Mrs. Hall McAllister sang beautifully and was very frenchy in her ways being a french woman that was not to be wondered at. Albert went away hunting with the Duke of Manchester and while he was gone I left for the East. . . . I was placed in the care of a Mrs. Rice of Cleveland, Ohio to return East. The week before I left California a steamship from the Sandwich Islands was ship wrecked on the Coast. The following morning Mr. Ver Miehr took me for a drive down to see it. One of the officers who had command of a life boat was the man my destiny had appointed for me to marry . . . there then began an acquaintance which ripened into a strong attachment which after seven years resulted in a marriage which has always proved to be a very happy one.[17]

The "little studio" Bierstadt had built on one of the high hills was described by *The Bulletin* as follows:

The studio wherein [*Donner Lake from the Summit*] was finished is a tall, slight frame-house, especially built for him on the very top of Clay street hill, and about 300 feet above sea level. This house, with its windows opening in every quarter, commands a magnificent view of the city below, and of the bay, from the Golden Gate in the west, to Mount Diablo in the east, including the whole sweep of its varied shore line and studding islands. Here Mr. Bierstadt has been studying rise and sunset effects, in addition to finishing his magnum opus. The large window—as big as the side of the house—which gives him the north light painters always want, commands at one glance a view of the whole passage from the Pacific Ocean to the inner bay, with the peninsular and Marin county shores, including Mount Tamalpais, a distance of six or seven miles. The light from other and small windows is shut off with curtains when not desired. Turning from the large one—which we may call a perpendicular skylight—and from the beautiful nature picture it reveals, the visitor to Mr. Bierstadt's unique atelier sees on a canvass the picture produced by his art.[18]

Meanwhile the Order of Saint Stanislaus of Russia (Fig. 167) had been bestowed on brother-in-law Albert for his services to Grand Duke Alexis, although *The Bulletin* reported that he had gotten it for *Mount Hood*, which had been exhibited in Russia. And early in the last year of his stay in California the picture that the artist had been working on since the first month he was there, *Donner Lake from the Summit*, was shown to the San Francisco public at the Art Association Gallery at 313 Pine Street. It received the best reviews yet: "It is a sublime painting of a sublime landscape," *The Chronicle* commented,[19] and *The California Art Gallery* was not far behind:

168. Bierstadt at forty-three. 1873. Drawing and engraving by H. X. Van de Casteele, from *California Art Gallery*, April 1873

The latest and most agreeable art-sensation of our city, was the painting of "Lake Donner" by Bierstadt, placed on exhibition for some days at the gallery of the Art Association. . . . Its chief charm is its realism, its careful faithful portraiture of, not only the great features of a California landscape, but all the minor distinctions that make its peculiarities. . . . It is a pleasure you can not exhaust in one or twenty visits. If you will take your lorgnette with you and look with an intelligent eye, you can discover new beauties every moment; and the oftener you see it, the more impressed you will be. . . . Many a time have I stood upon the summit and watched the glories of the matchless scene that lies along the Donner Lake over to the Truckee hills; I have walked too from the lake to the heights, gathering as I wandered, the delicate ferns growing along the silver brooks, and the wild flowers that are found in such profusion there in the open spaces; and I am familiar

169. *Donner Lake from the Summit.* 1873. Oil on canvas, 72 × 120″ (182.9 × 304.8 cm.). The New-York Historical Society, New York City. Also titled *View of Donner Lake, California*

170. *Autumn in the Sierras.* 1873. Oil on canvas, 72 × 120″ (182.9 × 304.8 cm.). The City of Plainfield, New Jersey. Formerly titled *The Rocky Mountains*

171. *Mount Brewer from Kings River Canyon, California.* 1872. Oil on canvas, 36 × 47″ (91.4 × 119.4 cm.).
Coe Kerr Gallery, New York City

with the view that Bierstadt has given in this picture. I am happy to offer my testimony as to the fidelity of his reproduction of one of the most charming and grand landscapes in the State, and I thank the artist for the hour of pleasure he has afforded me by one of the most striking paintings I ever saw, and which is to be, I judge, his magnum opus.[20]

Bierstadt soon sent *Donner Lake* to Huntington in New York, insuring it for $25,000. "If the picture should be damaged from water, or otherwise do not take it,"[21] he told his agent, W. O. Stoddard. He hoped Huntington, who had yet to see the picture, would see it in a frame, and the frame should be velvet with a plain gilt inside. He also spoke of a new mining property, and, if the assay was good, he wanted a large piece of it. Later, in May, he advised Stoddard to come out and look at the mineral prospects in Owens Valley.

Now Bierstadt busied himself with a new Yosemite canvas and a large picture of the South Sierra country, which he had visited with Clarence King the previous season. This latter he called *A View of the Kings River Mountains*. In April, he went south again, and *The Alta* quipped heavily: "Bierstadt is trying his hand at portrait painting—he is engaged on the head of Kings River."[22]

The Kings River picture was not finished in time for the reception opening the Art Association's exhibition on April 15. This was due to the artist's "recent accident."[23] There had been a stage accident on the trip into Inyo County. The driver had been killed, and Bierstadt was badly shaken up. *The Alta* and *The Chronicle* of May 16 both announced that there would be a "Kern's River picture" at the exhibition, as did *The Bulletin* on May 21. And both *Alta* and *Bulletin* reporters described it.[24] But it was not until May 28 that the Kings (not Kern) River painting was exhibited. *A View of the Kings River Mountains* had now become *Autumn in the Sierras*. Made from studies of the previous fall, when the artist was with King in the valley named after him, it showed the headwaters of the south fork of the river with Mount Brewer in the distance (Fig. 170). A separate, magnificent view of Brewer itself has recently been found (Fig. 171).

This time the artist's friend at *The Bulletin* seemed to have to strain to find something good to say. After a long scenario opening with "the landscape is a noble one," he ended: "Altogether the work is one of the most true and earnest which Bierstadt has produced."[25]

In June the artist wrote J. D. Whitney at Yale his praises of Mount Whitney and his joy that "the highest and finest mountain in the United States has been named after you . . . a sort of corner stone to the edifice of fame erected for yourself in the world of science."[26] Later the same month the artist's party made a farewell visit to Yosemite, registering at the Nevada Hotel on June 17. In August, on perhaps a farewell visit to the dear friends he had made, the artist and his sister-in-law drove down the Peninsula to the Ralstons, the Athertons, and a Major Rathbone. They returned to San Francisco by rail.

On October 11, 1873, after two years and three months in the West, Bierstadt and his wife took the train for Denver. There they stopped overnight and the next day went on to Chicago. By the twenty-seventh they were in Waterville with the Osbornes, and the artist was preparing a studio for a long winter's work. He had been renting Malkasten for the summers since 1869 to a New York physician named Prince. Prince and his family were there until 1874, after which the artist continued to rent the house to others.

NOTES: 1 *The San Francisco Bulletin*, July 29, 1871.

2 *Ibid.*

3 *The San Francisco Alta*, August 1, 1871.

4 Bierstadt to unknown addressee, August 11, 1871, California State Library, Sacramento.

5 *The San Francisco Bulletin*, September 18, 1871.

6 Bierstadt to Sherman, July 3, 1871, Manuscript Division, Library of Congress, Washington, D.C.

7 W. W. Belknap to Bierstadt, August 7, 1871, private collection.

8 Sheridan to Bierstadt, November 25, 1871, private collection.

9 *The San Francisco Bulletin*, January 6, 1872.

10 *The San Francisco Bulletin*, January 17, 1872.

11 From a May 1872 flyer in a private collection.

12 D. O. C. Townley, "Living American Artists," *Scribner's Monthly*, March, 1872, p. 605ff. This article is one of the least erroneous written about the artist during his lifetime, although it repeats, evidently from the flyer for the engraving of *The Rocky Mountains*, the erroneous date of 1858 for the trip made with Lander in 1859. It confirms what is evident to readers of contemporary criticism: that the artist's first big success was *Sunshine and Shadow*, and that *The*

Rocky Mountains and *The Base of the Rocky Mountains, Laramie Peak* established his reputation. The article also makes the curious point that the trip to Europe in 1867 was "to make studies for two paintings, commissioned by the Government, and to be placed in the Capitol at Washington." We know, as a matter of fact, that this project had fallen through four months before the artist left. But perhaps the project had not *really* fallen through, and the artist had been privately assured that it was merely put off. He finally did get the job, two years after the *Scribner's* article.

The article contains other mysteries. J. W. Kennard was said to own *Storm in the Rocky Mountains,* whereas the artist's niece wrote that Sir Herbert Peto was the owner. Perhaps Peto bought it and Kennard got it later; in any case, the article seems to eliminate the possibility that the painting had been burned (see Chapter 8, note 16). The owner of a painting called *Puget Sound* was, according to the article, A. A. Low of Brooklyn. We know that Bierstadt did not get to Puget Sound on his 1863 trip to the West, and to conjecture that he slipped up to Washington and back without anyone knowing it after he got to California is stretching the imagination too much. Probably the painting was incorrectly named; or possibly the artist had made an honest error and named a Columbia River view "Puget Sound."

13   *The San Francisco Bulletin,* March 5, 1872.

14   *Ibid.,* September 12, 1872.

15   On the second page of her notebook she says, "at this writing 1913," and on the eleventh page, "now at this date 1910."

16   Actually 1873.

17   From a notebook in the collection of Mrs. Orville DeForest Edwards, Dobbs Ferry, New York.

18   *The San Francisco Bulletin,* January 11, 1873.

19   *The San Francisco Chronicle,* January 12, 1873.

20   *The California Art Gallery,* February 1873.

21   Bierstadt to Stoddard, about February 16, 1873, Henry Francis du Pont Winterthur Museum, Winterthur, Delaware.

22   *The San Francisco Alta,* April 17, 1873.

23   Unidentified, May 16, 1873, clipping, collection Mrs. Orville DeForest Edwards, Dobbs Ferry, New York.

24   A Kern River picture, *Valley of Kern River, California,* has been said to be in the Hermitage, Leningrad, but as of 1966 it was not there. (I am grateful to J. D. Forbes of the University of Virginia for this information.)

25   *The San Francisco Bulletin,* May 29, 1873.

26   Bierstadt to Whitney, June 6, 1873, Yale University Library.

Ten

Declining Popularity

1873-1882

172. *Mount Corcoran.* 1875? Oil on canvas, 61 × 96¼″ (154.9 × 244.4 cm.). The Corcoran Gallery of Art, Washington, D.C.

THE TWO-STORY STUDIO into which Bierstadt snuggled for the winter months of 1873–74 had been built by his father-in-law, Amos Osborne, to the artist's specifications. It was next to the family house, and a fine example of Bierstadt's taste and intelligence (Fig. 173). The artist and his wife must have stayed with the Osbornes much of the winter, for late in January, 1874, the involved Corcoran Gallery negotiations had begun, and Joseph Henry, the secretary of the Smithsonian, wrote Bierstadt in Waterville: "Your letter in regard to the deposit of a picture in the Corcoran Art Gallery had been referred to the Committee on Art the Chairman of which will probably communicate with you on the subject."[1] This project, getting a picture into the Corcoran collection, did not bear fruit until 1877. Then he sold Corcoran a painting he called *Mount Corcoran,* said to have been the one called *Mountain Lake* at the National Academy of Design 1877 Annual (Fig. 172). Whatever range or peak the painting shows, "Mount Corcoran" is the name the artist gave to an outlier of Mount Whitney. Obviously he did it to flatter Corcoran. If Vanderbilt had been buying American art instead of European, it might have been offered to him with the name "Mount Vanderbilt." With the public taste now captivated by the Barbizon School of painting, and with expenses continuing high and income going down, the artist was reduced to public relations tricks that would have been beneath his dignity in the old days of *The Rocky Mountains* glory.

173. The Osborne home in Waterville, New York, with Bierstadt's studio at right. 1870s? Collection Mrs. Orville DeForest Edwards, Dobbs Ferry, New York

It may have been at this time, too, that Bierstadt decided to rent Malkasten perennially. When he went to New York, he stayed at the Brevoort Hotel. In 1875, 1879, and 1881 he spent so much time at the Brevoort that the New York directory of those years listed him as living there. In other years, until 1882, the Tenth Street Studio and/or Irvington were listed. The Waterville sojourn, which lasted into the fall of 1874, may have been decided upon for reasons of economy, although for his whole life the artist lived to within an inch of his income.

During this winter he set upon another scheme to sell his now largely unwanted pictures. At least one letter exists in which the artist proposed that a local art museum be established. He, the artist, would help things along by selling one of his paintings at a reduced figure. It seems possible that the letter he wrote on November 20, 1873, was only one of a series:

Mr. Dear Sir:
Knowing the interest you take in all matters I venture to ask you if you

233

174. *Mount Whitney.* c.1874.
Oil on canvas, 68 × 116″ (173 × 294.6 cm.).
The Rockwell Foundation, Corning, New York

think the present time would be a good one in which to agitate the subject of starting a fine public gallery. I take so much interest in the advancement of art that I would be glad to contribute a picture for such an enterprise. If therefore those gentlemen interested in such matters should desire it for such a purpose I would sell them my large picture "Autumn in the Sierras" . . . at half price. Sometimes men of large fortune whose age and bodily infirmities tell them they are soon to pass away like to leave some memorial behind them. That is the case with this Mr. Lick of San Francisco who has given about two million for scientific purposes.

Up to a certain moment they are anxious to accumulate all they can and then it must rapidly be disposed of. Such a man then may be in your city whose thoughts by your suggestion might be turned in this direction. I could aid you in collecting many fine works of art many too without cost simply as donations to the gallery. I would give a picture such as I get $2000 or more for and as I said before sell my large one at a very low price.

I regret that I did not have the pleasure of meeting you in New York. I expect to remain here till spring when I shall return to the city and finally to Irvington when I hope to have the pleasure of seeing you. Should you still care for the small picture . . . you may have it at your own price. If $300 is to [sic] much make it less.[2]

Evidently the artist's plans to move back into the house in Irvington did not materialize. In June he was at the Brevoort again, and early in September he was still in Waterville. Then a visitor from a newspaper in the neighboring city of Utica found him at home, working on a big new picture of the discovery of the Hudson River, which may not have been yet commissioned:

Mr. Bierstadt is just now engaged upon a large historical painting—a field of effort somewhat new to him. The scene is laid among the highlands of the Hudson and is designed to represent the forming of a treaty of peace between some of the early Dutch colonists and certain Indian tribes along the shores of that river. Mr. Bierstadt has leisure and much reserved power, which will doubtless be spent upon this

175. *Giant Redwood Trees of California.* Undated. Oil on canvas, 52½ × 43″ (123.4 × 109.2 cm.). The Berkshire Museum, Pittsfield, Massachusetts

◄ 176. *Mount Whitney* (detail of Fig. 174)

177. *Blue Clouds in the Rockies.* Undated. Oil on paper, 14 × 19″ (35.6 × 48.3 cm.).

canvas before the fruit of his labor will be exposed to the public eye. From what is shadowed forth in the uncompleted picture, I venture to predict that it will rank high among the works of this distinguished painter.

In response to the request of his visitor, he showed me a large number of his original sketches. These sketches, let me observe, are mostly in oil, upon loose sheets of canvass, and were made in the open air at all seasons of the year, not excepting winter. They are classified, for the most part, according to the country or district where they were made, and are arranged in separate portfolios kept in closets or trunks, so that any sketch which may be wanted for a particular purpose can be found without a moment's delay. The California sketches were most numerous. Here were groups and single specimens of the famous *Sequoia gigantea,* and of many other trees of that wonderful country. Here were the snowy Sierras and the waterfalls and strange mountain-forms of the Yosemite valley. As the contents of these portfolios were slowly turned over it required no laborious searching to discover the original materials of several of our artist's great California pictures.[3]

The studies of the *Sequoia gigantea* which the reporter saw were worked into a large picture, which was sent to Berlin for exhibition. The artist, always seeking illustrious patronage and "contacts," decided to offer it to the German emperor as a gift. He turned to his old friend George Bancroft, now American minister to Germany:

> I wanted very much to talk with you in regard to a picture which I have sent to Berlin and which I had thought of presenting to His Majesty, the Emperor, for whom I have the most profound admiration.
>
> I speak of it as a picture, but it might be more properly called a study from Nature. It is a portrait of the largest tree in California if not in the world, and they have named it there, "The King of the Mountains." It belongs to the group of Cedars called the Washingtonio Gigantea or Sequoia. I am well aware that crowned heads are not in the habit of accepting presents from their subjects or from the people of other countries, but knowing the great personal regard His Majesty

240

178. *Cloud Study.* Undated. Oil on paper, 6½ × 11¾″ (16.5 × 29.9 cm.). Thomas Gilcrease Institute, Tulsa

entertains for you and the terms of intimacy existing between you, I have thought you might present it for me if you consider it best, and thus possibly give him as much pleasure as I had when I first saw the grand original. The picture is an upright, three by four feet.

The tree is forty two feet in diameter, and three hundred feet in height—to say nothing of the four thousand years of history in its sealed trunk. In a few weeks I shall complete my picture the 'Discovery of the Hudson River' which I shall send to Washington, and hope to have the pleasure of showing it to you.

Mrs. Bierstadt joins me in kindest regards to Mrs. Bancroft and yourself.[4]

This painting is now unlocated. (The one with Galen Clark, Fig. 98, taken from studies made in 1863, may have been in progress in 1875.) Others, possibly done during the same period, are still with us (Fig. 175). In return for the painting, which the emperor accepted, the artist received a large autographed photograph of His Majesty.

Meanwhile, other paintings were under way. Among these, possibly, was one of the artist's finest westerns, *Mount Whitney* (Figs. 174 and 176). Others were *Mount Adams, Washington,* now in Princeton (Fig. 179), the Yosemite view at the Toledo Museum of Art (Fig. 182), and "an exquisite little view"[5] of Mount Saint Helens, which the artist gave to Horace Howard Furness. *Autumn in the Sierras* was traveling. In March it was on sale for $25,000 at Earle's in Philadelphia and was "undoubtedly the crowning effort of his life, thus far."[6]

Although Bierstadt had known George Bancroft for some years, his acquaintance was renewed at a dinner given in New York in October in honor of the first marquess of Dufferin and Ava, the governor-general of Canada. Bierstadt, along with Bancroft, may have met Dufferin then. Other notables present at the Brevoort dinner included Cyrus Field, John Jacob Astor, A. T. Stewart, Joseph Choate, Hamilton Fish, and Thurlow Reed. The Bierstadts gave the Dufferins a private tour of the artist's collection—possibly in both New York and Irvington—and the four were friends forever.

In March of the new year, 1875, Bierstadt placed on exhibition in the House of Representatives his nearly completed *Discovery of the Hudson* (Fig. 180), on which he had been working the previous fall when the Utica newspaper

179. *Mount Adams, Washington* [correct title?]. 1875. Oil on canvas, 54 × 83⅝″ (137.2 × 212.3 cm.).
The Art Museum, Princeton University, Princeton, New Jersey. (See CL-159.)

180. *The Discovery of the Hudson.* 1875. Oil on canvas, 72 × 122″ (182.9 × 309.9 cm.).
United States Capitol, Washington, D.C.

181. *Expedition under Vizcaino Landing at Monterey 1601.* 1875. Oil on canvas, 72 × 122" (182.9 × 309.9 cm.). United States Capitol, Washington, D.C.

correspondent had visited him in Waterville. Also on exhibition was his *King's River Canyon*, now lost. "I do not understand that they have yet been purchased by the Government," a reporter wrote, "but there is little doubt that they will be."[7] He was partly right: *Discovery of the Hudson* was bought at once for $10,000. The artist wrote that the painting had been commissioned in 1872, but specialists have not found such a record. The other Bierstadt painting in the Capitol, *Landing in Monterey* (now titled *Expedition under Vizcaino Landing at Monterey 1601*, Fig. 181), appears to have arrived in 1878, although it was under way in the fall of 1875, intended for the 1876 Centennial. Fifteen thousand dollars was appropriated "to purchase works of art for the Capitol Building."[8] Thomas Moran had also applied for a commission, but Bierstadt's painting was selected. On July 9, 1878, however, just before Bierstadt left for Europe, he wrote A. E. Spofford, the Librarian of Congress, in a letter now in the Library, that the purchase had not yet been made.

In the summer of 1875 the Bierstadts were at Malkasten. In July the Pennsylvania Academy of the Fine Arts, with its new building nearing completion, invited the artist to contribute a painting to the new gallery. With this request he heartily complied, sending *Mount Adams, Rocky Mountains*.

In October a 700-ton, 150-foot bark, named *Bierstadt* after the artist by its California owner, was launched in Wiscasset, Maine. "She has an exquisite

182. *El Capitan, Yosemite Valley.* 1875. Oil on canvas, 32¼ × 48″ (81.8 × 121.9 cm.).
The Toledo Museum of Art, Toledo, Ohio. Gift of Mr. and Mrs. Roy Rike

183. Lord Dufferin, governor-general of Canada. 1876. Collection Esther R. Bascom, Rosalie R. Rooks, Joyce R. Edwards, and Pauline R. Perry

184. Bierstadt at forty-six, in Charles I costume for 1876 Ottawa ball

185. Mrs. Albert Bierstadt at thirty-five, in Mary, Queen of Scots, costume for 1876 Ottawa ball

Figs. 184, 185: Collection Mrs. Orville DeForest Edwards, Dobbs Ferry, New York

figure-head," *The San Francisco Bulletin* reported, "most elegantly and elaborately carved, of full life-size, of Mrs. Bierstadt, the artist's wife, who is a lady of rare beauty and culture."[9]

Frenzied production of pictures ensued through the end of the year. *Landing in Monterey*, a Big Tree picture, a *King's River Canyon*, a view of San Francisco from San Rafael, and a view of the Hetch-Hetchy Valley were "nearly finished" by December 3,[10] and early in the next year a four-and-a-half-by-seven-foot *Mount Adams* was produced (see CL-159). The Big Tree picture, a Yosemite view, a *Mount Hood, Western Kansas*, and a painting called *California Spring* (evidently his National Academy picture of 1875 now titled *Sacramento Valley in Spring*, Fig. 193), were chosen by the artist for his part in the upcoming Philadelphia Centennial. *Landing in Monterey* was left out. Long before the Committee of Selection had met, John Sartain, the head of the Centennial Fair's Art Bureau, told Bierstadt he could have a space twelve by fifty-four feet—a significantly larger space than most other artists were given. Many of the Centennial paintings were for sale; Bierstadt wanted Sartain to help him sell one of the paintings, but Sartain declined.

The public reaction to the artist's Centennial works confirmed that many people now thought Bierstadt was passé. Led by John F. Weir, who was a judge and who wrote the official report of the art exhibition, the rejection was nearly

247

186. The earl of Dunraven.
1922. From his autobiography,
Past Times and Pastimes, 1922

188. The earl of Dunraven's English Hotel, Whyte's Lake, Colorado.
Collection William H. Jackson Photo-Library.
The State Historical Society of Colorado, Denver.
The site of this hotel is said to have been chosen by Bierstadt

187. Eliza Bierstadt, the artist's sister.
c.1864. Henry Francis du Pont
Winterthur Museum, Winterthur,
Delaware. Joseph Downs Manuscript
Collection (No. 64 × 39.1)

unanimous. The artist's works, Weir said, were sensational and meretricious, with "a loss of true artistic aim."[11]

Lord Dufferin (Fig. 183) and his wife, planning a great ball in Ottawa, now remembered the Bierstadts' courtesy of October, 1874. They invited the two to come to Canada for the event and be house guests of the governor-general and his wife during their stay. The invitation was accepted with alacrity. The ball was held at Government House on February 23, and was the social event of that or any Canadian season. Fifteen hundred notables were asked, and the Bierstadts were given places of honor. Albert, masked as Charles I, sparkled in his conversation, as did Rosalie, in both conversation and in dress, which was a version of Mary Queen of Scots (Figs. 184 and 185): "a puffed white satin petticoat studded with silver; black velvet train, richly worked in silver embroidery; white satin sleeves, studded with pearls; toque of the period, black velvet, white feather; ornaments of diamonds."[12]

The correspondent of a New York newspaper gave a colorful account of the entreé:

A more brilliant and entirely successful affair than that of Wednesday night has probably never been witnessed on this continent and but seldom in the older world.

Even before the hour appointed for the commencement of the ball

248

189. *The Rocky Mountains, Longs Peak.* 1877. Oil on canvas, 62 × 98″ (157.5 × 248.9 cm.).
Denver Public Library. Collection Western History Department

hundreds of sleighs were crunching the hard-frozen snow along the two miles which lie between the city and the hall, and the tinkle of their bells made the night lively till long past 5 the next morning. The night was cold enough to be a good specimen of a Canadian winter, but, cold as it was, sleigh after sleigh jingled up the well-lighted avenue and deposited its load of fair forms till about 9:30. The ball and ante rooms were crowded with as gay and fantastic a throng as any fancy ball could show. The noble proportions of the splendid room, with its exquisitely delicate tints of coloring on ceiling and walls, were brought out to their fullest extent by hundreds of wax candles grouped tastefully round the sides, in addition to the ordinary light afforded by gas chandeliers and brackets. Festoons of roses hung in graceful curves round the pilasters from the floor to the ceiling, while at the far end of the room stood, on a dais of three crimson steps, the throne, surmounted by an imperial crown.[13]

Arriving home on Ash Wednesday, Mrs. Bierstadt was agog with the memory. The Dufferins had invited them to come every year, "and fairly begged them to stay another week."[14] Telling of a dinner party given later, she could not understand why they should have been "so signally honored and favored."[15]

In New York in October, Dufferin had "a great crow" to pluck with Bierstadt: "Why did you not present me to your sister this morning according to your promise?"[16] This was Eliza (Fig. 187), "an unusually handsome young woman with marked individuality of character and distinction of manner,"[17] who was in the habit of cultivating celebrities herself. She had been busy for years collecting autographs, as well as people like the Frémonts, Frederick Church, and William H. Beard (from the latter two she solicited—but did not get—sketches). Eliza owned her brother's first big success, *Sunshine and Shadow*, until her death in 1896.

In 1876, the artist was commissioned by Windham Thomas Wyndham-Quin, the fourth earl of Dunraven (Fig. 186)—celebrated author, traveler, sportsman, politician, and bon vivant—to paint the glories of Longs Peak in Estes Park, Colorado. Bierstadt had known Dunraven for some time. The earl was a frequent visitor to the Brevoort Hotel, and a long-time admirer of Bierstadt's western scenes. Bierstadt, perhaps hoping for the commission, wined and dined the earl with a vengeance: there was a dinner party at the Brevoort on January

25, and another, perhaps near the same time. The latter was unexcelled, even at the Brevoort:

> Mr. Albert Bierstadt, the artist, gave a dinner on Wednesday evening last, at the Brevoort House, to the Earl of Dunraven, which brought together a distinguished company of gentlemen, and which, in point of style and in the character of the menu, has seldom if ever been excelled, even in that famous hostelry. The following is a full list of the guests present:—Earl of Dunraven, Major General W. S. Hancock, Professor Henry Draper, Lieutenant Colonel K. Rowan Niven, of the English Army; D. O. Mills, President of the Bank of California, San Francisco; General Cullum, Mr. John W. Hamersley, Mr. Wm. P. Douglass, Mr. James P. Kernochan, Mr. James Beekman, General L. P. deCesnola, Mr. Charles Whitehead, Mr. Henry Parker, Mr. Samuel Ward, Mr. John Ellis, Mr. P. B. DuChaillu, Mr. Joseph H. Choate, Mr. George A. Robbins, Colonel Tom A. Scott, of Philadelphia, President of the Pennsylvania Railroad, Mr. J. W. Garrett, of Baltimore, President of the Baltimore and Ohio Railroad.[18]

Either shortly before or shortly after this, apparently, the guest of honor and his host visited the Cesnola Collection on Fourteenth Street. (General Cesnola, who had been at the dinner party for Dunraven, had accumulated a large collection of ancient Greek artifacts, and later these became a nucleus of the Metropolitan Museum of Art.)

Dunraven had "discovered" Estes Park during an earlier, Christmastime visit to Denver at the "Delmonico's of the West," the famous Charpiot Hotel. He set about acquiring virtually the whole park—ten out of fifteen thousand acres of it—for himself. By means fair and foul—homesteaders and Coloradans thought foul, although many had approved the same methods when used by Americans—he began to buy. He was finally so involved in lawsuits that he was relieved to wash his hands of the project. But in 1876 his hopes were still high, and late in the year he took Bierstadt west to see the park. On the way, there was a Canadian moosehunt with Dunraven's cousin W. Montague Kerr. Then the three men went to Denver, where they registered at Charpiot's on the twenty-second. The next day they went to Estes Park, for a two weeks' stay. There they found the English Hotel on Fish Creek already under way. That is to

251

190. *Rocky Mountains, Colorado.* 1875–76? Oil on paper on masonite, 13¾ × 19½″ (34.9 × 49.5 cm.).
Museum of Fine Arts, Boston. M. and M. Karolik Collection

191. Bierstadt Lake,
Rocky Mountain National Park, Colorado.
Collection Albert Morton Turner, Orono,
Maine

say, the building materials were there, but the site was yet to be selected. The artist himself is said to have selected it on Whyte's Lake (Whyte was Dunraven's Colorado agent), which was yet to be created by damming the creek. The hotel (Fig. 188) was opened in the summer of 1877, with the artist and his patron present for the gala.

Besides numerous studies in and about Estes Park, among which is a painting of Whyte's Lake, the artist set to work on Longs Peak itself. The result, almost a year in the making, was the magnificent five-by-eight-foot *Rocky Mountains, Longs Peak* (Fig. 189), which today hangs in the Western Room of the Denver Public Library, from the windows of which, on a clear day, the original itself can be seen.

Back at Charpiot's in Denver on January 8 of the new year, 1877, Bierstadt did not linger. He was on his way east the next morning. This was the year he started taking his wife to Nassau for her health—her recurrent malaise had now been diagnosed as consumption—and after two months there and in Florida he was back in his New York studio hard at work on the picture for Dunraven. According to *Leslie's Illustrated* for June 16, it was "just finished," and the artist was planning to go back to Colorado for the grand opening of the English Hotel. He may have put finishing touches on his painting after his arrival, which *The Rocky Mountain News* reported on August 31. On the site, he began making sketches for other pictures. *The News*, with characteristic Victorian splendor, praised the beauties of the region and the artist's discrimination in deciding upon it:

He could not have found a more lovely spot than this Gem of the Rocky Mountains as the scene of the highest triumphs of his art. The massive grandeur and everlasting strength of the granite walls which environ this beautiful retreat, and the infinite variety and loveliness of landscape displayed throughout the park, have made so powerful an impression on the artist's mind that the subject has thoroughly absorbed his thought; and the bold and rugged, as well as the soft and beautiful features of this enchanting region, as they reappear on the glowing canvass, show at once the true artistic inspiration and the unerring touch of the master hand.[19]

Evidently *Leslie's* had been overstating the case when it reported in June that the picture was finished. The artist himself wrote on October 9 that it was "nearly completed,"[20] and in December he was arranging for it to have a short exhibition in Boston.[21] It was back in the artist's studio on February 27, 1878, and soon on its way to Europe, where it was exhibited at the Royal Academy before finally coming to a rest on the walls of Dunraven's house in Limerick. For his efforts the artist got $15,000, a mountain named after him, and his name on two other delightful bits of Colorado scenery, Bierstadt Lake (Fig. 191) and Bierstadt Moraine, both popular landmarks in Estes Park.

Constantly Bierstadt was involved in projects political and economic, far from the purpose of art. Reading in the paper that it had been proposed at a Cabinet meeting that government buildings should be built as near as possible to navigable waters so that they could be defended by gunboats against invasion, riots, etc., the artist proposed a canal—to be called the Hayes Canal, for the newly elected president—between Lake Erie and Lake Ontario. His eminence was so great in the eyes of his correspondent in Washington, General John Grant Mitchell, that the general wrote an aide: "Please issue a Ukase, in the absence of the President and order the work commenced—let him read it some Sunday."[22] There is no indication, however, that the project ever got beyond the aide's desk.

A whirlwind trip to San Francisco, whence he may have gone to check the terrain for his *Landing in Monterey*, placed in the Capitol the same year, 1878; a

192. The Rensselaer Building, 1271 Broadway and 32nd Street, with the Union Dime Savings Bank on the ground floor and Bierstadt's studio on the second floor

193. *Sacramento Valley in Spring.* 1875. Oil on canvas, 55 × 85″ (139.7 × 215.8 cm.).
California Palace of the Legion of Honor, San Francisco. Gift of Gordon Blanding.
(Formerly in the Montreal Museum of Fine Arts.)

194. Henry Blake, governor-general of the
Bahamas. c.1885. Collection Esther R.
Bascom, Rosalie R. Rooks, Joyce R. Edwards,
and Pauline R. Perry

tour with Dufferin, the governor-general of Canada, on a splendid panoplied visit to Montreal in February; a week's stay with the Hayeses in the White House later the same month; and again to Nassau in March; give some indication of the energy and ambitions of the artist. In March, he gave the newly formed Montreal Museum of Fine Arts a large painting, evidently the 1875 Academy Annual view of California in the spring. This the Montreal museum disposed of, and the painting has now, evidently, found its way into the California Palace of the Legion of Honor in San Francisco as *Sacramento Valley in Spring* (Fig. 193).

He was in Nassau with his "heart's treasure"[23] for six weeks, on a social round that regularly included the island's foremost dignitaries, among them the governor-general (Fig. 194) and his wife. His wife had been in Nassau for a while, and by the time she returned, in June, she had spent nine months there, in company with her sister Esther, who was to go to Europe with the Bierstadts. They had rented a house opposite the Royal Victoria Hotel, and the rent, Esther remembered, was a hundred dollars less a month than the house where they stayed in Paris the following year. While the artist was in Nassau, he sent a chitchat note to Hayes's son, Webb:

> I am here in Nassau where my hearts treasure is and as she is daily improving we shall go to Europe on the first of June. I may see you meanwhile however as I expect to be in Washington about the first of May.
>
> I have most agreeable recollections of my visit in your family where I found myself so fortunate as to make the acquaintance of your distinguished Father and his dignified and charming wife. I had a great deal of amusement over the glove that your Mother permitted me to secure the day of her last reception.
>
> Mrs Bierstadt's maid took my dress coat to brush it and finding it in the pocket brought it to her mistress.
>
> At first Mrs Bierstadt thought it was hers, but she soon discovered it was not and then the mystery was—whose was it. I was out at the time and when I returned she and her sister attacked me and it was not until I told all the circumstances and whose little hand it had encased that they let me off. Mrs Bierstadt then said that under the circumstances she would not be jealous and that she would have done the same herself

195. *Nassau Harbor.* 1877–plus.
Oil on panel, 14¾ × 20″ (37.5 × 50.8 cm.).
California Palace of the Legion of Honor,
San Francisco. H. K. S. Williams Fund

196. *Bahamas.* Undated.
Oil on paper on panel, 14 × 19″
(35.6 × 48.3 cm.). Collection L. J. Heaps,
London

had she been a man. Even as it is she says she thinks she would fall in love with Mrs. Hayes.

Mr Sessions you know has given twenty five thousand dollars to the Columbus Art gallery. If the President could only find time to write him a word it would do so much good. It would encourage further contributions of this nature and encourage Mr. Sessions who has a wife and Mother in Co.[lumbus] to contend with whenever he wants to contribute to art.[24]

The artist had written John Sartain in Philadelphia the previous July, telling him of plans for the Columbus gallery and asking Sartain for a copy of the Pennsylvania Academy's constitution and bylaws.

He left Nassau on April 24 and back in New York took a studio at 1271 Broadway, in the Rensselaer Building (Fig. 192). This place was to be, after three more years, his studio and home until his wife's death in 1893 and his remarriage the following year. He continued his correspondence, meanwhile, with the president's son, and was involved in an unexplained deal. Dufferin's brother, Lord Campbell, had written the artist; his letter was sent to Webb Hayes: "In regards to the enclosed if you can enlighten me, it would be strictly private of course."[25] Mrs. Bierstadt stayed in Nassau, on her doctor's orders—warm weather was the nineteenth century's specific for consumption—and her husband went down to Washington on his business with the president's son.

On July 20, 1878, the artist and his wife and sister-in-law, Esther Osborne, with Mrs. Bierstadt's Negro maid Harriet Claxton, boarded the White Star *Germanic* for Europe. They were gone for a year.

Our principal source of information about this trip is from Esther's memories of twenty years later. Details, particularly as to dates, were uninteresting to the writer and, as a consequence, unspecific to the historian. Early in August, from the Langham Hotel in London where they were staying again, the artist and his sister-in-law—his wife was ailing so much that she was more of a burden than a comfort on this trip—visited the James McHenrys at Oak Lodge. Here they saw *The Rocky Mountains* and *Vesuvius,* and found Mrs. McHenry deep in grief over the loss of thirteen (!) children. Then they went to Swansea, in Wales, to the duke of Manchester, whom they had seen in San Francisco five years before. They stayed several days, visited the Pendarvis

197. *The Wave.* 1887. Oil on canvas, 60 × 72″ (152.4 × 182.9 cm.).
Pioneer Museum and Haggin Galleries, Stockton, California. Haggin Collection.
Also called *The Surf* and *The Turquoise Sea*

Vivians—Vivian was a brother-in-law of Dunraven who was to use a number of Bierstadt's sketches in a book published the following year on the American West[26]—and returned to London in Vivian's private car. There they found Mrs. Bierstadt as sick as ever. Bret Harte, we are told, had called on her several times to cheer her up.

Esther seems to have thought that Mrs. Bierstadt sometimes acted a bit sicker than she was. Late that year, in Cannes, she wrote that Rosalie *seemed* to be too sick to go to a lunch. In Paris the following year she wrote, "I am sorry as I can be for Rose but if she would only let things go a little more she would be so much more comfortable and others too."[27]

While in London the artist talked about plans for a gallery of American art in that city, but nothing came of these. On the way to Cannes they stopped for a few weeks at the Hotel Meurice in Paris. Then Esther and Rosalie went on to Cannes, with Albert, detained by business in Paris, joining them later. Esther and her sister would have liked to have gone to a less fashionable place than Cannes, but "Albert had to go where there are rich people to sell his paintings to." At the Villa Marie Philippine, in Cannes, Bierstadt had oatmeal and baked apples for breakfast, his sister-in-law remembered. He was joined now, for a time, by his mother-in-law and sister-in-law Mary. They all had lunch with the Lords, Rosalie seeming too sick to go. The Lords were a New York family who had lived for years in London and whom Mrs. Bierstadt, when she was Mrs. Fitz Hugh Ludlow, had met in Florida in 1860, while spending the winter there.

Bierstadt knew the duke of Argyll, who was spending the winter in Cannes, and that was an open sesame for the travelers. The duke had six unmarried daughters, with one engaged to Lord Balfour. On January 7, the artist's birthday, his sister-in-law took to his studio "some green vases filled with potted plants and a lovely plaque." The artist habitually got to his studio at 9 A.M. It was heated by an immense white porcelain stove. In March, the artist was notified he had received a large loving cup (in Paris) from Grand Duke Alexis.

Back in Paris at the Continental Hotel, Rosalie indulged in a curious conceit. She found "a new plaything, a small child, of the people, whom she saw playing in the road. She bought him a suit of kilts, new boots, a mouchoir, toothbrush, big sailor hat." The Bierstadts and Esther then took an apartment on the Rue Roi du Rome.

While in Cannes they had expected to go to Egypt, but presumably did not.

260

198. *The Saint Lawrence River from the Citadel, Quebec.* 1881? Oil on paper mounted on canvas, 22 × 30½″ (55.9 × 77.5 cm.). Museum of Fine Arts, Boston. M. and M. Karolik Collection

They were in London in July and back to New York on August 3, 1879, aboard the *Brittanic*. In New York harbor the Ismays, the steamship line's owners, gave a lunch in a stateroom for twenty people, including the Bierstadts and their sister. The Leland Stanfords were there, and Mrs. Stanford wore "the *biggest emerald solitaire earrings* I ever saw." The artist and his wife then went to Washington for a few weeks, and Esther went back to Waterville. Back in New York the artist gave his celebrated lunch in honor of Dunraven and the son of the duke of Leeds, and soon Rosalie and her maid were off again to Nassau and the Royal Victoria.

Esther had been given a picture named, not altogether unexpectedly, *Lake Esther, Sierra Nevada Mountains,* with a somewhat inevitable islet in the center of the lake. This painting had been reproduced three years before in a western travel book.[28] It was one of Esther's fondest possessions until the day she died. "Esther Randall [her daughter] to have 'Lake Esther' from me," she wrote. "My other paintings just as you all want to divide them."[29]

That year, 1879, in G. W. Sheldon's *American Painters,* Bierstadt was said to be "a believer in Wagner's principle of the value of mere quantity in a work of art. . . . His style is demonstrative and infused with emotion."[30] The following year S. G. W. Benjamin found it "difficult to understand" that people were ever

199. Central diorama of the Museum of Science, Boston. The moose antlers are from a moose shot by Bierstadt about 1880, and are among the largest ever taken in America

200. *Dog's Head.* c.1882? Watercolor on paper, 7 × 7½" (17.8 × 19.1 cm.), oval. Collection Norma S. Lockwood, Cincinnati, Ohio

ecstatic over *The Rocky Mountains* and, curiously, thought *Storm in the Rocky Mountains* the "least sensational and most artistically correct of the artist's works."[31] About the same time, a reviewer climbed aboard the bored-with-Bierstadt bandwagon and wrote:

> Mr. Bierstadt's *Turquoise Sea* [Fig. 197] adds nothing to his reputation, or to the interest of the Exhibition. Setting aside the question of its artistic qualities, it represents a scene that is physically impossible. Surf is never of that color in any latitude. It is true one sees that tone in the Blue Grotto of Capri, or in the warm latitudes at a distance from the land. It is, furthermore, not possible for waves to break without leaving the beach covered with foam for a wide space as they flow back. But here we see a roller ninety to a hundred feet high, judging from the cliffs and the spar, actually tumbling on a dry beach! It is cause for genuine regret when an artist of such real talents forgets himself in absurdities like these, and when a committee have so little regard for his reputation as to admit a work that can only inure to his injury.[32]

Again his wife had a long stay in the Bahamas, returning evidently in June, 1880, after eight months, and just after Bierstadt returned from Canada. She was able to spend a short time with her husband, who was soon off to San

262

201. *Hunting Scene.* c.1880? Oil on paper, 14 × 18½″ (35.6 × 47 cm.). Collection Isabella Grandin, Boston

Francisco for five weeks sketching Shasta, the Sierras, and the coast, including Monterey. Immediately upon returning, in September they both went back to Montreal and Quebec. The marquess of Lorne, Victoria's son-in-law, had become governor-general of Canada, and the Bierstadts were cordially invited to visit him and his wife, Princess Louise. While there, or during a visit the following May, the artist may have made studies for one of the interesting paintings of his later career, *The Saint Lawrence River from the Citadel, Quebec* (Fig. 198). His wife returned to New York and was off to Nassau again, with Bierstadt continuing his hysterical activity. He now went across the continent to Tacoma, Vancouver in British Columbia, San Francisco, Denver, and Chicago, before getting back home in time to write his wife the following account of his trip, on December 26:

> I was wined and dined wherever I went in Vancouver, B.C., and at Tacoma where I remained about ten days making Studies. At Vancouver Mr. Abbott gave me his private car and my cook was one the Princess Louise had had, and I lived a la Prince! At Tacoma I met old and new friends and they sprinkled the ground with Champagne in my honor. Then to San Francisco where Madden, Alvord, Heuston and others did their best. The Clubs in all these places made it very pleasant for me. All enquired after you. . . . At Denver City they made dinners for me, Gov. Evans, Gen. Elbert and Bishop Warren;—Mrs. Warren ordered a picture. Then to Omaha. I stopped with Genl Patrick, two days in Chicago where I called on Pullman and Potter Palmer. Here I find many letters, dinners, receptions, the Astors, Roosevelt, Cutting, Mrs. Bliss, Gurnee Stuart, etc, etc.[33]

Sometime in 1880—possibly in the early months, since there does not seem to have been an occasion later—Bierstadt stalked and killed a moose in either New Brunswick near the Maine border or in Maine itself. He was a charter member of the Boone and Crockett Club, founded by his friend Theodore Roosevelt, whose one hundred members were made eligible by having "killed with the rifle, in fair chase, by still-hunting or otherwise, at least one individual of each of three various kinds of American large game."[34] "Fair chase" was taken to exclude "killing bear or cougar in traps, no 'fire hunting,' nor 'crusting' moose, elk or deer in deep snow, nor 'calling' moose."[35] Bierstadt's moose had the eighth

264

largest antlers in sporting history. These can now be seen on the body of the magnificent animal in the central diorama of Boston's Museum of Science (Fig. 199). The artist had given them to the New York Zoological Society, whence they came to Boston. Back in New York in early September, after another trip to California, Bierstadt continued his social life, including a dinner at Delmonico's in January, 1881, to which U. S. Grant accepted an invitation. He also planned, briefly, a house in Newport. Back with Lorne in June he went salmon fishing on the Gaspé Peninsula in a salmon stream which had been reserved for the governor-general and near which Dufferin, Lorne's predecessor, had built a fine house. During this time he may also have produced two recently discovered oils-on-wood of game birds and visited Nova Scotia.

About the middle of July he left New York for his first trip to Yellowstone Park.[36] There he stayed three months, collecting sketches and memorabilia, including a twenty-foot buffalo skin. "I purchased it while in the territories," the artist told a reporter later, "it being against my inclination, as you know, to kill anything when it is not absolutely necessary."[37] (Membership in the Boone and Crockett Club evidently came under the heading of absolute necessities.) In these hunting days Bierstadt also produced one of his rare watercolors (Fig. 200) and a hunting scene with a palette remarkably different from that customarily used (Fig. 201).

Most of what we know of the Yellowstone venture is the newspaper interview that the artist gave after he got back; from the John Sherman book (see below); and from a number of paintings. Although the reporter said that the artist had "caught the spray of the Bridal Veil" while he was away, evidently Bierstadt did not go to Yosemite this trip:

Yes, I have enjoyed myself—far more than I expected. I roughed it because it was necessary, and I think that I feel better for it. Why, I have become so accustomed to robust exercise that now I am in the midst of civilization, I hardly know what to do with myself. While I was in the Park we lived in tents almost exclusively. There are no houses anywhere near the geysers, and hence we found it sometimes very lonely. I say lonely because I did not find people to converse with; but, ah! how can one be lonely when one is surrounded by all the glories of a most glorious nature, and overhung by a sky unequaled by any in the

202. *On Route to Yellowstone Park, Company A's Camp of the 86th U.S. Army* [correct title?].
1881? Oil on paper mounted on canvas, 13 7/16 × 18¾″ (34.2 × 47.7 cm.).
Collection E. P. Richardson, Philadelphia

world? . . . This is not the first season I have spent about the Rocky Mountains, but it is my first introduction to the geysers of the Yellowstone. . . . We encamped near the geysers, and hence the heat of the boiling water warmed the atmosphere about us. The scene when looking from our tents out into the cool moonlight air, with the silvery spray of the geysers spreading out over the landscape, and the cascades falling from the cliffs in the distance, was very beautiful. I have several sketches here which I intend as jogs to my memory. . . . The Yellowstone Lake is not as clear as is popularly supposed, but is covered by a light film of green, due, in all probability, to the decayed vegetable matter at its bottom. It is very smooth, however, and is very rarely stirred to a storm. It is full of trout. The fish resemble the California trout to a noticeable degree, and sometimes are good eating. When I say sometimes I mean that the greater quantity of them are troubled, and, in fact ruined, by a parasitic worm. The fish are sometimes sixteen and eighteen inches long, and when caught have a worm which has eaten its way through the back. This is enough to disgust a person with the fish, as a dish is seldom very appetizing when one finds a worm eighteen inches long in the sauce. . . . The hunting through the park is very good, although it is against the law. But one does not heed the strict letter of the law when one is hundreds of miles away from civilization. . . . I shall be among the exhibitors at the academy next season. I do not regard the defection of the younger artists from the old Academy of Design as very fatal to either school. Artistic work in this country needs, as does business, a great deal of competition. The division has that effect, and I think it is by all means for the best. I am quite sure that all my brother-artists feel the same way, and although regretful that there has been any misunderstanding, are yet pleased to see the manly spirit of the growing artists.[38]

We know a bit more about Bierstadt's Yellowstone visit from the account in John Sherman's *Recollections of Forty Years*.[39] Sherman was one of the party who made the trip, along with General W. T. Sherman and others. The party formed in Chicago late in July, 1881, and from there went to Salt Lake City. There they stayed a few days before proceeding north through Ogden to Dillon and

Virginia City, Montana, and thence southeastward, evidently through the Madison River Valley, into Yellowstone. Bierstadt was one of the few members of the party to scale the 10,000 feet of Mount Washburn.

The party then left the park at Mammoth Hot Springs, near its northern border, traveled to Bozeman, Montana, and then back to Virginia City, Dillon, Ogden, Salt Lake City, and home. In spite of a number of Bierstadt paintings which dealers have given Grand Teton titles, the artist did not visit the Tetons on this, the only trip during which he approached the area.

After returning from Yellowstone on October 27, 1881, Bierstadt went up to Niagara Falls to greet the Lornes, who were on a state visit to the Falls before going west to Chicago, San Francisco, British Columbia, and, possibly, like their artist friend, to Yellowstone. "What beautiful sketches you must have brought back from that National Park of wonders," Lorne wrote Bierstadt the following spring.[40] He also thanked the artist for a painting of Montmorency, up the Saint Lawrence from Quebec. Lorne's wife, incidentally, had "much artistic ability, and is extremely fond of painting and drawing."[41]

Rosalie had returned from Nassau in the spring, and in November, 1881, she went back again for five months, returning in May, 1882. While in Nassau she stayed in great comfort at the Royal Victoria Hotel, partaking of the social life of the place with considerable relish. Whenever he could get away, her husband joined her—although his exact movements to and from Nassau in these years are unknown.

In September, 1882, Bierstadt was again in Niagara, where his brother Charles and two sisters lived, lunching and dining with Princess Louise. On his way up, he and his wife stopped to visit the in-laws in Waterville, and friends gave an elaborate reception for Rosalie. Two hundred guests were there, and "everything that would please the eye, ravish the ear, or tickle the palate was in abundance, and dispensed with admirable grace."[42]

NOTES: 1 Henry to Bierstadt, January 20, 1874, Manuscript Division, Library of Congress, Washington, D.C.

2 Bierstadt to unknown addressee, November 20, 1873, The New-York Historical Society. It has been said that this letter was written to a New Yorker and was part of an effort "to create such

an institution [as the Metropolitan Museum]" (Richard Shafer Trump, "Life and Works of Albert Bierstadt" [Ph.D. diss. (Columbus) Ohio State University, 1963]). But I think it clear that the letter was written to a resident of another city. Although Bierstadt regrets that he did not meet the addressee in New York, he refers to "your city," and this is an unlikely phrase for Bierstadt to use in referring to New York.

3   *The Utica Morning Herald and Daily Gazette,* September 17, 1874. Part of the piece was reprinted in *The San Francisco Bulletin*—Bierstadt's California friends remained interested in news about him for many years—on September 25. The article itself was dated September 11. The writer had "lately enjoyed a visit."

4   Bierstadt to Bancroft, October 17, 1874, Massachusetts Historical Society, Boston.

5   Furness to Bierstadt, February 9, 1874 (?), Henry Francis du Pont Winterthur Museum, Winterthur, Delaware.

6   *The Philadelphia Daily Evening Bulletin,* March 12 and 14, 1874.

7   Undated, but evidently March 1875, clipping, collection Mrs. Orville DeForest Edwards, Dobbs Ferry, New York.

8   Charles E. Fairman, *Art and Artists of the Capitol of the United States of America* (Washington: U.S. Government Printing Office, 1927), p. 271.

9   *The San Francisco Bulletin,* November 2, 1875.

10   *The New York Herald,* as quoted by *The San Francisco Bulletin,* December 3, 1875.

11   Quoted by James Thomas Flexner, *That Wilder Image* (New York: Bonanza Books, 1962), p. 299.

12   Clipping from Ottawa newspaper of February 24, 1876, collection Mrs. Orville DeForest Edwards, Dobbs Ferry, New York.

13   Unidentified clipping of dispatch dated February 25, 1876, and published in New York, perhaps the following day, collection Mrs. Orville DeForest Edwards, Dobbs Ferry, New York.

14   Rosalie Osborne Mayer to Mrs. Ross Taggart, undated, Museum of Fine Arts, Boston.

15   *Ibid.*

16   Dufferin to Bierstadt, October 1876, collection Mrs. Ralph Rooks, New London, Connecticut.

17   *The Philadelphia Press,* August 24, 1875.

18   Undated, but apparently early 1876, clipping, collection Mrs. Orville DeForest Edwards, Dobbs Ferry, New York.

19   *The Rocky Mountain News,* August 31, 1877.

20   Bierstadt to C. H. Brainard, October 9, 1877, Henry Francis du Pont Winterthur Museum, Winterthur, Delaware.

21   Bierstadt to unknown addressee, December 20, 1877, Boston Public Library.

22   Mitchell to "Rogers," August 10, 1877, Rutherford B. Hayes Library, Fremont, Ohio.

23   Bierstadt to Webb Hayes, April 21, 1878, Rutherford B. Hayes Library, Fremont, Ohio.

24   *Ibid.*

25   Bierstadt to Webb Hayes, April [—], 1878, Rutherford B. Hayes Library, Fremont, Ohio.

26   A. Pendarvis Vivian, *Wanderings in the Western Land* (London, 1879).

27   This and the following quotations dealing with the Bierstadts' travels in Europe in 1878–79 are taken from Esther Osborne's notebook of reminiscences, collection Mrs. Orville DeForest Edwards, Dobbs Ferry, New York.

28   Henry T. Williams, *The Pacific Tourist* (New York: H. T. Williams, 1876), p. 226.

29   This is at the end of the notebook of reminiscences.

30   G. W. Sheldon, *American Painters* (New York: D. Appleton, 1879), p. 149.

31   S. G. W. Benjamin, *Art in America* (New York: Harper & Bros., 1880), pp. 7–8.

32   *The American Art Review*, volume for 1880, p. 350.

33   Bierstadt to Rosalie Bierstadt, December 26, 1880, Museum of Fine Arts, Boston.

34   George Bird Grinnell (ed.), *American Big Game in Its Haunts* (New York: Forest and Stream Publishing Co., 1904), p. 486.

35   *Ibid.*

36   One of the more frustrating projects related to this work has been my attempts to trace a sketchbook the artist kept while in Yellowstone. It surfaced briefly in 1965 and has been unlocated since. A single note concerning it, "Yellowstone Camp, August 1881," is all that remains a part of recorded history.

37   *The New York Express*, October 28, 1881.

38   *Ibid.*

39   John Sherman, *Recollections of Forty Years* (New York: Werner, 1895), p. 823ff. (I am grateful to William H. Truettner for drawing this book to my attention.)

40   Lorne to Bierstadt, May 25, 1882, Henry Francis du Pont Winterthur Museum, Winterthur, Delaware.

41   Undated, but obviously 1881, clipping, collection Mrs. Orville DeForest Edwards, Dobbs Ferry, New York.

42   *The Rome* [N.Y.] *Republican*, September 9, 1882.

Eleven

The Decline Continues

1882-1893

203. Bierstadt at about
fifty-three. c.1883.
Collection Esther R. Bascom,
Rosalie R. Rooks,
Joyce R. Edwards, and
Pauline R. Perry

IN THE FALL OF 1882, Bierstadt, beset at once by unfriendly critics, a wife demanding constant, expensive care, and the responsibility of sustaining a life style worthy of a millionaire, was met with another disaster. On the morning of November 10 his house on the Hudson, Malkasten, burned to a shell, destroying property valued at $175,000, including a number of the artist's works.

The Tarrytown Argus said that the artist had not lived in the house for a number of years. The last time he regularly stayed there, judging from his correspondence, was in 1876. After that he wrote off and on from three addresses: the Brevoort, the Tenth Street Studio Building, and the 1271 Broadway studio. The New York City directory of 1877 listed him on Tenth Street and in Irvington. This was the last Irvington listing. The house had apparently been let by the summer, although the tenant for 1882, Henry T. Chapman, a broker, had stayed late in the season. He had, in fact, moved out with his family on November 9, the day before the fire.

Bierstadt's gardener, Peter Conrad, stayed in the house the night after the Chapmans left but swore that all the fires were out when he went home for breakfast early in the morning of the tenth. His account, told to a *New York Sun* reporter, is just a little ambivalent:

> I am sure that there was then [i.e., Thursday night] no fire in any part of the house. There had been a fire in the kitchen, on the northeast corner, in the dining room, and in the lady's room, but the family had used up all their fuel, and all the fires were out by noon. There was not a shovelful of coal left, and the last fire, to get breakfast by in the kitchen, was made with wood that soon burned out. Just a little before daylight I went home for my breakfast. A little after 7 o'clock I went back. I am sure nobody could have got into the house in my absence. When I entered the house I found the kitchen full of smoke. I ran for my fire extinguisher, and tried to use it, but the fire was already dropping down on me from overhead. It was between the floor and the ceiling, and between the stone wall and the pine lining of the studio, where I could not get at it. I ran out and cried Fire! and then ran back and saved what I could. Some of Jay Gould's men came over and helped me and some other persons, and after a while the firemen came, but they were too late to do any good. We saved twenty-two pictures and a

273

few other things. One picture I took out myself was big enough for four men to handle, and that, I think, was when I strained my back and my breast and my knee, but I was so excited then that I did not know it.[1]

Conrad talks about all the fires in the house being out by noon of the day the Chapmans left, on Thursday, and adds that among these was a little shovelful of wood coals in the kitchen. These had been used by the Chapmans to get breakfast with before they left. This was evidently after breakfast and before lunch, their last meal being breakfast. Assuming the weather to have been cold, since the Chapmans had fires in the dining room and the "lady's room," how did Conrad keep warm on Thursday night? Did he have no fire at all from Thursday noon on? He said that the Chapmans had used up all their coal, but evidently there was some wood left. It is easy to think that he had a wood fire in the kitchen before he went to bed, probably near the kitchen, and in the morning before he went home for breakfast. Would he have been content to stay all night in a cold house? Evidently his conscience hurt him.

Bierstadt's losses were in the neighborhood of $175,000, with the insurance covering all but about $35,000 or $40,000. The fire, then, left him with $125,000 or more. In a way, the holocaust must have been a relief. The house, with its taxes and maintenance—he evidently had a full-time caretaker—was likely as much a deficit as an asset, with the summer rentals scarcely covering the bills. It is also true that after a few years of luxuriating in its splendors, the house grew less attractive to the artist. Even in its early years, when Bierstadt was comfortably off and could well afford the expense, he often traveled or stayed in New York, even during the summer when the Irvington house was a tempting resort.

The artist's account of the fire is poignant. He was especially dismayed at the loss of his Western artifacts. For his whole life he was filled with nostalgia for the West and particularly for the glorious trip to the Wind River Mountains in 1859:

Mr. Bierstadt was in his studio over the Dime Savings Bank last night. "I was here," he said, "when a friend came in and told me my house was on fire. That was about 9 o'clock. I went up by the first train, but when I got there nothing was left standing but the walls. The building, which was of gneiss rock, taken out of the very spot where the house stood, and was finished with light granite trimmings, cost me $100,000. It was of no particular style of architecture, but erected to suit all the possible requirements of an artist. I could have painted a picture 40 feet long by 38 feet high in that studio. . . . Then the grounds outside were especially arranged with a view to painting animals under the best possible conditions of light and shade and background. The furniture in the house cost probably $10,000. There were also many paintings besides my own. The library was not a very large one, but contained many valuable works on art, and a large amount of patiently collected matters—that cannot be replaced—concerning the early history of this country, upon which I have been painting a good deal. The studio had in it not only some valuable paintings, but, what were to me almost priceless, the collection that I made during ten years in the Rocky Mountains of costumes, carvings, implements, and paraphernalia of various tribes of Indians and many objects of a branch of natural history in which I had deeply interested myself. I had made a study of the wild-horned animals of this country, and had many specimen heads of the deer, wapiti, mountain sheep, and goats from the time their horns start to grow until they are the most perfect specimens obtainable. For instance, I had fourteen pairs of wapiti heads. In the studio, also, were a great number of valuable studies and sketches, together with pictures completed and incomplete. . . . In some cases the loss in money would be almost nothing, yet in other regards very great. For instance, there was a book I had in my studio about early Indian wars that was copiously illustrated by Indians in their picture language, and some of the pictures in it were by Sitting Bull. I would not have taken a great deal for that.[2]

Among the Bierstadts lost, according to the artist, were an unfinished *Hetch-Hetchy Valley* and a *Niagara Falls.* The loss of these may not have caused much pain, since they had been started some time before. They had been left in a place where the artist seems not to have been comfortable for some years. And during the summer, at least, his tenants would not have particularly welcomed their landlord taking over the studio, nor would he have wanted to do so. A number of pictures were saved, however, and although the list the artist gave

The Sun was incomplete, it was substantial. But it is also true that of the works known to have been produced before the fire, nearly all are either located or have absences explained otherwise—such as an obscure foreign sale. Ten rescued pictures were named: *A Sunset in California; Glen Ellis Falls, N.H.; Portrait of J. B. Irving* (a fellow student at Düsseldorf)[3]; *The Wetterhorn; Autumn in the White Mountains; On the Pemigewasset River; Roman Scene; Moonlight in a California Forest; Coast Scene at Newport;* and *Sunset in* [sic] *a New York State Lake.*

Regrets poured in. Edmund Clarence Stedman wrote Mrs. Bierstadt: "I scarcely need write you to express my sorrow . . . not that I suppose you are so wedded to the place itself. . . ."[4] Lorne, in Vancouver: "I cannot tell you how grieved we were to see the telegram. . . . The Princess asks me especially to say how much she sympathizes with you, believe me, Dear Bierstadt. . . ."[5]

Fire or no fire, Mrs. Bierstadt was off to Nassau again at Christmastime. She went there for several months nearly every winter of the life that was left to her, occasionally returning to New York briefly in time to pack up for Europe. She was in Nassau the winters of 1883, 1884, 1885, 1886, 1887, 1891, 1892, and 1893, when she died. She was probably there in the other years—1888, 1889, and 1890—although there is no documentary evidence. During these years she went to Europe four times with her husband, in 1883, 1884, 1887, and 1891. Like her husband, she was not, one might say, a sedentary person. While in Nassau she lived in luxury at the Royal Victoria Hotel, and for all her illness managed quite a few sumptuous social occasions.

While she was gone, her husband busied himself with his own gadding. He was visiting Lorne in March, 1883, and wrote his mother-in-law a kind, warm letter:

> . . . the Governor wants me to spend a month with him. It is very charming here. . . . My visit recalls many charming occasions when Rose was here but alas I am afraid they will never be repeated again. . . . Dinner parties here every night; last night 48 dined here. Saturday night a large party on the ice, with 1000 lights; thermometer 18 below zero. Such is Canadian winter.[6]

He was back again with the Lornes in May:

Dear Mother,

I am having a nice time here. Her Royal Highness, the Princess Louise, is not only a clever artist but a charming woman in every way. We have picnics when we go out sketching and the weather is fine also. Everything is very free and easy except dinner at 8 1/4 when we all are in full dress. I take Her Royal Highness in to dinner most every day. The Governor is a right good fellow and takes good care of Canada. I wish we had a good government.[7]

Bierstadt sailed for Europe with his wife in June. Evidently he was now promoting the sale of a newly patented shotgun, for he showed it to the Japanese minister of war in Paris on June 23 and wrote that the minister was "much pleased."[8] A visit to Berlin, with possibly more gun promotion, followed in August, and the artist and his wife were back in New York in October. Then Mrs. Bierstadt wrote a two-installment letter to her sister, who was about to have a baby; first from off the Grand Banks and then, three days later, from New York:

. . . I hope for Father's sake it will be a boy—but I shall love it quite as well if it is a girl. Indeed if you should have six of them I should not think them too many. Perhaps in such an event you would let me have one of them to keep. . . . We have had a long and mostly stormy passage, but I have not once been seasick properly speaking. We have had Irving on board and Ellen Terry. . . . She is one of the most charming actresses of our age and so loveable off the stage. The Moscheles are on board. He is an artist and son of the composer. . . . They . . . sit at our table—Albert keeping the head and I the inside corner. . . . Albert sends much love as I do to you both. May God bless and keep you all. . . .[9]

In the fall of 1883, *Mount Whitney* and *Storm on Laramie Peak* were at the Louisville Exposition, and the Reverend Henry Whitney Cleveland thought that *Mount Whitney* was the "chief picture" of the show and "the fourth of the truly great landscapes of our country."[10] The other three, according to Cleveland, were Church's *Heart of the Andes* and *Niagara,* and Bierstadt's *The Rocky Mountains.* Although the critics did not much like Bierstadt now, amateurs, cultivated and otherwise, were still solidly in his camp.

During this year also the artist helped support a bill in Congress that would have placed works of art on a list free from import duty. He was later accused of wanting increased duty, and this confusion may have arisen from the fact that although a general tariff bill was passed raising the duties, the artist had vigorously supported the exclusion of art from the bill's provisions. He had, in fact, gone to Washington more than once to petition Congress to that effect. He made an excellent impression on some who saw him there.

> A tall, handsome man with a gray, waxed mustache [Fig. 203], and clear, piercing gray eyes, neatly-fitting Prince Albert coat buttoned tightly across his breast, is occasionally seen in the lobbies of the House and Senate. Just now he attracts the attention of those who do not know him, because of his handsome face and faultless carriage, and to those who do know him his name is a greater attraction than his face or figure. The small, neat card which he sends in by the door-keeper, bears the superscription "Albert Bierstadt, 1271 Broadway, New York." Those who know him point him out to their neighbors with a touch of pride, saying: "That is Bierstadt, the artist," whereupon Mr. Bierstadt is gazed upon by all who happen to be within earshot.[11]

The next year an interviewer from *The New York Spectator* found the artist "one of the most polite and cordial gentlemen . . . [German] but with little or no accent," hair beginning to turn "the least bit gray," and "the embodiment of health and good spirits."[12] An unidentified but penetrating writer of the time gives us another good picture of the famous artist:

> Mr. Bierstadt seems quite oblivious to his [reputation]. . . . Neither does he affect any singularity of costume as a necessary insignia of genius. The long locks, the long beard, the outre collar, the dingy and dilapidated garments which give to many artists not only a distingue but a very dirty appearance, all are wanting. Yet he has a marked presence, and an intellectual beauty of pose, dependent upon neither outline nor coloring. The gray eyes are remarkably clear and kind, even gentle in their expression. His manner is singularly free from self-consciousness. It is not the manner of a "man of society," but of a nature simple and sincere, yet somewhat isolated and introspective, which has formed

itself. It is the manner of a man who says very little simply for the sake of making himself agreeable, but who means always to be true and kind.[13]

The *Spectator* reporter was told that the artist had sent one of his Big Tree pictures to a London gallery, where, after it had been received, it was "remembered" that only dead artists were shown in that gallery. "Mr. Bierstadt," the reporter wrote, "told the managers that rather than die just then he would take the picture back."[14] It seems unlikely that such a definite policy would be remembered only after a picture had braved the Atlantic to get there.

In April, 1884, Bierstadt sent Chester Arthur some paintings of Yellowstone for the White House, and, as a result, it has been said, Arthur visited the park. Needing money later, the artist tried to get an appropriation to pay for the paintings. In June, 1886, and as late as November, 1893, he was still trying. "I am at this moment," he wrote to a Washington contact in 1888, "in want of money . . . cannot you raise for me ten thousand dollars . . . with the pictures as security. I would make a discount. . . . I have an investment I wish to make. . . ."[15] "I have been told," the artist had written the preceding year, "that in order to have the bill passed for the purchase of my works in the White House that a 'lobbyist' is necessary . . . can you give me some information on this point."[16] According to Harrison papers in the Library of Congress, Bierstadt made further efforts to persuade Cleveland's successor, Benjamin Harrison. He had left the pictures in the White House, he told Harrison, at President Arthur's "earnest request." He commended Arthur's secretary, still in Washington, as his agent. Two years later he tried again, just after his wife died.

Hard times reduced the artist to other undignified extremities. Through a contact he had close to the shah of Persia he tried, in effect, to sell the office of Persian Consul General in the United States:

. . . the party near the Shah who gives this office wants twenty five thousand dollars for it. You would have to call it $30,000 so as to have a margin. There is money in it as Persia would give all contracts—etc—etc —through that office and I would like to get a man who would look at the business part of it as well as the social. Some of the Washington people would like to be the first representative of a power like this This

279

must be kept very quiet and not get into print as there are plenty of people who want it at double the price. . . . I am told by some people that there are millions in it. Persia has no debt wants all modern improvements, etc—etc. If a good man is found I would cable his name and get answers if he would be accepted. if accepted the proper papers would come through the State Dept.[17]

The first American minister to Persia was the historian S. G. W. Benjamin, whom Bierstadt knew well. It is likely that Benjamin was the artist's "party near the Shah."

In 1885 and again in 1888 the artist wrote President Cleveland directly, introducing him to two distinguished visitors. Earlier in the latter year he introduced the inventor of a new gun, Henry Schulhof, to the President. He had had Schulhof to dinner at the Union League Club and was very enthusiastic about the new gun and pistol. "I think this matter is almost as good as the Edison inventions, as the European powers are bound to have them."[18] In spite of this, however, he told a *Tribune* reporter that he was not interested in a financial way but rather because of his years in the wilderness, where a gun was "a most valuable companion."[19]

In 1884, the artist and his wife visited Italy, Switzerland, Paris, and London, and stayed four or five months; in 1887, there was a very brief visit, evidently not more than a month; in 1891, they were in London, Brussels, Cologne, Berlin, and the Isle of Wight, where they visited the Lornes. This time he stayed two months, and possibly his wife did not go with him. In the summer of 1886 he visited the Wisconsin Dells and the Lake Superior region (Figs. 204 and 207). Returning from this trip, he found waiting for him a decoration from the sultan of Turkey, the Order of Medjid. The sultan had been given the artist's painting of a Yellowstone geyser by a Constantinople banker, and it now hung on the walls of a palace on the Bosporus alongside others fancied by the ruler, including works by Gérôme and Meissonier.

Late the same year the immensely popular Hungarian painter Mihály von Munkácsy stayed with Bierstadt and painted in his studio. He was given a dinner at Delmonico's by the Hungarians of the city, to which Bierstadt was invited along with Carl Schurz, Joseph Pulitzer, Henry Ward Beecher, Abram Hewitt, Chauncey Depew, Perry Belmont, Jesse Seligman, D. O. Mills, Whitelaw Reid,

280

204. *View of Duluth* [correct title?]. 1886. Oil on paper mounted on canvas, 18½ × 28″ (47 × 71.1 cm.).
Collection Jeno F. Paulucci, Duluth, Minnesota

205. *The Last of the Buffalo.* 1888.
Oil on canvas, 71¼ × 119¼″ (181 × 302.9 cm.).
The Corcoran Gallery of Art, Washington, D.C.
(Compare CL-254.)
In 1888, the year of this painting, there are said
to have been 541 buffalo in the United States

206. Buffalo skull evidently used in
The Last of the Buffalo. The American
Museum of Natural History, New York City

and Daniel Huntington. Both Bierstadt and Huntington, among others, made speeches.

Several days later Huntington, responding to Bierstadt's invitation to serve on a committee of artists to select American works for an English exhibition the following year, declined the honor. Seven or eight of the artist's works finally appeared in the show, which was under the management of John Sartain, the Philadelphia engraver and head of the art bureau of the 1876 Centennial. Huntington suggested others, including Frederick Dielman, who later made his own suggestions to Bierstadt.

One of those suggested was William Sartain, John's son, a well-known landscape painter. A letter of January 11, 1889, from William to his father,[20] is the earliest documentary evidence of Bierstadt's last famous work, *The Last of the Buffalo* (Fig. 205). Sartain suggested to his father that the painting should be "etched," and that he thought his father could get fifteen hundred dollars for the job.

Bierstadt had prepared the work for, and submitted it to, the selection committee for the Paris Exposition of 1889. As a Chevalier of the Legion of Honor he was entitled to a place in the Paris Salon of that year, and he took it, loaning *The Last of the Buffalo*. But when the work was shown to the group of American artists in New York who were choosing works for the Paris Exposition, it was rejected. One of them, J. G. Brown, later said that it was principally because the painting was too big—it was six by ten feet—but also because it did not represent Bierstadt at his best. Surely the principal reason was because the artists thought that it did not represent American art at its best.

Joseph Pulitzer's *World* was at its sarcastic best in reporting the affair:

The Committee of seventeen distinguished artists who were appointed to select pictures for the American exhibit at the Paris Exposition paid a high compliment to Mr. Albert Bierstadt by rejecting his superb canvas, "The Last of the Buffalo." It is to Mr. Bierstadt's great credit that the vote in the negative was unanimous.

Those who have seen the collection forwarded by this eminent galaxy can best appreciate the delicate tribute paid the artist in question. Mr. Bierstadt's great picture was so singularly different from those chosen by the Committee, both in merit and value, that its rejection was

207. *On Lake Superior—Sand Island.* 1886? Oil on paper, 14 × 19″ (35.6 × 48.2 cm.).
Meredith Long & Co., Houston

imperative—the more urgently because nineteen-twentieths of the exhibit were selected by said Committee from the works of its own members. The blasphemy of placing a canvas worth only $25,000 beside works of art worth at least $10 a square yard is so evident that the justification of the Committee in its seemingly ruthless course of discrimination becomes clearly apparent. The only unpleasant feature of the whole matter is that Mr. Bierstadt, being a Chevalier of Legion d'Honneur, a medallist of the French Academy and Knight of half a dozen Royal Orders, has the privilege of sending his magnificent picture to the Exposition—American Art Committee withstanding or not—and has cruelly availed himself thereof.[21]

The exclusion of the artist from a Washington exhibition in this same month called forth equal scorn:

What manner of pigmies of pigment are these alleged artists who are seeking a notoriety beyond the reach of their daubs by forming "committees" from their petty little selves and then giving wide publication to the fact that they have "rejected" one of Albert Bierstadt's pictures? The latest bit of this idiotic impertinence was the exclusion from a Loan Exhibition in Washington of a fine canvas which had not been loaned but actually given, most generously, by Mr. Bierstadt for the benefit of the charity for which the exhibition was held. The only excuse for this amazing impudence furnished by the "artists" in charge was that Mr. Bierstadt "did not belong to their school of art." This same thin excuse was also given by the learned committee of chromo-tinkers who selected their own nightmares for the Paris Exposition, insulted Mr. Inness and "rejected" Mr. Bierstadt's magnificent work, "The Last of the Buffalo."[22]

The villain, of course, was not the American committee, or the European Committee, or even Bierstadt. The taste of Düsseldorf and Munich had been left far behind, and now the Barbizon painters were being pushed out of fashion by what *The World* called the "greenery-yallery Impressionist school."[23] Rejected in the sixties, when Bierstadt was having his first successes, the Impressionists were now beginning to take over the mainstream of fashion and in any case had

208. *Autumn Woods.* 1886. Oil on canvas, 54 × 84″ (137.1 × 213.3 cm.). The New-York Historical Society, New York City

generally monopolized the critics of the avant-garde. Pulitzer's optimism about an early end to the "Gallic craze," was, however, abysmally blind:

It is also pleasant to see that the Impressionist school had now reached the color-blind stage of staggers in art, and this year's crop of freaks [in the National Academy Annual] is so appalling that the end happily cannot be far off.[24]

For all this, Elizabeth Gardner Bouguereau sent her consolations and added a comment or two of her own about the "young men of the slap-dash school":

My darling Rosalie
My last letter to Albert answered your inquiries with regard to his large painting at the Salon. It looked finely in certain lights, but certainly many of its best qualities could not be appreciated without a nearer view. It was not hung high, nor was it quite on the line. I showed it to *many* persons, and it was much liked. . . . The American jury took both the lion's and the pig's share for themselves. From the men who composed it I anticipated they would not favor me, so I sent my new work to the Salon. Of the three good paintings I sent them they accepted the two largest, refusing a small canvas just for the sake of showing their power. They will succeed in their desire and *will obtain high recompenses* for themselves. The international jury is largely composed of young men of the slap-dash school. A few Members of the Institute are there as figure heads, but they will be outnumbered by the others. As I expected nothing, I am in no wise disappointed. I *love* my art. . . . Especially I disdain the journals, it disturbs one's peace of mind.[25]

The artist himself must have been deeply hurt. It is obvious he had done his best, and that best was now rejected by his fellow artists. It is difficult to believe that it was, as he told a reporter, "a matter of indifference" to him:

"It is a matter of indifference to me," said Albert Bierstadt, "but I cannot understand why they should refuse my picture, for there is only one, 'The Last of the Buffalo.' . . . They were the jury appointed to select works of art by resident American artists for the Paris Exposition.

209. *White Horse in the Sunset.* Undated. Oil on paper, 11½ × 15½″ (29.2 × 39.4 cm.).
Buffalo Bill Historical Center, The Whitney Gallery of Western Art, Cody, Wyoming

210. *The King of the Forest*. 1880s.
Oil on canvas, probably about 60 × 48″. Whereabouts unknown.
Formerly at the Free Public Library, New Bedford, Massachusetts

211. *The Moose*. Undated.
Oil on canvas, 49⅝ × 42½″ (126 × 107.9 cm.).
Pioneer Museum and Haggin Galleries, Stockton, California.
Haggin Collection

In their circular they say that this is the first opportunity to display in Europe the art of this country since 1878, and give utterance to the belief that American art has made great advance during the past ten years, which is undoubtedly true. All works produced by an American citizen since 1878 were to be eligible, and artists were urged to send their best work.

"I was, of course, anxious to aid the art jury, and designated 'The Last of the Buffalo' because it was one of my latest and was considered by my friends and competent critics as among my best efforts. Since then I have heard nothing more about the matter until I read the cable despatch in to-day's World. . . . Why my picture was rejected I, of course, do not know.

"I have endeavored to show the buffalo in all his aspects and depict the cruel slaughter of a noble animal now almost extinct. The buffalo is an ugly brute to paint, but I consider my picture one of my very best. To tell you the truth, I am not surprised because I have received more recognition in Europe than in America. My paintings sell better over there. Two are in the Imperial gallery at St. Petersburg, and there is another in the royal gallery at Berlin, while the Sultan of Turkey has another. That autograph photograph of Emperor William was given me by him in 1883, framed just as it is. You may imagine that it gratifies an artist to find his pictures commanding high prices, even though he does not always get the money."[26]

212. Bierstadt at about fifty-eight. c.1888. The Whaling Museum, New Bedford, Massachusetts

The Last of the Buffalo had an additional significance. It was apparently the immediate stimulus for the first official census of America's remaining buffalo. It is estimated that at the time of the discovery of America, there were 60 million buffalo and in 1850, forty years before Bierstadt's painting, 20 million. But at the time of *The Last of the Buffalo* the total number of cows, bulls, and calves in America was estimated to be only 551. Now, with government protection, that number has grown to 25,000.

On another trip West in August the artist wrote his wife back in New York from Banff, Alberta, to which he had gone on the newly completed Canadian Pacific Railroad: "I saw several train loads of Buffalo bones," he wrote. The bones were being sent East for use in sugar refineries, and Indians were hired to

291

gather them at four dollars a ton. "Here in reality was the last of the Buffalo. . . . Shall I send you a ton?"[27]

For miles the woods around Banff were afire, and the artist could not sketch the scenery because of the smoke. He felt "just like painting" and hoped he would soon get the chance. Near Banff he made studies for a large painting of Mount Sir Donald, honoring Donald Alexander Smith, the Canadian entrepreneur who built the railroad. This work was shown at the Union League Club the following January and is now in the public library of Bierstadt's home town, New Bedford (Fig. 214). Arriving in Victoria the following week, the artist sailed on a coastwise steamer, the *Ancon*, for a visit to Alaska. At Loring, Alaska, on Revillagigedo Island, the *Ancon* met disaster. At three o'clock in the morning the ship was backing off the wharf:

> . . . swinging on her stern line, to hold her off the reef. An excited Chinese, seeing the line slack, before the vessel's weight had come on it, cast the light [*sic*] off the wharf pile. Before another line could be passed ashore the Ancon was carried by the tide on to the reef. When the tide fell she broke her back.[28]

From shore the artist painted the ship lying wrecked, with felicitous results (Fig. 213). Unfortunately he and the other passengers had to stay in Indian huts and salmon canneries for five days, until the next steamer brought them back to Vancouver. Meanwhile, however, he made fifty studies, some of which survive.[29]

While in the Northwest the artist went again to Portland, where he made sketches of Mount Hood. "It will pay," he wrote his wife.[30] He was also in Tacoma, making studies for a *Mount Tacoma* and two or more showing Mount Tacoma (now Rainier) from the banks of the Puyallup River (Figs. 220 and 221).

Soon the artist sold *The Last of the Buffalo* to Colonel J. T. North, the nitrate king, for a reported $50,000 and was off to Europe on his 1891 gala. He visited Spain, Italy, and Portugal, making studies for his contribution to the upcoming World's Columbian Exposition, a celebration of the four-hundredth anniversary of Columbus's landing in the New World (Figs. 222–224). He also made an Isle of Wight visit to Princess Louise and her mother, Victoria. He showed the queen photographs of his latest work. Later she was said to have been pleased to say that she would like to own some of them. Why she did not bring her desire to fruition is anybody's guess. Later in the same year he went to San Salvador

213. *Wreck of the "Ancon," Loring Bay, Alaska.* 1889. Oil on paper mounted on panel, 14 × 19¾″ (35.5 × 50.2 cm.).
Museum of Fine Arts, Boston. M. and M. Karolik Collection

214. *Rocky Mountains in the Selkirk Range, near the Canadian Border, Mount Sir Donald.* 1889? Oil on canvas, 83½ × 57½″ (212.1 × 146 cm.). Free Public Library, New Bedford, Massachusetts

215. *Alaskan Coast Range* [correct title?].
Undated. Oil on paper, 13¼ × 19″
(33.7 × 48.2 cm.). National Collection of
Fine Arts, Smithsonian Institution,
Washington, D.C.
Gift of Mrs. Orrin Wickersham June

217. Northwest Indian artifact
collected by Bierstadt.
The American Museum of Natural
History, New York City

216. *Indian Canoes, Puyallup River,
Washington.* 1880?/1889? Oil on paper,
13¾ × 18½″ (34.9 × 47 cm.).
Kennedy Galleries, New York City.
May have been painted either during
Bierstadt's 1880 visit to the area or
during his 1889 visit

218. *Cloud Study.* 1889? Oil on paper mounted on board, 8 × 8⅜″ (20.3 × 21.3 cm.).
Collection Paul Hollister, Jr., New York City. Possibly a Canadian Rockies study

219. *The Conflagration.* Undated. Oil on paper, 11¼ × 15⅛″ (28.6 × 38.4 cm.).
Worcester Art Museum, Worcester, Massachusetts. Not a scene of the burning of Malkasten

220. *Puyallup River and Mount Rainier.* 1880?/1889? Oil on paper mounted on board, 13¾ × 19″ (34.9 × 48.2 cm.). Collection Henry Melville Fuller, New York City. This painting, as well as Fig. 221, may have been done either during Bierstadt's 1880 visit to the area or during his 1889 visit

(Watling's Island), where Columbus was believed to have landed, and sketched it. Rosalie had been doing research for him on the problem and had enlisted the aid of the governor of Nassau in the definition of the proper spot, which was, the governor wrote, "a sweeping coral beach on the S. E. point of Watling Island."[31] Either on a trip to Chicago or from photographs, he also made a study of the *Niña* and the *Santa Maria,* which had been reconstructed for the Fair and were lying at anchor in Jackson Lake, Chicago (Fig. 225).

In May, 1892, the work was ready, and Bierstadt produced a typical New York "afternoon." A liveried usher escorted visitors into a "magnificent" and "brilliantly illuminated" anteroom, where they found a

> . . . typical high-class gathering of the city, a couple of dignified divines, two or three artists with Velásquez beards, one or two literary people, a half dozen society men and women and a celebrated beauty. This, with a musician, is the proper admixture for a correct "afternoon." That is, to be very small and select, and for the entertainment of clever people. . . . After a few moments spent in the anteroom we went into the large studio where the great picture, unveiled, stood on an easel in a favorable northern light. The first

298

221. *Mount Rainier.* 1880?/1889?
Oil on canvas, 54 × 84"
(137.2 × 213.4 cm.). Union League
Club, New York City. Formerly called
Mount Shasta

impression is of a glowing, riotous, golden sunlight of the tropics, so different from our polar light. A brilliant blue sky is reflected in craters as blue, against whose horizon loom the white sails of the Spanish ships. The foreground is a clearing of the jungle, like woods near the shore. Cocoanut palms, in whose branches monkeys wrangle, and tangled tropical vegetation of wonderful coloring, add to the warmth of color scheme. The artist has chosen the moment when Columbus, with a few attendants, is just landing on the yellow beach from a small boat. The discoverer, taking possession of the country in the name of his king, has evidently just set his feet upon the golden sand, and swarming Indians are hurrying through the wood toward him, leaving a neglected fire in the clearing, to prostrate themselves at his feet. This is the first impression. After a little you begin to notice that one of the Indians possesses but a single brown leg, the other being indicated in white chalk. You see other mysterious white chalk outlines, all over the picture, but so powerful and startling is the remarkable work that you forget entirely at first its unfinished state, so strong is the effect of the blaze of color and the power of the conception and you realize that this will indeed be one of the most important attractions of the world's fair.

299

222. *The Landing of Columbus.* 1893. Oil on canvas, 80 × 120″ (203.2 × 304.8 cm.). The City of Plainfield, New Jersey

223. *The Landing of Columbus.* 1893?
Oil on canvas, 72 × 121″
(182.9 × 307.3 cm.).
The Newark Museum,
Newark, New Jersey

224. *The Landing of Columbus.* 1892.
Oil on canvas, 108 × 204″
(274.3 × 518.2 cm.).
The artist's wedding gift to his
second wife; his largest painting.
Formerly in the American Museum of
Natural History, New York City;
destroyed by order of the director,
March 1960

225. *The "Niña" and the "Santa Maria."* 1893? Oil on paper, 13½ × 18½″ (34.3 × 47 cm.). M. Knoedler & Co., New York City. Study for *The Landing of Columbus,* possibly sketched from photographs of the reconstructed ships in Jackson Lake, Chicago

Everyone was wondering, "If it is so great now, what will it be when it is completed?"[32]

On another such occasion the artist had as his guests of honor a descendant of Sebastian Cabot and of Admiral Pinzon, who commanded one of Columbus's ships.

The artist's guests were often favored with delightful souvenirs from his hand. In Nassau these were little seashells with a few strokes of paint inside; in New York they were the famous "Bierstadt butterflies" (Fig. 227). His technique in charming the ladies with little Bierstadts of their own was described by the lady reporter who had been titillated by the artist's New York "afternoon":

We women were so glad we *were* women that afternoon, for Mr. Bierstadt presented each lady with a souvenir. This is how he made them. We all clustered about the table and he took out a palette, a knife and some large slips of cartridge paper. Two or three daubs of pigment on the paper, a quick fold, and holding it still folded against a pane of glass, he made two or three strokes of that wizard-like palette knife on the outside, and hey, presto! a wonderful Brazilian butterfly or moth, even the veining on the wings complete! A pencil touch added the

302

antennae, the artist's autograph was added to the corner, and now we each of us own a painting by Bierstadt.[33]

The studio at 1271 Broadway, where these gatherings were held, was considered the finest in the city. At the "afternoon" described above, a young clergyman present read a chapter from a forthcoming novel, *The Greek Madonna,* in which the artist, under the pseudonym of Bradley Outerbridge, played an important part. Of interest to the historian in this impossible novel is the description it gives of the artist's studio:

Bradley Outerbridge's studio was located in the second story of a marble building on Fifth Avenue, the ground floor being used as a general picture-gallery and art salesroom. The studio itself, one of the most elegant in the city, was reached by both an elevator and a flight of marble steps. Bradley Outerbridge was a landscape painter of world-wide celebrity, his paintings adorning the palaces of the Emperor of Germany, the Czar of Russia, long lists of English castles and country-houses, and even the presence chambers of the Sultan of Turkey.

It was to Bradley Outerbridge's studio that Shelton Chauncey betook himself one afternoon late in October of his middle year in the Seminary, on a different errand from that of any previous visit. Not bothering himself to call the elevator boy, he climbed the marble staircase of this thoroughly fire-proof building. A liveried servant answered the bell call at the studio entrance. The door opened into a vestibule, at the opposite end of which still another door conducted to an ante-room. Beyond this apartment was the reception-room, which was carpeted with Wilton of white groundwork, and fitted out with elegant court furniture imported from Europe for the Irvington villa and saved unharmed from the wreck of the conflagration. Bear-skin rugs, the trophies of Bradley Outerbridge's hunting expeditions in the Rocky Mountains, were disposed here and there about the floor.

The walls of the reception-room were hung with some of the artist's finest California landscapes, and on the mantel stood a large-sized autograph picture of his friend, the Emperor of Germany, in black and

226. *Butterflies with Riders.* Undated.
Oil on paper, 10 × 14″ (25.4 × 35.6 cm.).
Private collection, New York City

white, with the royal crest emblazoned on the top of the gold frame. A small bookcase in ebony was surmounted by a somewhat similar souvenir from the Grand Duke Alexis. The photograph was taken imperial size and bore the Grand Duke's signature underneath. Costly bronzes were grouped on the mantel, in front of which stood a pair of immense Japanese vases of an intricate pattern. At the right of the vestibule opening into the reception-room, a pair of doors, partially of glass, admitted the visitor to what he most wanted to see—the studio proper. At first one seemed confronted by theatrical scenery, yet more artistic than seen on any stage, the paintings near the doorway being of such Titanic size that they reached from the floor nearly up to the high ceiling. One of these gigantic creations depicted the peaks of the Matterhorn. Another, the artist's masterpiece, two of the colossal trees of the California forest. On shelves at each end of the studio, in line with the frieze, stood white, stuffed Rocky Mountain goats. Indian relics and curios bedecked the spacious gallery, which seemed given over to naturalness.

At an easel, in range with the tall trees of the Mariposa Grove, sat Bradley Outerbridge, the mellow October sunlight streaming in

227. *Butterfly.* 1873–plus. Oil on paper, 6½ × 9¾″ (16.6 × 24.8 cm.). Florence Lewison Gallery, New York City

through the side windows of the well-lighted studio. As the porter announced Shelton Chauncey's coming, Bradley Outerbridge arose from the herd of buffaloes which he was painting, and shaking hands cordially with his visitor beckoned him to a seat in one of the sumptuous Gothic chairs.[34]

With *The Landing of Columbus* ready and waiting for its Chicago unveiling, the artist suffered the loss of his wife. Rosalie Osborne Bierstadt died at the Royal Victoria Hotel in Nassau, the Bahamas, on March 1, 1893, at the age of fifty-two. Her body arrived in New York on March 11, and the next day the funeral was held in Waterville. Her husband and his brother Edward and son, and other Bierstadts from New York and Niagara Falls were there. The local obituary recalled the deceased's charms:

> Mrs. Bierstadt from childhood was of a sunny and joyous nature, endowed with beauty of person and of mind, and in manner was winning and attractive. She had a rare literary taste and culture, and was a favorite in social life, for which she was especially fitted by her exquisite tact and easy adaptability. Delicate in health for many years she struggled bravely with disease and was patient and uncomplaining, enjoying much herself and making joyful all about her by her cheerful conversation sparkling with incident and adventure which her ready memory had always at command, and in her absence by her sprightly correspondence in which she was specially gifted. . . . After reaching Nassau where she had spent so many winters in the genial climate and warm sunshine she loved so well and with the many friends who had always anticipated her coming and by loving words and deeds had so greatly endeared themselves to her, she seemed slowly but surely to improve, and warmest hopes were raised that health would be restored and life prolonged. These flattering promises were of short duration and an illness of four days proved a strain too exhausting for the little strength she had gathered and so death came unexpectedly at last.[35]

The artist is said to have carried a miniature of his wife about with him after she died and set it beside him wherever he dined. Rosalie had been a beloved wife and a major asset to her husband in his career of knowing, entertaining, and winning over the "right" people. She was undoubtedly an excellent hostess and conversationalist. But in her last years she had been a burden, too, and in spite of her husband's grief, he must have felt a certain relief.

NOTES: 1   *The New York Sun*, November 11, 1882.

2   *Ibid.*

3   Bierstadt did few "finished" portraits. His *Martha Simon* of 1857 (Fig. 28); *The Cavalier* (Fig. 6); the J. B. Irving portrait listed as saved from the fire; an 1867 copy of an ambrotype of a black woman, Lucinda Seton Chase, which is said to have belonged to Augustus Saint Gaudens (I am grateful to Lois Fink for drawing this portrait to my attention); a portrait of his wife in her Mary, Queen of Scots, costume; a portrait of Oliver Hazzard Perry—not the naval hero—which I have been told about but have not seen; and another portrait in private hands which I have been told about but also have not seen—these comprise the list. A number of slighter, "unfinished" portraits were also painted. Several of these were reproduced in Fitz Hugh Ludlow's book, *The Heart of the Continent* (Fig. 89); others of a scout, possibly Jim Bridger (Figs. 60 and 61), and one of John Tyndall (CL-115), are reproduced here.

4   Stedman to Rosalie Bierstadt, November 12, 1882, private collection.

5   Lorne to Bierstadt, November 14, 1882, Henry Francis du Pont Winterthur Museum, Winterthur, Delaware.

6   Bierstadt to Mrs. Amos Osborne, March 7, 1883 (transcript), Museum of Fine Arts, Boston.

7   Bierstadt to Mrs. Amos Osborne, May 5, 1883 (transcript), Museum of Fine Arts, Boston.

8   Bierstadt to "Barttell," June 23, 1883, Archives of American Art, New York City.

9   Rosalie Bierstadt to her sister Esther, October 18, 1883, collection Mrs. Orville DeForest Edwards, Dobbs Ferry, New York,

10   From a seven-page critique by the Rev. Henry Whitney Cleveland of Louisville, Kentucky, in the New-York Historical Society. Cleveland was an author and journalist who lived in Louisville at the time of the Exposition. I have not determined if his critique of Bierstadt's painting was for publication or for self-edification.

11   *The St. Louis Post-Dispatch*, apparently May 4, 1883.

12   *The New York Spectator*, April 26, 1884.

13   Unidentified clipping, collection Mrs. Orville DeForest Edwards, Dobbs Ferry, New York.

14   *The New York Spectator*, April 26, 1884.

15   Bierstadt to unknown addressee, November 9, 1888, Historical Society of Pennsylvania, Philadelphia.

16   Bierstadt to unknown addressee, February 8, 1887, Historical Society of Pennsylvania, Philadelphia.

17   Bierstadt to "Mr. Bruce," February 21, 1888, Historical Society of Pennsylvania, Philadelphia.

18   Bierstadt to "Col. Woodworth," August 9, 1888, Archives of American Art, New York City.

19   *The New York Tribune,* undated clipping, collection Mrs. Orville DeForest Edwards, Dobbs Ferry, New York.

20   In the Sartain Collection, Historical Society of Pennsylvania, Philadelphia.

21   *The New York World,* March 17, 1889.

22   *Ibid.,* March 31, 1889.

23   *Ibid.*

24   *Ibid.*

25   Elizabeth Gardner Bouguereau to Rosalie Bierstadt, June 29, 1889, private collection.

26   Undated, but March 1889, clipping from *The New York World,* clippings album, collection Mrs. Orville DeForest Edwards, Dobbs Ferry, New York.

27   Bierstadt to Rosalie Bierstadt, August 5, 1889 (transcript), Museum of Fine Arts, Boston.

28   Will Lawson, *Pacific Steamers* (Glasgow: Brown, Son & Ferguson, 1927), p. 199.

29   I am grateful to Mrs. Patricia Roppel of Ketchikan, Alaska, for considerable precise information about the *Ancon* voyage.

30   Bierstadt to Rosalie Bierstadt, September 18, 1889 (transcript), Museum of Fine Arts, Boston.

31   Governor-General Blake to Rosalie Bierstadt, November 19, 1889, private collection.

32   *The Detroit Free Press,* May 15, 1892.

33   *Ibid.*

34   Shelton Chauncey [Charles W. de L. Nicholls], *The Greek Madonna* (New York: G. W. Dillingham, 1893), p. 157ff.

35   March 1893 clipping, collection Mrs. Orville DeForest Edwards, Dobbs Ferry, New York.

Twelve

Final Years

1893-1902

228. *The Morteratsch Glacier, Upper Engadine, Pontresina.* 1895? Oil on canvas, 72 × 119⅛″ (182.9 × 302.6 cm.).
The Brooklyn Museum, New York City.
Gift of Mary S. Bierstadt. The artist's 1895 Christmas gift to his second wife

Now bierstadt's indomitable energy helped him. Soon after his wife's death in 1893, he became involved in a project to establish a National Academy of Art in Washington, with Congress expected to give ten or fifteen acres for it. To this effect he tried to tap various wealthy ladies for a million dollars as a "corner stone."[1] We do not know what men were solicited, but the artist thought it would be a fine idea if a woman started the ball rolling. There were few women who could afford to do it, he wrote. These included Mrs. George Hearst—the artist had heard she had twenty million and she would not miss one million—and Miss Mary Garrett of Baltimore, the Baltimore and Ohio heiress. He expected to see Mrs. Hearst and would not directly ask her for the money but simply suggest a National Academy to her as a good idea for the country. Miss Garrett, he thought, might be interested in doing it for Baltimore. "She would like to do something better than Walters can do," the artist wrote, "who is not a gentleman. (the Garretts do not like him.) (Private.)"[2]

His fellow conspirator in this project was Kate Field, author of *Kate Field's Washington* who had published a tribute to Bierstadt's wife. "She has solved the problem," Miss Field wrote, suggesting that Rosalie had found "The Answer in the Great Beyond." "But as you say," Bierstadt replied, "this side of it is for us to solve."[3] The following year, at the time of his second marriage, he renewed his subscription to Miss Field's paper and, always thoughtful of others, sent a subscription to his sister Eliza in Niagara Falls. (In June, 1896, while the artist was in Europe, Eliza died, and Bierstadt went into mourning.)

His social life seems to have gone on unabated by mourning over the death of his wife. Invitations to General Sherman to a dinner at the Union League—"very tempting, &—yes—I will . . . "[4] and one to Edmund Clarence Stedman to the same occasion are extant. A Dr. Cassimati, the eighty-year-old ex-president of the Greek Senate, was evidently to be guest of honor. Clarence King, his old friend of Mount Whitney days, who was then staying at the Union League, was also to be there, in spite of the constant pain of a spinal affliction. Late in 1893, in a final effort to realize something from his five White House pictures, he was able to have a bill introduced authorizing their purchase for $65,000. "Really, Mr. Bierstadt," *The Art Amateur* jibed, "this is carrying a joke too far."[5]

A letter late in the year to President Cleveland described the artist's position concerning duty-free art, and the great number of fakes about:

311

Dear President-Cleveland:

Sometime ago when I had the pleasure of meeting you in our club, I spoke of the tariff on Art. out of 1400 Artists only 17 favor this tariff thus leaving 1383 who want no protection.

This great country has for years been aiding the Artists of foreign lands by telling the world that our Artists need protection. it is a great mistake. The only persons benefitted have been the dealers in Art. they prefer to pay the duty and armed with this document from the Custom house show it to the customer as an evidence of the genuiness [sic] of his goods which in many cases are clever imitations.

The Artists both here and abroad wish to protect the liberal picture buyer and aid him in his desire to posess only the best pictures wether [sic] by foreign or native artists. It is well known that fully one half of the pictures imported are frauds. Free Art would of course send us a ship load of these frauds, but this quantity would send the price down to five dollars each and that is the present value of most of them. Every man would have a Corot or Diaz and a host of others, although dead they still work by proxy. Corot left 700 pictures and sketches, out of this number twelve thousand according to a Paris paper have been sold in the Hotel Druot and when we reflect that most of them came to this Country we are not happy.

Give us free Art. good pictures we are not afraid of. it is the imitations. counterfits [sic] that injure not only the Artist but the buyer.

Most Sincerely Yours
Albert Bierstadt[6]

Bierstadt's efforts to elicit support for a National Academy of Art may have somehow led him to his acquaintance with Mary Hicks Stewart. "The Widow Stewart," as some of the artist's relatives called her, was the widow of David Stewart, the millionaire banker, father of the celebrated Isabella Stewart Gardner of Boston. Mrs. Stewart had been married before she married Stewart and had had two children. She was a member of the famous Hicks family of Brooklyn. Albert Bierstadt now became her third husband. Family legend has it that she married him for the people he knew and that he married her for the comfortable living she could give him. Inevitably, when a poor man marries a

229. Bierstadt and his second wife on the balcony of, perhaps, a Saratoga hotel. 1894–1901. Collection Albert Morton Turner, Orono, Maine

rich widow the explanation is money; few think that there is love, and money is never a coincidence.

The wedding took place at the bride's house in Brooklyn on March 7, 1894. She gave her age as fifty-one (it was actually fifty-seven), and he gave his as sixty-four. The pastor of St. Thomas Church, the Reverend Dr. J. W. Browne, officiated, and the witnesses were two of the bride's brothers, Edgar and Henry. Few of the groom's relatives were there, but one of these was his nephew Oscar Albert, son of the artist's brother Edward. Oscar Albert's wife, however, was not invited. The invitation has come down to us:

My dear Nephew.
Your father will hand you this. I want you to come to 322 Fifth Ave on Wednesday Mar 7th at 4 1/2 o'clock to meet and make the acquaintance of your aunt that is to be, Godwilling. It is to be a very quiet affair otherwise your wife would be included in this invitation

Yours truly
Albert[7]

313

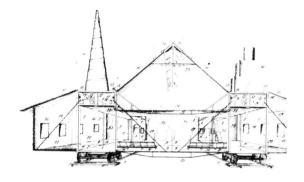

230. Bierstadt patent 559966, for railway cars designed to be adapted for use as a fort, a church, etc., filed June 26, 1893, granted May 12, 1896

Three-twenty-two Fifth Avenue was to be the Bierstadts' home until the artist's death, after which his widow moved into the Plaza Hotel.

For a wedding gift, the artist gave his new bride a version of his *Landing of Columbus*. It was nine by seventeen feet, the largest painting he ever made (Fig. 224). In 1909, seven years after he died, his widow gave it to the American Museum of Natural History. There it hung in the power plant until 1960, when it was inexplicably destroyed by order of the director.

The artist and his second wife are said to have spent several months of each year in Europe, and for the first four years of their marriage this seems to be correct. On their wedding trip, the first year, they were said to have been entertained by Queen Victoria on the Isle of Wight. If that is what the new bride wanted—to meet the "right people"—she was having her way. When in New York, the legend relates, they drove about in an open landau, she looking her way and he his. This picture of their life together cannot easily be squared with the obvious pleasure the two are having in a hotel balcony photograph (Fig. 229). Nor can it be squared with our knowledge of the artist's character: Bierstadt enjoyed life to its fullest and surely would not have married a woman who would not at least have been good company. The legend of indifference, not unexpectedly, comes from the first Mrs. Bierstadt's family, as does the statement that the marriage was a marriage of convenience. Young Oscar Albert's son has told me that he remembers Aunt Mary being very happy to see him, making him feel at home and giving him petit fours to eat.

He also remembers being shown a little model of a railroad car and being allowed to handle it. This was evidently the model for one of a series of patents the artist took out in the 1890s. There were six of them, three applied for in June, 1893, two more in May, 1894, and another in May, 1896.[8] All concerned improvements on railway cars, which were made to open out to form dwellings, chapels, theaters, art galleries, shops, etc., or to join with other such cars for the same purpose (Fig. 230). Although Bierstadt wrote Stedman that Pullman's "head man in Chicago"[9] had come to see his plans and was much interested, I have found no record of their having gone into production.

Sometime between May and August, 1896, Bierstadt wrote Henry Huttleston Rogers, in Fairhaven, Massachusetts, asking him to recommend a man to take hold of the railway car proposition. "All I want is an honest man who is willing and competent, as for me I am willing to let the man make a fortune. I

314

cannot afford to waste time making money"[10]—which seems an odd remark from a man who had spent most of his life doing little else. As a lagniappe, the artist sent along his portrait of Martha Simon, Rogers's "ancient neighbor" (Fig. 28).

Although the new Mrs. Bierstadt was a millionairess (she left more than one million when she died in 1916, though not a cent to a Bierstadt), the artist did not expect his new wife to take over his obligations. These included $10,000 he had borrowed in May, 1892, and $4,000 he had borrowed in September, 1894, after he had remarried. He assigned his entire property on January 17, 1895, to a referee for sale to the satisfaction of his creditors. The sheriff seized a hundred and fifty paintings to satisfy the $10,000 obligation, but the artist's lawyer, a Mr. Phelps, was sure that a sale would easily cover the obligations.

That summer the Bierstadts must have been in Europe, for at Christmastime of 1895 the artist gave his wife a magnificent Christmas present, a painting of the Morteratsch Glacier in the Engadine Alps, and signed it "Merry Christmas to Mary" (Fig. 228). The previous Christmas, Bierstadt had given his wife a Western scene; this painting has recently been rediscovered. In 1896 he was again in Europe—Budapest, Lucerne, etc. The Bierstadts were in Switzerland again in 1897 and apparently did not go again during the artist's lifetime. When getting ready to go in 1896, Bierstadt thought he might stay there:

> I may stay a year. I may make my home over there. I am boxing my things so as to have them sent if I want them. . . . Life here is getting to be a burden instead of a pleasure. It is just as bad for the people with money as it is with those who have nothing.[11]

Before he went abroad in May, 1896, Bierstadt became interested in promoting the gas and electrical projects of Charles Sanders Peirce, the mathematician-logician-philosopher. He gave Peirce half interest in a picture to be sold and the money used for patents on an acetylene invention of Peirce's. He tried to promote the invention in Europe, including Russia, but was unsuccessful. The following year, however, 1897, an English prospect materialized, and both the artist and Peirce got "thirty thousand dollars at least." "When it comes make some good investments," he admonished Peirce, "as the interest on that alone is a nice thing to have in [sic] a rainy day."[12] Bierstadt

315

evidently closed up his studio at 1271 Broadway in the spring of 1897, for in April he made arrangements for Peirce to have a sofa bed from the place.

The previous December the artist's nephew, Edward Hale Bierstadt, a book collector and bibliographer, died. The artist wrote the widow a kind letter, touching on his views on religion, a subject concerning which we have little information:

My dear Niece.
Would to God I could say my dear Nephew as well but alas he has left us and on Angel wing has gone to another and better world where we all hope to meet him and other dear ones as well.

This news I got as we returned from Church by a telegraph message. I replied at once saying our sincere sympathy. Command me if I can serve you. will come to you tomorrow.

May God in his great love comfort you. and do not forget that you and the dear little boy are dear to me as well as to other members of the family and as I said in my telegram to my brother command me if I can serve you. My wife joins in sympathy God bless you and your dear boy.[13]

During the years Rosalie was alive and ailing the artist spoke of his prayers for her recovery and the "Great Future" which God had prepared:

"I try to do my best and every day I read something from the Good Book, besides prayers for my Rosalie" [Bierstadt wrote]. One day when he had been reading from 1st Corinthians he wrote "How I wish I were able to use the beautiful language of St. Paul, and do as much good as he has done." In another letter "I firmly believe in the Great Future which God has prepared for us and I trust each day I am coming nearer to the life that will be in harmony with his."[14]

In July, 1897, from Switzerland, Bierstadt was still trying to promote the Schulhof gun, and wrote McKinley about it; in January, 1898, he interceded with the president for a friend who wanted an appointment at the Paris 1900 Exposition; in July, 1898, he sent the president a newspaper clipping from Bar Harbor, where he was staying; and the following month, he sent simply "good

316

wishes" from West End, New Jersey. In 1899 he tried to persuade the government, through the good offices of John Hay, the secretary of state, to buy an area on the Island of Corfu and its castle, Achillon, lately owned by the empress of Austria. The artist thought that if the United States owned it, it could be offered to Queen Victoria for her regular three-month spring outing, "and when the heads of two great nations come together it means peace."[15] Victoria regularly went to the South of France, but since there was then hostility between France and England, the queen might be exposed to embarrassment. She could go through Germany to Corfu and could bypass France. The artist had previously written McKinley himself, suggesting the use of the island as a naval base; evidently getting nowhere with the president, he decided to contact the secretary of state. But the United States did not act, and Victoria was deprived of her projected American hospitality.

Meanwhile Bierstadt's painting, now evidently done in the house at 322 Fifth Avenue, though diminished, was regular. In 1898 he painted a big *Golden Gate* and in 1899 a three-by-five *Destruction of Pompeii and Herculaneum*. Both of these went into his brother Edward's collection and were sold at the Edward Bierstadt sale in 1908. They were also exhibited at the third annual exhibition of the Worcester Art Museum which opened on June 3, 1901. There they were "greatly admired."[16] Late in the same year the artist tried to get back his 1858 painting *The Roman Fish Market* from the Boston Athenaeum and give the Athenaeum another in its place. But the Athenaeum would have none of this, "as Bierstadt's late work is not as good."[17]

On the morning of February 18, 1902, after returning from a walk to the Union League Club, Bierstadt complained of feeling ill and asked a servant to bring him a stimulant. He then went to his room, and when the servant came, he found the artist dead. His body was taken to the vault at Woodlawn, where it was kept until spring, when it was taken to New Bedford. There it was buried beside the bodies of Henry and Christina Bierstadt, his mother and father, in the New Bedford Rural Cemetery.

NOTES: 1 Bierstadt to Kate Field, May 14, 1893, Boston Public Library.

          2 *Ibid.*

231. The artist's studio. 1902? Vose Galleries of Boston

232. The artist's studio. 1902? Vose Galleries of Boston.
The New-York Historical Society's *Autumn Woods* can be identified, as well as a forest sunset scene to the right of *Autumn Woods*.
The Boston Museum of Science moose antlers and the stuffed mountain goats which the artist painted can also be seen

3   *Ibid.*, April 3, 1893, *loc. cit.*

4   Sherman to Bierstadt, September 4, 1893, Henry Francis du Pont Winterthur Museum, Winterthur, Delaware.

5   *The Art Amateur,* October 1893.

6   Bierstadt to Cleveland, November 29, 1893, Manuscript Division, Library of Congress, Washington, D.C.

7   Bierstadt to Oscar Albert Bierstadt, March 2, 1894, private collection.

8   Application nos. 559962, 559963, 559964, 559965, and 559966, all granted on May 12, 1896; and 566127, granted on August 18, 1896.

9   Bierstadt to Stedman, September 4, 1893, Archives of American Art, New York City.

10   Bierstadt to Rogers, undated, Millicent Library, Fairhaven, Massachusetts. Bierstadt speaks of having been allowed five patents. Five were allowed in May, 1896, with a sixth being allowed in August of that year. Thus the letters must have been written between the two dates.

11   Bierstadt to unidentified addressee, undated, private collection.

12   Bierstadt to Peirce, January 5, 1897, Houghton Library, Harvard University, Cambridge, Massachusetts.

13   Bierstadt to Mrs. Edward Hale Bierstadt, December 20, 1896, collection Mr. and Mrs. Albert Morton Turner, Orono, Maine.

14   Rosalie Osborne Mayer to Mrs. Ross Taggart, undated, Museum of Fine Arts, Boston. Miss Mayer was quoting from Bierstadt's letters, which were before her as she wrote but which are now unlocated.

15   Bierstadt to Hay, February 20, 1899, Manuscript Division, Library of Congress, Washington, D.C.

16   *The Worcester Daily Telegram,* June 5, 1901.

17   From a note of November 21, 1901, Boston Athenaeum accession records.

Chronology

1830   JANUARY 7: Albert Bierstadt born near Düsseldorf, Germany

1832   FEBRUARY 22: Arrives with family in New Bedford, Massachusetts

1850   MAY 13: Offers course in monochromatic painting, his first known art venture

1851   First known exhibitions, in New Bedford and Boston

      AUGUST 14: First known sale

1853   Goes to Europe to study in Düsseldorf

1856   JUNE (?): Leaves Düsseldorf, travels through Germany and Switzerland to Italy

1857   *Martha Simon*
      AUGUST: Leaves Italy and returns to New Bedford

1857–58   Resumes teaching and painting in New Bedford, exhibits, and takes trips to White Mountains, Newport, etc.

1858   APRIL: First "official" exhibition—*Lake Lucerne* and others—at National Academy of Design, New York City
      JULY 1: Organizes New Bedford's first art exhibition
      C. DECEMBER: First historical painting, *Gosnold at Cuttyhunk, 1602*

1859   APRIL: Leaves with F. S. Frost for trip through West with Lander's Expedition
      JULY 10: In Wyoming, writes long letter to *The Crayon*
      SEPTEMBER 3: In Wolf River, Kansas, writes letter to *The New Bedford Daily Mercury*
      C. DECEMBER: Moves to Tenth Street Studio, New York City

1860   FEBRUARY: *Wind River Country*
      C. APRIL: *The Base of the Rocky Mountains, Laramie Peak*

1862   *Sunshine and Shadow*

1863   C. MARCH: *The Rocky Mountains, Lander's Peak*
      C. APRIL (?): *The Bombardment of Fort Sumter*
      APRIL: With Fitz Hugh Ludlow, leaves for West to visit Nebraska, Colorado, Utah, California and Oregon
      AUGUST: Enters Yosemite Valley for the first time

1864   *Valley of the Yosemite*, first known Yosemite painting
      APRIL: *The Rocky Mountains*, at New York Sanitary Fair, elicits high praise (the artist rivals Frederick Church for the first time) and dissent
      C. MAY: *Mount Hood*

1865–66   Builds home, Malkasten, in Irvington on Hudson, New York

1866   C. JANUARY: *Storm in the Rocky Mountains*
      NOVEMBER 21: Marries Rosalie Osborne Ludlow, Fitz Hugh Ludlow's divorced wife, in Waterville, New York

1867   APRIL: *The Domes of the Yosemite*
      JUNE 22: Sails with wife for two-year stay in Europe, to visit England, France, Germany, Austria, Switzerland, Italy, and Spain. Awarded Legion of Honor by Napoleon III

1868   JULY 9: Host in London to spectacular dinner in honor of Longfellow

1870   *The Emerald Pool* completed
      FEBRUARY: Thompson sale and scandal

1871   JULY: Leaves with wife for two-year stay in California
      SEPTEMBER–DECEMBER: Arranges entertainment for Grand Duke Alexis of Russia

1873   C. JANUARY: *Donner Lake from the Summit*
      MAY: *Autumn in the Sierras*
      OCTOBER 11: Leaves California with wife for return to East

1875   c. MARCH: First national painting, *The Discovery of the Hudson*, finished

1876   FEBRUARY: Prominent guest, with wife, at Government Ball in Ottawa
Exhibits a Big Tree picture, a Yosemite view, a *Mount Hood*, *Western Kansas*, and *California Spring* at Philadelphia Centennial

1877   c. OCTOBER: *Rocky Mountains, Longs Peak*, commissioned by the earl of Dunraven, finished
Begins regular visits to Nassau for wife's health

1878   FEBRUARY: Stays at White House with Hayeses
JULY 20: Leaves with wife for a year in Europe

1880   c. JUNE: Goes to California
c. NOVEMBER: Goes to Washington, Vancouver, California, etc.

1881   JULY–OCTOBER: Visits Yellowstone Park

1882   NOVEMBER 10: Irvington home burns to ground

1883   c. MAY: Supports duty-free works of art
JUNE: Visits Europe, promoting sale of newly patented shotgun to foreign governments

1884   MAY 28: Leaves for Europe with wife

1886   Visits Wisconsin and Lake Superior region
Receives Order of Medjid from Sultan of Turkey

1887   Visits Europe with wife

1888   *The Last of the Buffalo*

1889   *The Last of the Buffalo* rejected for Paris Exposition
AUGUST–SEPTEMBER: Visits Canadian Rockies and Alaska

1891   Visits Spain, Italy, Portugal, and West Indies, making studies for *The Landing of Columbus* for World's Columbian Exposition

1892   MAY: *The Landing of Columbus*

1893   MARCH 1: Mrs. Bierstadt dies in Nassau
MAY: Promotes establishment of a National Academy of Art

1893–96   Patents for improvements on railway cars

1894   MARCH 7: Marries Mary Hicks Stewart

1895   JANUARY: Bankruptcy

1899   FEBRUARY: Promotes sale of island of Corfu to U.S.

1901   FEBRUARY 22: Last known work, a watercolor, signed and dated
JUNE 3: Last known exhibition during his lifetime, at Worcester Art Museum, Massachusetts

1902   FEBRUARY 18: Dies in New York City

Check List of Paintings by Bierstadt

IN PUBLIC COLLECTIONS IN THE UNITED STATES

I have tried to make this list as exhaustive as possible and have examined the large majority of the works listed. In several cases I decided that works attributed to Bierstadt were not authentic. So that it may not be thought that I have omitted these works inadvertently, I list the collections in which they are found: Oakland Museum, Oakland, California; Colby College Museum of Art, Waterville, Maine; Fruitlands Museum, Harvard, Massachusetts; Heckscher Museum, Huntington, New York; Andrew Dickson White Museum of Art, Ithaca, New York; The Metropolitan Museum of Art, New York City; Parrish Art Museum, Southampton, New York; R. W. Norton Art Gallery, Shreveport, Louisiana; and the Whitney Gallery of Western Art, Cody, Wyoming.

Titles are those supplied by owners, even if I believe these to be incorrect. Dubious titles are followed by the notation "correct title?" in brackets. Whenever possible, I have placed what I believe to be the correct title in brackets following the "official" title. Where I have not been able to supply correct titles, I have written "incorrect title" in brackets.

The dating is my own and sometimes differs from the owners'. In the case of paintings not dated by the artist himself, I have based the dates on other evidence. When dates are not given, it can be assumed that this evidence was too thin even for an estimate. I have avoided dating finished pictures to correspond with the dates of the studies: such pictures could have been produced much later. I have also avoided dates made on the basis of the stylistic or technical development of the artist's technique.

When "ABierstadt" appears, it should be assumed that the "A" and "B" are in monogram, with the right leg of the "A" identical with the spine of the "B". I have indicated the few exceptions. I have tried to retain original punctuation, capitalization, lineage, etc., although I have sometimes had to rely on imprecise information from owners.

Not all signatures are believed to be the artist's. I have sometimes indicated this, but there are a number of other cases in which signatures are evidently not authentic. Most of these were added to sketches or studies, and a number are remarkable for their naïveté. In general, I am skeptical of finished works without signatures, as well as signatures on sketches and studies: Why should the artist fail to sign a work he had finished and, on the other hand, sign a work he had not finished?

The collections are listed alphabetically by state and city in which they are located; works in each collection are listed chronologically. Dimensions are given with heights before widths. "LR" means lower right, "LL" lower left, "UR" upper right, and "UL" upper left.

G.H.

ARIZONA
Phoenix
Phoenix Art Museum:

CL-1. *Rocky Mountains*
Oil on canvas, 18 × 26½" (45.8 × 67.3 cm.).
LR: ABierstadt
Gift of Mr. Max W. Frendel

A preliminary study for this work has recently come to light (Fig. 107).

CALIFORNIA
Berkeley
*The Bancroft Library,
University of California:*

CL-2. *Covered Wagons* 1859?
Oil on illustration board,

14 × 11″ (35.5 × 27.9 cm.).
LR: ABierstadt   The Robert B. Honeyman, Jr., Collection. Reproduced by permission of The Director, The Bancroft Library

CL-3.   *Lake Tahoe, California* [correct title?]   1863?
Oil on canvas, 14 × 19″ (35.5 × 48.3 cm.).
LR: ABierstadt   The Robert B. Honeyman, Jr., Collection. Reproduced by permission of The Director, The Bancroft Library

University of California Art Museum:

CL-4.   *Yosemite Winter Scene*   1872
SEE FIG. 156
Oil on canvas, 32⅛ × 48⅛″ (81.6 × 122.2 cm.).
LR: ABierstadt/1872   Gift of Henry D. Bacon

Los Angeles
Los Angeles County Museum of Art:

CL-5.   *Lander's Peak, Wyoming*
Oil on canvas, 36½ × 26¼″ (92.8 × 66.7 cm.).
LR: ABierstadt   Gift of Mr. and Mrs. Henry M. Bateman

CL-6.   *Redwood Trees*
Oil on paper mounted on canvas, 30 × 21½″ (76.2 × 54.7 cm.).
Gift of Dr. Robert C. Major

Oakland
The Oakland Museum:

CL-7.   *Yosemite Valley*   1868
Oil on canvas, 36 × 54″ (91.4 × 137.2 cm.).
LL: ABierstadt/1868

CL-8.   *Owens Valley, South Sierra*   1871
Oil on canvas mounted on Masonite, 9⅜ × 12¾″ (23.8 × 32.4 cm.).
On reverse, in ink: Cala—Owens Valley S. Sierra, 1871

CL-9.   *California—Indian Camp: Scene near Mariposa*   1871–73
Oil on canvas mounted on Masonite, 14 × 21″ (35.6 × 53.4 cm.).
LL: ABierstadt

CL-10.   *The High Sierras*
Oil on millboard, 12 × 18″ (30.5 × 45.7 cm.). LR: ABierstadt

CL-11.   *Mountain Scene*
Oil on cardboard, 13¾ × 19″ (34.9 × 48.2 cm.).

CL-12.   *Ox*   SEE FIG. 50
Oil on cardboard, 11½ × 18¼″ (29.2 × 46.3 cm.). LL: AB

CL-13. *The Pacific Coast (The Bay of San Francisco)*
Oil on board, 13 × 20″ (33 × 50.8 cm.). LL: ABierstadt

CL-14. *Seals on the California Coast*
Oil on millboard, 16½ × 23″ (41.9 × 58.4 cm.). LR: ABierstadt

CL-15. *View of Oakland*
Oil on canvas mounted on cardboard, 6¾ × 10¼″ (17.1 × 26 cm.). LL: ABierstadt

San Diego
Fine Arts Gallery of San Diego:

CL-16. *View of the Wetterhorn from Grindelwald*
Oil on paper, 28½ × 19¾″ (72.4 × 50.2 cm.).
On reverse, in pencil, in artist's hand: The Wetterhorn/with the Valley of Grundelwald/Switzerland/A. B.
Gift of Mr. Edmund T. Price, 1958

The Timken Art Gallery, The Putnam Foundation:

CL-17. *Camping in the Yosemite* 1864
SEE FIG. 1
Oil on canvas, 34 × 27″ (86.4 × 68.6 cm.). LL: ABierstadt/1864

San Francisco
California Historical Society:

CL-18. *On the Merced River*
Oil on canvas, 36½ × 52½″ (92.7 × 133.4 cm.). LR: ABierstadt

California Palace of the Legion of Honor:

CL-19. *Farallon Islands* 1872
SEE FIG. 158
Oil on cardboard mounted on canvas, 14 × 19″ (35.6 × 48.3 cm.). On reverse before relining: Cala. 1872 Farallone Islands Pacific Ocean   Trustee Funds

CL-20. *Sacramento Valley in Spring* 1875
SEE FIG. 193
Oil on canvas, 55 × 85″ (139.7 × 215.8 cm.).
LR: ABierstadt   Gift of Gordon Blanding

This is evidently the painting given by the artist to the Montreal Art Association, the forerunner of the Montreal Museum of Fine Arts, which disposed of it (Chap. 9). It was one of the artist's National Academy pictures in 1875.

CL-21. *Nassau Harbor* 1887–plus
SEE FIG. 195
Oil on panel, 14¾ × 20″ (37.5 × 50.8 cm.). LR: ABierstadt
H.K.S. Williams Fund

Santa Barbara
Santa Barbara Museum of Art:

CL-22. *Mirror Lake, Yosemite Valley* 1864
Oil on canvas, 22 × 30¼″ (55.9 × 76.5 cm.).
LR: ABierstadt
Preston Morton Collection

This painting was used for an engraving for a frontispiece for Ludlow's *Heart of the Continent*. In another printing of the book, *Camping in the Yosemite* (Fig. 1, CL-17) was used.

Stockton

Pioneer Museum and Haggin Galleries:

CL-23. *Sunset in the Yosemite Valley* 1868
SEE FIG. 103
Oil on canvas, 35½ × 51½" (90.2 × 130.8 cm.). LL: ABierstadt/1868
Haggin Collection

CL-24. *Forest Monarchs* 1875–plus
Oil on canvas, 31½ × 47½" (80 × 120.7 cm.). LR: ABierstadt
Haggin Collection

Wright & Gardner's stretchers, patented January 19, 1875.

CL-25. *Cloud Effect, Estes Park* 1876–77
Oil on canvas, 15¾ × 20¾" (40 × 52.7 cm.). LL: ABierstadt
Haggin Collection

CL-26. *The Wave* 1887 SEE FIG. 197
Oil on canvas, 60 × 72" (152.4 × 182.9 cm.). LR: ABierstadt
Haggin Collection

Other titles are *The Surf* and *The Turquoise Sea.*

CL-27. *Canadian Rockies* 1889?
Oil on canvas, 27 × 18½" (68.6 × 47 cm.). LL: ABierstadt
Haggin Collection

CL-28. *Mount Sir Donald* 1889?
Oil on canvas, 27⅜ × 19½" (69.5 × 49.5 cm.). LL: ABierstadt
Haggin Collection

CL-29. *Evening on Oneida Lake* [*Oneida Lake*]
Oil on canvas, 32 × 45" (81.3 × 114.3 cm.). LL: ABierstadt
Haggin Collection

CL-30. *In the Yosemite Valley*
Oil on canvas, 23⅜ × 31⅜" (59.3 × 79.7 cm.). LL: ABierstadt
Haggin Collection

CL-31. *Lake in the Yosemite Valley*
Oil on canvas, 44 × 34¼" (111.8 × 87 cm.). LL: ABierstadt
Haggin Collection

CL-32. *The Moose* SEE FIG. 211
Oil on canvas, 49⅝ × 42½" (126 × 107.9 cm.). LL: ABierstadt
Haggin Collection

CL-33. *Yosemite Valley*
Oil on canvas, 36½ × 52¼" (92.8 × 132.7 cm.). LL: ABierstadt
Haggin Collection

Yosemite
Yosemite National Park Museum:

CL-35. *Night at Valley View* 1864
SEE FIG. 114
Oil on canvas, 34 × 27⅛" (86.4 × 69
cm.). LL: ABierstadt/64

The former title was *Moonlight on
the Merced.*

COLORADO
Colorado Springs
Colorado Springs Fine Arts Center:

CL-36. *Rocky Mountain Landscape*
Oil on paper mounted on canvas,
12½ × 18" (31.8 × 45.7 cm.).
LR: ABierstadt Gift of Mrs.
Earle E. Partridge, Mrs. Marshall
Sprague, and Mrs. John Wolcott
Stewart

CL-37. *Teton Range, Moose, Wyoming* [in-
correct title]
Oil on paper mounted on canvas,
12¼ × 18½" (31.1 × 47 cm.).
LR: ABierstadt [not by artist]
Purchase Funds of Mrs. A. E.
Carlton

Denver
Denver Art Museum:

CL-38. *The Rocky Mountains*
Oil on canvas, 13¼ × 18¼" (33.7 ×
46.3 cm.). LL: ABierstadt

Denver Public Library:

CL-39. *The Rocky Mountains, Longs Peak*
1877 SEE FIG. 189
Oil on canvas, 62 × 98" (157.5 ×
248.9 cm.). LL: ABierstadt
Collection Western History Department

University of Denver:

CL-40. *Weeping Oaks, Clear Creek*
[California] 1880
Oil on canvas, 35½ × 51½" (90.2 ×
130.8 cm.). LL: ABierstadt

Bierstadt visited Clear Lake, near
Mount Shasta, in August, 1880. On
his way home he stopped in Denver, where he called on Bishop
Warren and his wife. Mrs. Warren
ordered a picture. Perhaps Mrs.
Warren's picture was not forthcoming until 1891, when her husband
announced this gift from the artist
to the University.

CONNECTICUT
Hartford
Wadsworth Atheneum:

CL-41. *On the Beach at Capri* 1857
Oil on academy board, 10⅛ × 12¾"
(25.7 × 32.4 cm.). LL: ABierstadt
The Ella Gallup Sumner and Mary
Catlin Sumner Collection

CL-42. *In the Yosemite Valley* 1866
Oil on canvas, 35 × 50" (88.9 × 127
cm.). LR: ABierstadt 1866

CL-43. *The Yosemite Valley* [incorrect title]
1867 SEE FIG. 104
Oil on canvas, 35⅜ × 49⅝" (89.8 ×
126 cm.). LR: ABierstadt

CL-44. *The Hetch-Hetchy Valley, California*
SEE FIG. 165
Oil on canvas, 37¼ × 58¼" (94.6 ×
147.9 cm.). LL: ABierstadt

New Britain
*The New Britain Museum of
American Art:*

CL-45. *Wasatch Mountains, Wind River
Country, Wyoming* 1861
SEE FIG. 75
Oil on canvas, 26½ × 40½" (67.3 ×
102.9 cm.). LR: ABierstadt/1861

CL-46. *Seal Rocks, Farallon Islands* 1873
or 1875 SEE FIG. 159
Oil on canvas, 30 × 45″ (76.2 ×
114.3 cm.). LR: ABierstadt

An 1888 "scenario" of this painting
identifies it with the Farallon Islands. The artist was finishing a
Farallon Islands painting early in
1873 and another early in 1875.
Either date is appropriate for this
work.

New Haven
Yale University Art Gallery:

CL-47. *The Trappers' Camp* 1861
SEE FIG. 82
Oil on millboard, 13 × 19″ (33 ×
48.3 cm.). LR: ABierstadt/1861
The Whitney Collections of
Sporting Art

CL-48. *Yosemite Valley, Glacier Point Trail*
c. 1872? SEE FIG. 162
Oil on canvas, 54 × 84¾″ (137.2 ×
215.3 cm.). LL: ABierstadt
Gift of Mrs. Vincenzo Ardenghi

CL-49. *Indian Sunset: Deer by a Lake*
Oil on canvas, 30⅜ × 44½″ (77.2 ×
113 cm.). Bequest of Evelyn A.
Cummins

New London
Lyman Allyn Museum:

CL-50. *Italian Costume Studies* 1856–57

Oil on paper, 11¼ × 18″ (28.6 ×
45.7 cm.). LR: ABierstadt; UL, in
artist's hand: Italian Costume
Studies

CL-51. *Mountain Landscape with Sunset*
Oil on paper, 3¼ × 3¾″ (8.2 × 9.5
cm.).

DELAWARE
Wilmington
Delaware Art Museum:

CL-52. *Canyon and River*
Oil on academy board, 12 × 18″
(30.5 × 45.7 cm.).

DISTRICT OF COLUMBIA
Washington
The Corcoran Gallery of Art:

CL-53. *The Buffalo Trail: The Impending*

Storm 1869
Oil on canvas, 29½ × 49½″ (74.9 ×
125.7 cm.). LL: ABierstadt/1869

CL-54. *Mountainous Landscape by Moonlight*
1871 SEE FIG. 166
Oil on canvas, 30 × 50″ (76.2 × 127
cm.). LR: ABierstadt/1871

CL-55. *Mount Corcoran* 1875?
SEE FIG. 172
Oil on canvas, 61 × 96¼″ (154.9 ×
244.4 cm.). LR: ABierstadt

It has been said that this painting is
the same as the artist's *Mountain
Lake*, painted in 1875, shown at the
National Academy of Design's 1877
Annual, and renamed to flatter
Corcoran. I have not seen the
evidence for this (Chap. 10).

CL-56. *The Last of the Buffalo* 1888
SEE FIG. 205
Oil on canvas, 71¼ × 119¼″ (181 ×
302.9 cm.). LR: ABierstadt

Although this work is usually dated
1889, a brochure for its exhibition
is dated January, 1889. Thus, late
1888 is logical for its completion.
(Compare CL-254.)

*The Hirshhorn Museum and Sculp-
ture Garden:*

CL-57. *Scene in Tyrol* 1854
Oil on board, 9⅜ × 12¾″ (23.8 ×
32.4 cm.). LR: AB/1854 On
reverse, in artist's hand: "Scene in
Tyrol/Mr. B. P. Shillaber. with the /
Compliments of A. Bierstadt."

Shillaber was a Boston friend of the
artist who wrote homespun humor
under the pseudonym "Mrs. Part-
ington."

CL-58. *European Landscape*
Oil on paper, 19 × 26½″ (48.2 × 67.3 cm.).

CL-59. *Farralones Island, Pacific* [*Farallon Islands, Pacific*]
Oil on canvas, 16¼ × 19¼″ (41.2 × 48.9 cm.). LR: ABierstadt On reverse, in artist's hand: Farralones Islands. / Pacific Ocean

CL-60. *Gathering Storm*
Oil on paper, 7⅛ × 10″ (18.1 × 25.4 cm.).

CL-61. *Grey Tempest*
Oil on paper, 6 × 8¾″ (15.2 × 22.2 cm.). On reverse, in artist's hand: White Mts—N. H.

CL-62. *Iceberg*
Oil on paper, 5⅝ × 9″ (14.3 × 22.9 cm.).

CL-63. *Shady Pool White Mountains New Hampshire* [correct title?]
Oil on canvas, 22½ × 30″ (57.2 × 76.2 cm.). LR: ABierstadt

CL-64. *Study in Grey*

Oil on paper, 7¾ × 10″ (19.7 × 25.4 cm.).

CL-65. *West Indies Coast Scene*
Oil on paper mounted on board, 13½ × 18½″ (34.3 × 47 cm.). LL: ABierstadt

National Collection of Fine Arts, Smithsonian Institution:

CL-66. *Alaskan Coast Range* [correct title?]
SEE FIG. 215
Oil on paper, 13¼ × 19″ (33.7 × 48.2 cm.). Gift of Mrs. Orrin Wickersham June

CL-67. *Sunset, Sierra Nevada* [correct title?]
Oil on paper, 13¼ × 19″ (33.7 × 48.2 cm.). Gift of Mrs. Orrin Wickersham June

United States Capitol:

CL-68. *The Discovery of the Hudson*   1875
SEE FIG. 180
Oil on canvas, 72 × 122″ (182.9 × 309.9 cm.). LR: ABierstadt

CL-69. *Expedition under Vizcaino Landing at Monterey 1601*   1875
SEE FIG. 181

Oil on canvas, 72 × 122″ (182.9 × 309.9 cm.). LR: ABierstadt

FLORIDA
Coral Gables
The Lowe Art Museum, University of Miami:

CL-70. *Yosemite Valley*
Oil on paper mounted on canvas, 16 × 20″ (41.7 × 50.8 cm.). LL: ABierstadt
Barker Collection of American Art

GEORGIA
Athens
Georgia Museum of Art, The University of Georgia:

CL-71. *Yellowstone Falls* 1881
Oil on paper mounted on canvas, 19¼ × 13½″ (48.9 × 34.3 cm.). LL: ABierstadt   Eva Underhill Holbrook Memorial Collection of

Atlanta
High Museum of Art:

CL-72. *Pioneers of the Woods, California*
Oil on canvas, 19 × 25¾″ (48.3 × 65.4 cm.). LL: ABierstadt   Gift of the Exposition Foundation, 1971

ILLINOIS
Chicago
The Art Institute of Chicago:

CL-73. *Princess Louisa Inlet, British Columbia* [correct title?]   1889?
Oil on canvas, 29 × 43¾″ (73.7 × 109.3 cm.). LR: ABierstadt
Charles H. and Mary F. S. Worcester Collection

INDIANA
Indianapolis
Indianapolis Museum of Art:

CL-74. *Alaska*   1889?
Oil on canvas, 14 × 20″ (35.6 × 50.8 cm.). LR: ABierstadt   Gift of Mrs. Addison Bybee

KANSAS
Lawrence
University of Kansas Museum of Art:

CL-75. *Sunset on the Plains*
Oil on canvas, 19 × 26″ (48.2 × 66 cm.). LR: ABierstadt   Gift of the Honorable Charles V. Kincaid in memory of his wife, Edith T. Kincaid

KENTUCKY
Louisville
J. B. Speed Art Museum:

CL-76. *Mountain Landscape*
Oil on paper mounted on canvas,
11 × 15″ (27 × 38.1 cm.).
LL: ABierstadt

LOUISIANA
Shreveport
The R. W. Norton Art Gallery:

CL-77. *Emigrants Resting at Sunset* 1861?
SEE FIG. 80
Oil on canvas, 37 × 58″ (94 × 147.3
cm.). LL: ABierstadt

Possibly the painting titled *Emigrants Camping,* exhibited at the
National Academy of Design Annual in 1861.

CL-78. *Morning in the Rocky Mountains*
1862 SEE FIG. 66
Oil on paper mounted on canvas,
8½ × 11½″ (21.6 × 29.2 cm.).
LL: ABierstadt/62

Note the close relationship to *Wasatch Mountains, Wind River Country,
Wyoming* (Fig. 75, CL-45), which is
dated the previous year.

MARYLAND
Baltimore
The Walters Art Gallery:

CL-79. *The Blue Grotto, Capri*
Oil on cardboard, 6⅞ × 8¾″ (17.4
× 22.2 cm.). LL: AB

MASSACHUSETTS
Amherst
*Amherst College,
Mead Art Building:*

CL-80. *Campfire* 1863
Oil on canvas, 17 × 24½″ (43.2 ×
62.2 cm.). LR: ABierstadt 1863

CL-81. *Boston Harbor at Night*
Oil on canvas, 18 × 22⅞″ (45.7 ×
58.1 cm.).

Jones Library:

CL-82. *Platte River, Nebraska* 1863
SEE FIG. 70
Oil on canvas, 36 × 57½″ (91.4 ×
146 cm.). LR: ABierstadt/1863 On
loan from the Jones Library to the
Mead Art Building, Amherst College

Andover
*Addison Gallery of American Art,
Phillips Academy:*

CL-83. *The Coming Storm* 1869
SEE FIG. 141
Oil on panel, 9½ × 13″ (24.2 × 33
cm.). LR: AB/69

CL-84. *The Snow Mountain*
Oil on panel, 14 × 18″ (35.6 × 45.7
cm.). LR: ABierstadt

Boston
Museum of Fine Arts:

CL-85. *Fishing Boats at Capri* 1857
SEE FIG. 26
Oil on paper mounted on canvas,
13½ × 19½″ (34.3 × 49.5 cm.).
LR: Capri/June 14 1857/ABierstadt
M. and M. Karolik Collection

CL-86. *The Portico of Octavia, Rome* 1858
SEE FIGS. 31, 32
Oil on canvas, 28½ × 37″ (72.4 ×
94 cm.). LR: ABierstadt
Deposited by the Boston Athenaeum
Titled by the artist *Roman Fish
Market;* also called *The Arch of
Octavius* (Chap. 3).

CL-87. *Thunderstorm in the Rocky Mountains* 1859 SEE FIGS. 56, 57 Oil on canvas, 19 × 29"(48.2 × 73.7 cm.). LL: AB 59. Given in memory of Elias T. Milliken by his daughters, Mrs. Edward Hale and Mrs. John Carroll Perkins

CL-88. *Indians near Fort Laramie* 1859? SEE FIG. 59 Oil on paper on cardboard, 13½ × 19½" (34.3 × 49.5 cm.). LL: ABierstadt M. and M. Karolik Collection

CL-89. *View from the Wind River Mountains, Wyoming* 1860 SEE FIG. 53 Oil on canvas, 30¼ × 48½" (76.8 × 123.2 cm.). LL: ABierstadt/1860 On reverse, in artist's hand: "View looking Northwest from the Wind River Mountains. the Wahsatch Mountains seen in the distance. Sketched from nature July 1st 1859. Painted in New York 1860." M. and M. Karolik Collection

The Wasatch Mountains are not northwest from any point in the Wind River Range.

CL-90. *Valley of the Yosemite* 1864 SEE FIG. 99 Oil on prepared millboard, 11¾ × 19¼" (29.8 × 48.9 cm.). LR: ABierstadt/64 M. and M. Karolik Collection

CL-91. *Seal Rocks, Farallones [Farallon Islands]* 1872 Oil on paper mounted on cardboard, 13½ × 19" (34.3 × 48.2 cm.). LL: ABierstadt On reverse before mounting: Farralone Is Pacific 1872

CL-92. *Rocky Mountains, Colorado* 1875–76? SEE FIG. 190 Oil on paper on Masonite, 13¾ × 19½" (34.9 × 49.5 cm.). LR: ABierstadt On reverse before relining: Rocky Mts. Colo. M. and M. Karolik Collection

CL-93. *The Ambush* 1876? SEE FIG. 78 Oil on canvas, 30 × 50½" (76.2 × 128.3 cm.). LL: ABierstadt M. and M. Karolik Collection

This is possibly the picture called *Attack on Wagon Train by Indians* when it was shown at the Century Association in New York City in November, 1876.

CL-94. *Moose Hunters' Camp, Nova Scotia* 1880? Oil on canvas, 26½ × 36½" (67.3 × 92.2 cm.). On reverse, in artist's hand: Moose Hunters Camp/Nova Scotia/A. Bierstadt M. and M. Karolik Collection

CL-95. *Geyser, Yellowstone Park* 1881 Oil on paper mounted on cardboard, 14 × 19½" (35.5 × 49.5 cm.). LR: ABierstadt On reverse before mounting: Yellowstone M. and M. Karolik Collection

CL-96. *The Saint Lawrence River from the Citadel, Quebec* 1881? SEE FIG. 198 Oil on paper mounted on canvas, 22 × 30½" (55.9 × 77.5 cm.). LL: ABierstadt On reverse before mounting: "View of the Citadel, Quebec." M. and M. Karolik Collection

Dufferin Terrace, shown in this picture, was evidently completed about 1880, although the uniforms are those of twenty years previous (letters from the curator of the Quebec Museum, in the Museum of Fine Arts, Boston).

CL-97. *Interior of a Library, Minneapolis* 1886? Oil on canvas, 19¾ × 14½" (50.2 × 36.9 cm.). LL: ABierstadt M. and M. Karolik Collection

This painting was in the Edward Bierstadt sale of April 27, 1905.

CL-98. *Wreck of the "Ancon," Loring Bay, Alaska* 1889 SEE FIG. 213 Oil on paper mounted on panel, 14 × 19¾" (35.5 × 50.2 cm.). LR: ABierstadt M. and M. Karolik Collection

See Chap. 11. I am grateful to Mrs. Patricia Roppel of Ketchikan, Alaska, for pointing out that Loring is the name of the fishing village where the *Ancon*'s party was stranded, and, so far as any map shows, not the name of a bay.

CL-99. *Banana Trees*
Oil on canvas mounted on Masonite, 19¼ × 13½″ (48.9 × 34.3 cm.).
LL: ABierstadt   Bequest of Maxim Karolik

CL-100. *The Black Horse*
Oil on paper mounted on board, 13½ × 19¼″ (34.3 × 48.8 cm.).
M. and M. Karolik Collection

CL-101. *Study of a Brown Horse*
Oil on panel, 14½ × 19¾″ (36.8 × 50.2 cm.). LR: ABierstadt
Bequest of Maxim Karolik

CL-102. *The Buffalo Trail*
Oil on canvas, 32 × 48″ (81.3 × 121.9 cm.). LR: ABierstadt
M. and M. Karolik Collection

CL-103. *Grove of Trees*
Oil on paper on cardboard, 13½ × 19″ (34.3 × 48.2 cm.).
LR: ABierstadt
M. and M. Karolik Collection

CL-104. *Indian Camp*
Oil on canvas, 13¼ × 17¾″ (33.6 × 45.1 cm.). LL: ABierstadt
M. and M. Karolik Collection

CL-105. *Lake Tahoe, California*
Oil on canvas, 22 × 30″ (55.9 × 76.2 cm.). M. and M. Karolik Collection

CL-106. *Niagara from the American Side*
Oil on paper mounted on canvas, 14 × 19½″ (35.5 × 49.5 cm.).
LL: ABierstadt   Bequest of Maxim Karolik

CL-107. *Palm Trees with a Domed Church*
Oil on paper mounted on canvas, 14 × 19½″ (35.5 × 49.5 cm.).
LL: ABierstadt   M. and M. Karolik Collection

It has been said that this work may be of the Southwest (*M. and M. Karolik Collection of American Paintings,* Cambridge, 1949), but the artist did not visit the Southwest, and the church has been excluded from California's Missions (letter from the director of the California Society of Pioneers). The West

Indies—and therefore Nassau, the most natural site—has also been ruled out (*M. and M. Karolik*, ibid.). Perhaps it is Spain, but we know no other Spanish works by the artist; perhaps it is the French Riviera.

CL-108. *Sail Boats*
Oil on cardboard, 13¾ ×19" (34.9 × 48.2 cm.). LL: ABierstadt
Bequest of Maxim Karolik

CL-109. *Snow Scene with Buffalo*
Oil on prepared millboard, 18 × 24" (45.7 × 60.9 cm.).
LL: ABierstadt
M. and M. Karolik Collection

CL-110. *Storm in the Mountains*
SEE FIG. 138
Oil on canvas, 38 × 60" (96.5 × 152.4 cm.). M. and M. Karolik Collection

This has been called a scene of the Grosser Wachtman, near Berchtesgaden.

CL-111. *Yosemite*
Oil on canvas, 13½ × 19" (34.3 × 48.2 cm.). LL: ABierstadt
Bequest of Maxim Karolik

Cambridge
The Fogg Art Museum, Harvard University:

CL-112. *The Trout Brook*   1859
Oil on cardboard, 9⅛ × 11¾" (23.2 × 29.8 cm.). LL: AB 59

CL-113. *Rocky Mountains, "Lander's [Frémont's?] Peak"* [incorrect title] 1863
Oil on canvas, 44⅜ × 36½" (112.7 × 92.7 cm.). LR: ABierstadt/63

If *The Rocky Mountains* (Fig. 108, CL-170) in the Metropolitan Mu-

seum is taken as Bierstadt's idea of Lander's or Frémont's Peak, it is obvious that this painting does not represent the same locale: neither the mountains' profiles, the path of the glacier, the waterfall, nor the foreground terrain corresponds to the Metropolitan picture.

CL-114. *Landscape*   1868
Oil on canvas, 12⅞ × 16" (32.7 × 40.7 cm.). LR: AB 68

This painting was probably inspired by an Alpine conglomerate, with a lively bit of imagination thrown in.

CL-115. *Portrait of John Tyndall*   1893?
Watercolor with overglaze of oil and varnish on paper, 5¼ × 3¾" (13.3 × 9.5 cm.). UR: John Tyndall /AETAT 45 by AB

Evidently taken from an 1865 photograph—Tyndall was 45 in that year—and published in an American magazine on Tyndall's death in 1893. This work is something of a mystery. The motivation is obscure: Bierstadt must have agreed to copy the photograph for some personal reason; the technique is not characteristic; watercolors by the artist are nearly unknown.

Fairhaven
Millicent Library:

CL-116. *Martha Simon* 1857 SEE FIG. 28
Oil on cardboard, 19 × 13″ (48.2 × 33 cm.). LR: Martha Simon, the last of the Naragansetts, 1857 AB

See Chap. 3.

Harvard
Fruitlands Museum:

CL-117. *Ascutney Mountain from Claremont, New Hampshire* 1862
Oil on canvas, 41½ × 71″ (102.9 × 180.4 cm.). LR: ABierstadt/62

CL-118. *San Rafael, California* 1875?
Oil on canvas, 31⅞ × 48″ (83.5 × 121.9 cm.). LR: ABierstadt

This is evidently the painting formerly in the Art Institute of Chicago, and the one called *Near San Rafael, California* at the National Academy 1875 Annual.

New Bedford
Free Public Library:

CL-119. *Sunset Light, Wind River Range of the Rocky Mountains* 1861
SEE FIG. 101

Oil on canvas, 39 × 60″ (99.1 × 152.4 cm.). LR: ABierstadt

CL-120. *Rocky Mountains in the Selkirk Range, near the Canadian Border, Mount Sir Donald* 1889? SEE FIG. 214
Oil on canvas, 83½ × 57½″ (212.1 × 146 cm.). LR: ABierstadt

This was evidently done from sketches made during the artist's 1889 trip through the Canadian Rockies. Sir Donald Alexander Smith (1820–1914) was the builder of the Canadian Pacific Railway.

CL-121. *Sunset near the Platte River* or *Salt Lick at Sunset Glow*
Oil on canvas, 27½ × 39″ (69.8 × 99.1 cm.). LL: ABierstadt

The Whaling Museum:

CL-122. *Gosnold at Cuttyhunk, 1602* 1858
SEE FIG. 35
Oil on canvas, 28 × 49″ (71.1 × 124.5 cm.). LR: ABierstadt/1858
Gift of Miss Emma B. Hathaway

Northampton
Smith College Museum of Art:

CL-123. *A Wilderness Lake* 1861
Oil on canvas, 25 × 39⅛″ (63.5 × 99.4 cm.). LL: ABierstadt./1861.

CL-124. *Florida Landscape* [correct title?]
Oil on paper, 13¾ × 19⅛″ (34.9 × 48.5 cm.). LL: ABierstadt

CL-125. *Yosemite Valley*
Oil on paper mounted on canvas, 13¾ × 18¾″ (34.9 × 47.6 cm.). LL: ABierstadt

Pittsfield
The Berkshire Museum:

CL-126. *Connecticut River Valley, Claremont, New Hampshire* 1868
Oil on canvas, 27 × 44″ (68.6 × 111.8 cm.). LL: ABierstadt/1868

Although formerly called a New Bedford view, it is almost the same as *Ascutney Mountain from Claremont, New Hampshire* (CL-117).

CL-127. *Giant Redwood Trees of California*
SEE FIG. 175
Oil on canvas, 52½ × 43″ (123.4 × 109.2 cm.). LL: ABierstadt

South Hadley
Mount Holyoke College Art Museum:

CL-128. *Hetch Hetchy Cañon, California*
Oil on canvas, 51½ × 42″ (130.3 × 106.7 cm.). Gift of Mrs. A. L. Williston and Mrs. E. H. Sawyer in 1876, wives of two trustees upon the opening of the Art Gallery in old Williston Hall.

Springfield
The Springfield Museum of Fine Arts:

CL-129. *The Hetch Hetchy Valley, California*
Oil on canvas, 26⅛ × 36¼″ (66.3 × 92.6 cm.). LL: ABierstadt
Bequest of Mr. Luke S. Stowe

George Walter Vincent Smith Art Museum:

CL-130. *The Brothers' Burial* [or *The Brother's Burial*] 1861 SEE FIG. 74
Oil on canvas, 18 × 32½″ (45.7 × 82.6 cm.). LL: ABierstadt/1861

CL-131. *Sunrise in the Hetch Hetchy Valley, California*
Oil on canvas, 29¾ × 43¾″ (75.5 × 111.1 cm.). LR: ABierstadt

Weston
Regis College:

CL-132. *Italian Coastal View* [*Amalfi?*] 1861
Oil on canvas, 19½ × 24″ (49.5 × 60.9 cm.). LL: ABierstadt/1861

Worcester
Worcester Art Museum:

CL-133. *The Conflagration* SEE FIG. 219
Oil on paper, 11¼ × 15⅛″ (28.6 × 38.4 cm.).

CL-134. *Yosemite Falls*
Oil on canvas, 36 × 26⅛″ (91.4 × 66.3 cm.).

MICHIGAN
Detroit
The Detroit Institute of Arts:

CL-135. *The Wolf River, Kansas* 1859?
SEE FIG. 63
Oil on canvas, 48¼ × 38¼″ (122.5 × 97.1 cm.). LR: ABierstadt
The Dexter M. Ferry Jr. Fund

CL-136. *Yosemite Falls* [incorrect title]
Oil on paper mounted on canvas, 19 × 14″ (48.3 × 35.6 cm.).
LR: ABierstadt
Gift of Carl F. Clarke

MINNESOTA
Minneapolis
The Minneapolis Institute of Arts:

CL-137. *Lakeshore Landscape*
Oil on canvas, 13⅝ × 18⅝″ (34.6 ×
47.3 cm.). LR: ABierstadt

MISSISSIPPI
Laurel
*Lauren Rogers Library and
Museum of Art:*

CL-138. *Autumn in New Hampshire*
Oil on canvas, 13¾ × 19¾″ (34.9 ×
50.2 cm.). LR: ABierstadt

MISSOURI
Saint Louis
Saint Louis Art Museum:

CL-139. *Olevano*   1856 or 1857
SEE FIG. 22
Oil on canvas mounted on panel,
19 5⁄32 × 26½″ (48.6 × 67.3 cm.).
LR: ABierstadt   Along bottom
edge, left to right: "Volatre Olivano
Roco, San Stafano Kapr [—?] ani-
ka".   Eliza McMillan Fund

Contemporary spellings make the

places in the inscription Velatre,
Olevano, Rocca San Stefano, and
Capranica. The finished painting,
for which *Olevano* was evidently a
study, has recently come to light
(Fig. 23).

CL-140. *Surveyor's Wagon in the Rockies* [in-
correct title] 1859? SEE FIG. 36
Oil on paper mounted on canvas,
7¾ × 12⅞″ (19.7 × 32.7 cm.).
LR: ABierstadt   Gift of J.
Lionberger Davis

It has often been said that the
artist's 1859 trip west was with
Lander's "surveying" expedition.
Evidently this is the source of the
error in this title. Lander's mission
was to "improve" a road already
well established (Chap. 4).

CL-141. *Nooning on the Platte* [correct title?]
1859?   SEE FIG. 49
Oil on paper mounted on canvas,
6¾ × 12⅞″ (17.2 × 32.7 cm.).
LL: Bierstadt [*sic*. The "A" is no
longer present, having been rubbed
off by the frame.]   Gift of J.
Lionberger Davis

NEBRASKA
Omaha
Joslyn Art Museum:

CL-142. *Dawn at Donner Lake, California*
1871–73
Oil on canvas, 21¼ × 29″ (51.4 ×
73.7 cm.). LL: ABierstadt
Gift of Mrs. C. N. Dietz

CL-143. *Storm on the Matterhorn*
Oil on canvas, 53¾ × 83½″ (136.5
× 212.1 cm.). LL: ABierstadt
Gift of Ben Gallagher

CL-144. *The Trappers, Lake Tahoe*
Oil on canvas, 19½ × 27¾″ (49.5 ×
70.5 cm.). LR: ABierstadt
Gift of Mrs. Harold Gifford

CL-145. *Valley of the Yosemite*   SEE FIG. 105
Oil on canvas, 14 × 19″ (35.6 × 48.3
cm.). LR: ABierstadt
Gift of Mrs. C. N. Dietz

NEW HAMPSHIRE
Manchester
The Currier Gallery of Art:

CL-146. *View of Moat Mountain, Intervale,
New Hampshire*
Oil on canvas, 19 × 25⅞″ (48.3 ×
65.7 cm.). LR: ABierstadt

NEW JERSEY

Montclair
Montclair Art Museum:

CL-147. *Brook in Woods*
Oil on canvas, 20 × 30″ (50.8 × 76.2 cm.). LL: ABierstadt

New Brunswick
Rutgers University Art Gallery:

CL-148. *Buffalo Hunter*   1888?
Oil on canvas, 26 × 36″ (66 × 91.4 cm.). LR: ABierstadt

CL-149. *Waterfall* [*Minnehaha Falls, Minneapolis, Minnesota*]
Oil on canvas, 22 × 30″ (55.8 × 76.2 cm.). LL: ABierstadt

CL-150. *Waterfall Landscape*
Oil on canvas, 40 × 30″ (101.7 × 76.2 cm.). LR: ABierstadt

Newark
The Newark Museum:

CL-151. Study for *Sunshine and Shadow*
1855   SEE FIG. 8
Oil on paper, 19 × 13″ (48.2 × 33 cm.). LR: Cassel july 1855; LL: ABierstadt   Gift of J. Ackerman Coles, 1920

We know from Worthington Whittredge's account books in the Archives of American Art that Bierstadt was in Cassel in 1855. He apparently was there at no other time.

CL-152. *Mount Whitney* [incorrect title]
1869
Oil on canvas, 36 × 54″ (91.4 × 137.1 cm.). LR: ABierstadt/1869

In 1869 few people had yet seen Mount Whitney, and the artist was not to see it for several years (Chap. 9).

CL-153. *The Landing of Columbus*   1893?
SEE FIG. 223

Oil on canvas, 72 × 121″ (182.9 × 307.3 cm.). LR: ABierstadt

CL-154. *Bison*
Oil on canvas, 14 × 19″ (35.6 × 48.2 cm.). LR: ABierstadt

CL-155. *Lake at Franconia Notch, White Mountains*
Oil on canvas, 13½ × 19½″ (34.3 × 49.5 cm.). LR: ABierstadt

CL-156. *Landscape*
Oil on canvas, 13 × 18¾″ (33 × 47.6 cm.). LL: AB

Plainfield
The City of Plainfield:

CL-157. *Autumn in the Sierras*   1873
SEE FIG. 170
Oil on canvas, 72 × 120″ (182.9 × 304.8 cm.). LR: ABierstadt

Formerly titled *The Rocky Mountains*. The signature, although evidently authentic, is curious. The artist may have been in pain while finishing this picture (Chap. 9); surely it is one of his least successful works. Its "scenario" corresponds closely with the account of *Autumn in the Sierra* (or *Sierras*) in *The San Francisco Bulletin*, May 29, 1873.

CL-158. *The Landing of Columbus*   1893
SEE FIG. 222
Oil on canvas, 80 × 120″ (203.2 × 304.8 cm.).
LL: Albert Bierstadt./1893

Princeton
The Art Museum, Princeton University:

CL-159. *Mount Adams, Washington* [correct title?]   1875
SEE FIG.179
Oil on canvas, 54 × 83⅝″ (137.2 × 212.3 cm.). LR: ABierstadt./1875

Although this painting is clearly dated 1875, a work called *Mount Adams on the Columbia River, Oregon*, of the same width, was in a private collection in Washington, D.C., not later than 1872. Perhaps *Mount Adams, Washington* is the same painting and was not dated until 1875, but if so, this is the only known case of Bierstadt's dating a painting several years after its completion.

NEW MEXICO
Santa Fe
Museum of New Mexico:

CL-160. *Wyoming* [incorrect title]
Oil on canvas, 19¼ × 26½″ (48.9 × 67.3 cm.). LL: ABierstadt
Fine Arts Permanent Collection

Wyoming could not have presented such neat farms and carefully cultivated fields during any time Bierstadt was in the state. More likely this is a White Mountains scene.

NEW YORK
Buffalo
Albright-Knox Art Gallery:

CL-161. *The "Marina Grande" in Capri with the Faraglioni Rocks in the Background*   1859   SEE FIG. 73
Oil on canvas, 42 × 72″ (106.7 × 182.9 cm.). LR: ABierstadt./1859

Canajoharie
Canajoharie Library and Art Gallery:

CL-162. *El Capitan*
Oil on paper mounted on fabric, 21 × 28″ (53.3 × 71.1 cm.).
LL: ABierstadt

Dobbs Ferry
The Masters School:

CL-163. *Moonlight on the Lake*
Oil on paper mounted on board, 4¼ × 7¾″ (10.8 × 19.8 cm.).
Presented by the Orville DeForest Edwards Family

Elmira
Arnot Art Museum:

CL-164. *Approaching Storm*   1854
SEE FIG. 12
Oil on canvas, 16⅜ × 20½″ (41.6 × 52.1 cm.). LR: ABierstadt/1854

This is another view of the farmhouse in *Westphalian Landscape* (CL-241).

Ithaca
Herbert F. Johnson Museum of Art, Cornell University:

CL-165. *Swiss Mountain Scene*   1859
Oil on canvas, 24 × 34″ (60.9 × 86.4 cm.).   LL: ABierstadt/1859

This painting is one of those formerly belonging to the Swain School of Design in New Bedford and is evidently one of those damaged by fire at the school.

CL-166. *Finsterhorn*
Oil on canvas, 11½ × 7¼″ (29.2 × 18.4 cm.).   LL: ABierstadt

CL-167. *Spur at the Edge at Sunset, Grindel-wald*
Oil on canvas, 7½ × 10″ (19.1 × 25.4 cm.).

New York City
The Brooklyn Museum:

CL-168. *The Morteratsch Glacier, Upper Enga-dine, Pontresina* 1895?
SEE FIG. 228
Oil on canvas, 72 × 119⅛″ (182.9 × 302.6 cm.). LL: ABierstadt./ Merry Christmas to Mary 1895
On the waterfall in the right center distance:Mary / Al[be]rt / I A[nn?]/ 14/ 95
Gift of Mary S. Bierstadt

A memento of a shared 1895 trip seems appropriate for an 1895 Christmas gift. If the inscription on the waterfall is a reference to the artist's first anniversary of his wedding to his second wife, it is curious, since that event took place on March 7, 1894. Perhaps it was the anniversary of their meeting. I am grateful to Linda Ferber of the Brooklyn Museum for finding this second inscription.

CL-169. *Encampment in the Rockies* [*Encampment near Mount Shasta*]

Oil on paper mounted on canvas, 14 × 19⅞″ (35.6 × 50.5 cm.).
LL: ABierstadt   Dick S. Ramsay Fund

The peak here is evidently Mount Shasta, in the Cascades in Northern California. This range is only rarely spoken of as part of the Rockies.

The Metropolitan Museum of Art:

CL-170. *The Rocky Mountains* 1863
SEE FIGS. 108–10
Oil on canvas, 73½ × 120¾″ (186.7 × 306.7 cm.). LR: ABierstadt/1863
Rogers Fund, 1907

CL-171. *Merced River, Yosemite Valley* [incorrect title] 1866
Oil on canvas, 36 × 50″ (91.4 × 127 cm.). LR: ABierstadt/1866
Gift of the sons of William Paton, 1909

CL-172. *Sunrise on the Matterhorn* 1878–plus?
Oil on canvas, 50½ × 42⅝″ (128.3 × 108.3 cm.). LL: ABierstadt
Gift of Mrs. Karl W. Koeniger, 1966

National Academy of Design:

CL-173. *On the Sweetwater near Devil's Gate, Nebraska* 1859
Oil on canvas, 12¼ × 18″ (31.1 × 45.8 cm.). On reverse, in artist's hand: on the Sweet water near the Devil's Gate / Sketched 1859. / Nebraska / price $100, with frame.

The New-York Historical Society:

CL-174. *Indian Encampment, Shoshone Village* 1860   SEE FIGS. 64, 65
Oil on canvas mounted on board, 24 × 19″ (60.9 × 48.2 cm.). LR: ABierstadt   On reverse, in artist's hand: Shoshone Village, among the cottonwood/Trees on the sweetwater river, Wind-river mountains/in the distance.

CL-175. *Donner Lake from the Summit* 1873   SEE FIG. 169
Oil on canvas, 72 × 120″ (182.9 × 304.8 cm.). LL: ABierstadt

Also titled *View of Donner Lake, California*

CL-176. *Autumn Woods* 1886
SEE FIG. 208
Oil on canvas, 54 × 84″ (137.1 × 213.3 cm.). LR: ABierstadt
On reverse, on a label, in ink, in artist's hand: "Autumn Woods Head of Susquehanna/River/N.Y. State/A Bierstadt/1271 [Broad]way New York."

The sources of the Chenango and Unadilla rivers, both of which might be said to be heads of the Susquehanna, are within a few miles of Bierstadt's wife's home in Waterville, New York. The first account of *Autumn Woods* appeared in a newspaper report of April 2, 1887; thus the date.

CL-177. *Indian Beauty*
Oil on canvas, 22½ × 17½″ (57.2 × 44.5 cm.).
The tablet on this painting reads, in part: "Painted by Albert Bierstadt c1840 [sic]". Since the artist was ten years old in 1840, and did not see his first Indian until 19 years later, this date is impossible.

CL-178. *Indians* [*Indians and Wampum*]
Oil on academy board, 13½ × 19″ (34.3 × 48.2 cm.). LR: ABierstadt

The first, third, and fourth Indians from the left are named by the artist. The third and fourth are possibly "Kaniac" and "Barbage." On the reverse is a pencil sketch of an Indian with a drawn bow on a running horse.

CL-179. *Indians*
Oil on academy board, 13¼ × 18¾″ (33.7 × 47.6 cm.). LR: ABierstadt
Beneath the Indians, left to right: Mudzumana Morona/Moose hunter Tom/Untergonod [?] Partq [?] Owecho/Yellow beads

The Whitney Museum of American Art:

CL-180. *Rock and Log on a Hilltop* c. 1859
Oil on paper, 10⅛ × 13⅛″ (25.7 × 33.3 cm.).

Rochester
Memorial Art Gallery of the University of Rochester:

CL-181. *Conway, New Hampshire*

Oil on paper, 9½ × 12⅛″ (24.2 × 30.7 cm.). LR: ABierstadt
On reverse, not in artist's hand: Con/way N.H./James Andrews/ Portsmouth, N.H.

Syracuse
Syracuse University Art Collection:

CL-182. *Albino Doe and Two Fawns in a Forest*
Oil on canvas, 21½ × 29″ (54.6 × 73.7 cm.). LL: ABierstadt

Yonkers
Hudson River Museum:

CL-183. *The Burning Ship*
Oil on paper mounted on cardboard, 9¾ × 13¾″ (24.8 × 34.9 cm.). LL: AB   Mrs. Edwin H. Finken and Miss Madeline Wolfenz

NORTH CAROLINA
Winston-Salem
Reynolda House, Inc.:

CL-184. *Sierra Nevada*
Oil on canvas, 38½ × 56½" (97.8 × 143.5 cm.). LL: ABierstadt

OHIO
Cincinnati
Cincinnati Art Museum:

CL-185. *Bow River Valley, Canadian Rockies* 1889?
Oil on canvas, 19 × 27" (48.2 × 68.6 cm.). LR: ABierstadt
The Edwin and Virginia Irwin Memorial

The locale of this painting has been identified by Vern Paschal.

Cleveland
The Cleveland Museum of Art:

CL-186. *Half Dome, Yosemite Valley* 1866
Oil on canvas, 38 × 56" (96.5 × 142.2 cm.). LR: ABierstadt/66
Hinman B. Hurlbut Collection

Formerly called *Mount Starr King.*

CL-187. *Mount Aetna* [*Vesuvius*] 1868
SEE FIG. 135
Oil on canvas, 17⅛ × 24" (43.5 × 60.9 cm.). LR: ABierstadt Gift of S. Livingstone Mather, Philip Richard Mather, Katherine Hoyt (Mather) Cross, Katherine Mather McLean, and Constance Mather Bishop.

The "scenario" of this painting corresponds closely to descriptions of the artist's *Vesuvius* (Chap. 8).

Columbus
Columbus Gallery of Fine Arts:

CL-188. *Landscape on the Platte River*
Oil on panel, 18 × 24½" (45.7 × 62.2 cm.).
Gift of Francis C. Sessions

CL-189. *Yosemite Valley* [incorrect title]
Oil on canvas, 27¾ × 39½" (70.5 × 100.3 cm.). LL: ABierstadt
Bequest of Rutherford H. Platt

Oberlin
Allen Memorial Art Museum, Oberlin College:

CL-190. *Sphinx Rock*
Oil on canvas, 5 × 5¾" (12.7 × 14.6 cm.). LL: Sphinx Rock

Toledo
The Toledo Museum of Art:

CL-191. *El Capitan, Yosemite Valley* 1875
SEE FIG. 182
Oil on canvas, 32¼ × 48" (81.8 × 121.9 cm.). LL: ABierstadt
On reverse: El Capitan Yosemite Valley/1875. Also: El Capitan Yosemite Valley Cal. painted 1875/A. Bierstadt Gift of Mr. and Mrs. Roy Rike

Youngstown
The Butler Institute of American Art:

CL-192. *The Oregon Trail* 1869
SEE FIG. 94
Oil on canvas, 31 × 49″ (78.7 × 124.5 cm.). LR: ABierstadt

This is a close parallel to *Emigrants Crossing the Plains* (CL-194).

OKLAHOMA
Oklahoma City
The National Cowboy Hall of Fame and Western Heritage Center:

CL-193. *Scout [Jim Bridger?]* 1859
SEE FIG. 61
Oil on composition board, 10 × 7″ (25.4 × 17.8 cm.). LR: ABierstadt

CL-194. *Emigrants Crossing the Plains* 1867 SEE FIG. 93
Oil on canvas, 60 × 96″ (152.4 × 243.8 cm.). LR: ABierstadt/67

A close parallel to *The Oregon Trail* (CL-192).

CL-195. *Rams in Dunraven* 1876
Oil on board, 7¼ × 9⁵⁄₁₆″ (18.4 × 25.6 cm.). LR: AB

Produced when the artist was visiting Colorado with the earl of Dunraven.

CL-196. *California Landscape*
Oil on board, 22 × 30″ (56 × 76.2 cm.). LL: ABierstadt

Tulsa
Philbrook Art Center:

CL-197. *Rocky Mountain Scene*
Oil on canvas, 30 × 44″ (76.2 × 111.7 cm.). LL: ABierstadt

CL-198. *Sunset Glow* SEE FIG. 130
Oil on canvas, 26 × 36″ (66 × 91.4 cm.). LL: ABierstadt

Possibly a view of the Hudson River.

Thomas Gilcrease Institute:

CL-199. *Trapper* 1859? SEE FIG. 62
Oil on paper, 19 × 13″ (48.2 × 33 cm.). LL: ABierstadt

CL-200. *Wind River Mountains* 1859?

Oil on paper, 7 × 12″ (17.8 × 30.5 cm.). On reverse: a pencil sketch of an Indian encampment. Also, in artist's hand: Wind River Mts./Nebraska

CL-201. *Wind River Mountains, Rocky Mountain Chain* 1859?
Oil on paper, 10 × 13″ (25.4 × 33 cm.). LR: ABierstadt

CL-202. *Mountain and River Scene* 1864
Oil on canvas, 14 × 20″ (35.6 × 50.8 cm.). LR: AB/64

CL-203. *Sierra Nevada Morning* 1870
SEE FIG. 145
Oil on canvas, 56 × 84″ (142.2 × 213.5 cm.). LR: ABierstadt/1870

CL-204. *Antelope* SEE FIG. 69
Oil on pasteboard, 9 × 15″ (22.8 × 38.1 cm.). LR: ABierstadt [possibly not by artist]

CL-205. *Black Hills, Colorado* SEE FIG. 142
Oil on paper mounted on board, 14 × 19″ (35.6 × 48.2 cm.).

CL-206. *Boats of the Far North*
Oil on paper mounted on board, 14
× 18″ (35.6 × 45.7 cm.).
LR: ABierstadt

CL-207. *Buffalo*
Oil on paper, 20 × 28″ (50.8 × 71.1
cm.). LR: ABierstadt

CL-208. *Buffalo Chase* SEE FIG. 92
Oil on canvas, 20 × 28″ (50.8 × 71.1
cm.).

CL-209. *Buffalo Studies*
Oil on paper, 13 × 19″ (33 × 48.2
cm.). LR: ABierstadt

There is a very slight profile of an
Indian brave in upper left.

CL-210. *Canoes*
Oil on paper, 13 × 18½″ (33 × 47
cm.) [cropped]. LR: ABierstadt

CL-211. *Cloud Study* SEE FIG. 178
Oil on paper, 6½ × 11¾″ (16.5 ×
29.9 cm.). LL: ABierstadt

CL-212. *Indian Brave*
Oil on paper, 12 × 18″ (30.5 × 45.7
cm.). LL: AB

CL-213. *Landscape* [1]
Oil on paper, 14 × 19″ (35.6 × 48.2
cm.). LR: ABierstadt

CL-214. *Landscape* [2]
Oil on canvas, 14 × 19″ (35.6 × 48.2
cm.). LR: ABierstadt

CL-215. *Mountain Range*
Oil on paper, 7½ × 9″ (19 × 22.9
cm.).

CL-216. *Multnomah Falls*
Oil on canvas, 44 × 30″ (111.7 ×
76.2 cm.). LR: ABierstadt

CL-217. *Niagara Falls*
Oil on canvas, 25 × 20″ (63.5 × 50.8 cm.).

CL-218. *Northern River*
Oil on paper, 13 × 19″ (33 × 48.2 cm.). LR: ABierstadt

CL-219. *Oakland, California*
Oil on paper mounted on board, 9½ × 13½″ (24.2 × 34.3 cm.). LR: ABierstadt

CL-220. *On the High Plains*
Oil on paper, 9 × 16″ (22.9 × 40.7 cm.).

CL-221. *On the Platte River, Nebraska*
SEE FIG. 48
Oil on pasteboard, 8 × 10″ (20.3 × 25.4 cm.). LL: ABierstadt

CL-222. *Pioneer Camp* [*Indian Camp*]
Oil on paper, 14 × 19″ (35.6 × 48.2 cm.). LR: ABierstadt

Although the artifacts in this painting are Indian—possibly Mariposan—the figure at the right is not obviously an Indian, thus the incorrect title. But a comparison of this figure with the lefthand figure of *Indian Camp* (CL-104) indicates that this figure is indeed an Indian, possibly the same person. This figure appears to have been added at a later date by the artist—or a dealer—wanting to make a more "complete," saleable picture. Other examples of this practice are the figures in *On the High Plains* (CL-220), *Encampment in the Rockies* (CL-169), *Longs Peak, Colorado* (CL-235), *Grove of Trees* (CL-103), *Rocky Mountain Landscape* (CL-36), and in various paintings in private collections.

CL-223. *Point Lobos*
Oil on canvas, 46 × 32½″ (116.8 × 82.5 cm.). [cropped].
LR: ABierstadt

CL-224. *Portrait Sketches of Indians*
Oil on paper, 14 × 19″ (35.6 × 48.2 cm.). LL: ABierstadt

CL-225. *Rocky Mountains*
Oil on paper, 13 × 18″ (33 × 45.8 cm.). LR: ABierstadt [partly torn away]

CL-226. *Sierra Nevada Mountains [Yosemite Valley from Inspiration Point]*
Oil on canvas, 18 × 24″ (45.7 × 60.9 cm.). LR: ABierstadt

This may have been painted from a photograph.

CL-227. *Sierra Nevada Mountains in California*
Oil on canvas, 21 × 30″ (53.3 × 76.2 cm.) [severely cropped].
LR: ABierstadt

CL-228. *White Mountains, New Hampshire*
SEE FIG. 146
Oil on paper, 11 × 15″ (27.9 × 38.1 cm.).

OREGON
Portland
Portland Art Museum:

CL-229. *Mount Hood* 1869 SEE FIG. 163
Oil on canvas, 36⅛ × 60¼″ (91.7 × 153 cm.). LR: ABierstadt/69

Not to be confused with the 1864 *Mount Hood,* which is unlocated.

CL-230. *Mountain Landscape with River and Sailboat*
Oil on board, 13¼ × 19″ (23.7 × 48.2 cm.). LL: ABierstadt

CL-231. *Seal Rocks, San Francisco* [correct title?]
Oil on cardboard, 15¼ × 28″ (38.7 × 71.1 cm.).

PENNSYLVANIA
New Wilmington
Westminster College:

CL-232. *Forest Sunrise*
Oil on canvas, 31 × 49″ (78.8 × 124.5 cm.).

This painting came to Westminster College untitled. The present title is one I have given it.

RHODE ISLAND
Providence
*Museum of Art,
Rhode Island School of Design:*

CL-233. *Landscape* 1856
Oil on canvas, 24 × 30″ (60.9 × 76.2 cm.). LL: ABierstadt/1856

TEXAS
Dallas
Dallas Museum of Fine Arts:

CL-234. *The Matterhorn*
Oil on paper mounted on canvas, 21½ × 29½″ (54.7 × 74.9 cm.).
LL: ABierstadt

Fort Worth
Amon Carter Museum of Western Art:

CL-235. *Longs Peak, Colorado* 1876–77
Oil on paper mounted on canvas,
13⅞ × 19¼″ (35.3 × 48.9 cm.).
LR: ABierstadt

CL-236. *Lake Tahoe* [correct title?]
Oil on paper mounted on canvas,
13⅜ × 19″ (33.9 × 48.2 cm.).
LL: ABierstadt

CL-237. *Mont Blanc*
Oil on canvas, 22⅛ × 30¼″ (56.2 ×
76.9 cm.). LR: ABierstadt

CL-238. *Sunrise, Yosemite Valley*
Oil on canvas, 36¼ × 52¼″ (92.1 ×
133.8 cm.). LR: ABierstadt

Houston
The Museum of Fine Arts:

CL-239. *Mountain Lake*
Oil on canvas, 36½ × 52 5⁄16″ (92.7
× 132.8 cm.). LL: ABierstadt
Gift of the Joseph C. Cullinan
Family

VERMONT
Saint Johnsbury
Saint Johnsbury Athenaeum:

CL-240. *The Domes of the Yosemite* 1867
SEE FIG. 122
Oil on canvas, 116 × 180″ (294.6 ×
502.9 cm.). LR: ABierstadt

Shelburne
Webb Gallery of American Art,
Shelburne Museum Inc.:

CL-241. *Westphalian Landscape* 1855
SEE FIG. 11
Oil on canvas, 26 × 34½″ (66 ×
87.6 cm.). LL: ABierstadt/1855

This is another view of the cottage
in *Approaching Storm* (CL-164).

CL-242. *The Burning Ship* [*The Confederate
Cruiser "Shenandoah" Burning Whal-
ers in the South Pacific?*] 1867?
Oil on canvas, 30¼ × 50″ (76.5 ×
127 cm.). LL: ABierstadt/1867?

CL-243. *Sunset, Ice Breaking Up* [*Alaska
Revillagigedo Island?*] 1889?
Oil on canvas mounted on board,
10½ × 17¾″ (26.7 × 45.1 cm.).
LR: ABierstadt

See Chap. 11.

CL-244. *Landscape with Hills*
Oil on canvas, 13¼ × 18½″ (33.7 ×
47 cm.). LR: ABierstadt—

VIRGINIA
Richmond
Virginia Museum of Fine Arts:

CL-245. *A Quiet Valley [Westphalian Landscape]* 1855
Oil on canvas, 33½ × 42¼″ (85.1 × 106.7 cm.). LR: ABierstadt. 1855

WASHINGTON
Seattle
Charles and Emma Frye Art Museum:

CL-246. *The Great Salt Lake* 1863?/1881?
SEE FIG. 96
Oil on paper mounted on board, 14 × 19½″ (35.6 × 49 cm.).
LR: ABierstadt

May depict Bierstadt's and Ludlow's visit to Great Salt Lake in 1863, although Bierstadt visited the area again in 1881 (Chaps. 6 and 10).

Seattle Art Museum:

CL-247. *Beach Scene*
Oil on paper mounted on fiberboard, 13¼ × 18½″ (33.7 × 47 cm.). LR: ABierstadt   Gift of

Mrs. John McCone in memory of Ada E. Pigott

WISCONSIN
Milwaukee
Milwaukee Art Center:

CL-248. *Grizzly Bears (American Black Bears)* 1859?   SEE FIG. 68
Oil on paper mounted on canvas, 14 × 16″ (35.6 × 45.7 cm.).
LL: ABierstadt   Layton Art Gallery Collection

CL-249. *Wind River Mountains, Nebraska Territory* 1862
Oil on composition board, 12 × 18½″ (30.5 × 47 cm.).
LL: ABierstadt/1862
Layton Art Gallery Collection

WYOMING
Cody
Buffalo Bill Historical Center, The Whitney Gallery of Western Art:

NOTE: Many of The Whitney Gallery's photographs are cropped; sight-sizes are given for all paintings in this collection.

CL-250. *Wind River, Wyoming* 1870
Oil on canvas, 52½ × 83⅛″ (133.4 × 211.1 cm.). LR: ABierstadt/70

CL-251. *Old Faithful* 1881
Oil on paper, 18⅛ × 12¾″ (46 × 32.4 cm.). LR: ABierstadt

CL-252. *Yellowstone Falls* 1881
Oil on canvas, 43½ × 29¾″ (110.5 × 75.5 cm.). LR: ABierstadt

CL-253. Sketch for *The Last of the Buffalo* 1888
Oil on paper, 13½ × 18″ (34.3 × 45.7 cm.). LR: ABierstadt

CL-254. *The Last of the Buffalo* (alternate version)   1888
Oil on canvas, 60 × 96″ (152.4 × 243.8 cm.). LR: ABierstadt

Compare the Corcoran painting (CL-56): the principal difference between the two is the standing buffalo at the left in the Corcoran painting.

CL-255. *Buffalo Head*
Oil on paper, 12⅝ × 14⅝″ (32.1 × 37.2 cm.). LL: ABierstadt

CL-256. *Deer*
Oil on paper, 13¼ × 18¾″ (33.7 × 47.6 cm.). LL: ABierstadt

CL-257. *Deer in Mountain Home*
Oil on paper, 13 × 18⅝″ (33.1 × 47.3 cm.).   LR: ABierstadt

CL-258. *Elk*
Oil on paper, 12¼ × 18½″ (31.1 × 47 cm.). LR: ABierstadt

CL-259. *Elk*
Oil on paper, 13⅝ × 18½″ (34.6 × 47 cm.). LR: ABierstadt

CL-260. *The Grand Tetons* [incorrect title]
Oil on paper, 13½ × 23″ (34.3 × 58.4 cm.). LL(scratched in paint): ABierstadt

Evidently the artist never visited the Tetons (Chap. 10).

CL-261. *In the Foothills*
Oil on paper, 13½ × 18⅝″ (34.3 × 47.3 cm.). LR: ABierstadt

CL-262. *In the High Mountains*
Oil on paper, 13⅛ × 17⅝″ (33.3 × 44.7 cm.). LL: ABierstadt

CL-263. *Indian Buck, Squaw and Papoose*
Oil on paper, 15⅞ × 10⅞″ (40.3 × 27.6 cm.). LR: AB

CL-264. *Indian Encampment: Evening*
Oil on paper, 13 × 18⅝″ (33 × 47.3 cm.). LR: ABierstadt

CL-265. *Indian Hunters in Canoe*
Oil on paper, 13¾ × 18½″ (34.9 × 47 cm.). LR: ABierstadt

CL-266. *Indian Scout*
Oil on paper, 11¾ × 7⅝″ (29.8 × 19.3 cm.). LR: ABierstadt

CL-267. *Landscape near Claremont, N.H.*
Oil on paper, 10¼ × 12¾″ (26 × 32.4 cm.). LR: ABierstadt

The Whitney Gallery's name for this painting is simply *Landscape*, but M. Knoedler & Co.'s records indicate the title given above.

CL-268. *Majesty of the Mountains*
Oil on canvas, 53¾ × 83⅝″ (136 × 212.4 cm.). LL: ABierstadt

The presence and style of the cottage suggest a European scene.

CL-269. *Mountains*
Oil on paper, 9⅝ × 13⅜″ (24.4 × 34 cm.). LL: ABierstadt

CL-270. *Mountains*
Oil on paper, 10½ × 14⅝″ (26.7 × 37.1 cm.). LL: ABierstadt

CL-271. *Summer Snow on the Peaks*
Oil on paper, 13 × 18½″ (33 × 47 cm.). LR: ABierstadt

CL-272. *Sunset on Peak*
Oil on paper, 13⅝ × 19″ (34.6 × 48.3 cm.). LR: ABierstadt

CL-273. *Trapped*
Oil on paper, 10⅝ × 14⅝″ (27 × 37.1 cm.). LL: ABierstadt

CL-274. *Two Horses*
Oil on paper, 13⅝ × 19″ (34.6 × 48.3 cm.). LR: ABierstadt

CL-275. *Two Horses*
Oil on paper, 13½ × 19″ (34.3 × 48.3 cm.). LR: ABierstadt

CL-276. *Wagon Train*   SEE FIG. 95
Oil on paper, 13½ × 18⅞″ (34.3 × 47.9 cm.). LR: ABierstadt

CL-277. *White Horse in the Sunset*
SEE FIG. 209
Oil on paper, 11½ × 15½″ (29.2 × 39.4 cm.). LL: ABierstadt

CL-278. *A Wild Stallion*
Oil on paper, 12⅝ × 18¾″ (32.1 × 47.6 cm.). LR: ABierstadt

CL-279. *Wooded Landscape*
Oil on paper, 12⅝ × 18″ (32.1 × 45.7 cm.). LL: ABierstadt

Likely a White Mountains scene.

CL-280. *Yosemite Valley*
Oil on paper, 15½ × 18¾″ (39.4 × 47.6 cm.). LR: ABierstadt

Bibliography

BOOKS:

Henry T. Tuckerman. *Book of the Artists.* New York: G. P. Putnam and Son, 1867, p. 387ff.

G. W. Sheldon. *American Painters.* New York: D. Appleton, 1879, p. 149.

S. G. W. Benjamin. *Art in America.* New York: Harper & Bros., 1880, p. 97ff.

Sadakichi Hartmann. *A History of American Art.* Boston: L. C. Page & Company, 1902, p. 69.

Samuel Isham. *The History of American Painting.* New York: Macmillan Company, 1905, p. 251.

Mrs. H. J. Taylor. *Yosemite Indians and Other Sketches.* San Francisco: Jonck and Seeger, 1936, p. 80ff.

California Art Research, II, First Series. Washington, D.C.: Works Progress Administration, 1936–37, p. 98ff.

E. P. Richardson. *American Romantic Painting.* New York: E. Weyhe, 1944, p. 25.

Clara Endicott Sears. *Highlights Among the Hudson River Artists.* Port Washington, N.Y.: Kennikat Press, 1947, p. 143ff.

Wolfgang Born. *American Landscape Painting.* New Haven: Yale University Press, 1948, p. 69.

Virgil Barker. *American Painting.* New York: Bonanza Books, 1950, p. 587.

Harold McCracken. *Portrait of the Old West.* New York: McGraw Hill, 1952, p. 137ff.

E. P. Richardson. *Painting in America.* New York: T. Y. Crowell, 1956, p. 229ff.

Alexander Eliot. *Three Hundred Years of American Painting.* New York: Time Inc., 1957, p. 95.

James Thomas Flexner. *That Wilder Image.* New York: Bonanza Books, 1962, p. 294ff.

James Thomas Flexner. *Nineteenth Century American Painting.* New York: G. P. Putnam, 1970, p. 134ff.

Barbara Novak. *American Painting of the Nineteenth Century.* New York: Praeger, 1971, *passim*.

James Biddle, Carl Carmer, and John K. Howat. *The Hudson River and Its Painters.* New York: Viking Press, 1972, pp. 47–48.

Larry Curry. *The American West.* New York: Viking Press, 1972, p. 40.

ARTICLES:

"Albert Bierstadt." *Zeitschrift für Bildende Kunst,* 1870, p. 65ff.

D. O. C. Townley. "Living American Artists." *Scribner's Monthly,* March 1872, p. 605ff.

"Albert Bierstadt." *California Art Gallery,* April 1873, p. 49ff.

William Newton Byers. "Bierstadt's Visit to Colorado." *Magazine of Western History,* January 1890, p. 237ff.

Benjamin Poff Draper. "Albert Bierstadt." *Art in America,* April 1940, p. 61ff.

Yosemite Nature Notes, May 1944, p. 49ff.

Gerhard G. Spieler. "A Noted Artist in Early Colorado." *American-German Review,* June 1945, p. 13ff.

Ruth Gilette Hardy. "A Mountain Traveler." *Appalachia,* June 1950, p. 63ff.

E. S. Wallace. "Albert Bierstadt, Artist." *The Westerners New York Brand Book,* 1955, pp. 1, 20–21.

Joseph W. Snell. "Some Rare Western Photographs by Albert Bierstadt." *The Kansas Historical Quarterly,* Spring 1958, p. 1ff.

Florence Lewison. "The Uniqueness of Albert Bierstadt." *The American Artist,* September 1964, p. 28ff.

Gordon Hendricks. "The First Three Western Journeys of Albert Bierstadt." *The Art Bulletin,* September 1964, p. 333ff.

Gordon Hendricks. "Bierstadt's Western Journeys." *Auction,* March 1970, p. 42ff.

Gordon Hendricks. "Bierstadt's *The Domes of the Yosemite.*" *The American Art Journal,* Vol. III, no. 2 (Fall 1971), p. 23ff.

Gordon Hendricks. "Bierstadt and Church at the New York Sanitary Fair." *Antiques Magazine,* November 1972, p. 892ff.

EXHIBITION CATALOGUES:

A Selection of Paintings by Albert Pinkham Ryder and Albert Bierstadt, Swain School of Design, New Bedford, Mass., April 23, 1960.

An Art Perspective of the Historic Pacific Northwest,

353

Montana Historical Society, Helena, August 1963.

The Creative Core of Bierstadt, Florence Lewison Gallery, New York, 1963.

Man, Beast and Nature, Florence Lewison Gallery, New York, 1964.

Albert Bierstadt, Santa Barbara Museum of Art, Santa Barbara, Calif., August 5, 1964.

Bierstadt, His Small Paintings, Florence Lewison Gallery, New York, 1968.

Gordon Hendricks, *ABierstadt,* The Amon Carter Museum of Western Art, Fort Worth, Tex., January 27–March 19, 1972; The Corcoran Gallery, Washington, D.C., April 2–May 14, 1972; The Whaling Museum, New Bedford, Mass., May 28–July 5, 1972; The Whitney Museum of American Art, New York, September 11–November 5, 1972; The Pennsylvania Academy of the Fine Arts, Philadelphia, November 15, 1972–January 3, 1973.

Gordon Hendricks, *Albert Bierstadt,* M. Knoedler & Co., New York, September 15, 1972.

MISCELLANEOUS:

The M. and M. Karolik Collection of American Paintings, Boston, 1949, p. 74ff.

Richard Shafer Trump, "Life and Works of Albert Bierstadt," Ph.D. dissertation, Ohio State University, Columbus, 1963.

Index

NOTE: Public collections are not indexed unless referred to in the text; they are arranged alphabetically by state and city in the Check List.

LIST OF CREDITS

The author and publisher wish to thank the libraries, museums, and private collectors for permitting the reproduction of paintings, prints, photographs, documents, and maps in their collections. Photographs of all works have been supplied by their owners or custodians except for the following, whose courtesy is gratefully acknowledged:

Amon Carter Museum of Western Art, Fort Worth, Tex., Fig. 117; Angle, Lee, Fort Worth, Tex., Figs. 29, 101, 106, 107, 123, 177, 197, 201, 223; Beville, Henry B., Alexandria, Va., Figs. 54, 166; Blackwell, William R., Louisville, Ky., CL-73; Blomstrann, E. Irving, New Britain, Conn., Figs. 75, 159, CL-42; Bowers, W. L., Colorado Springs, Colo., CL-36; Burstein, Barney, Boston, Mass., Figs. 10, 13; Castelli, Guido, New York City, Fig. 87; Clements, Geoffrey, New York City, Figs. 64, 65, 81, 108–110, 154, 208, 218, 227, CL-57–65; Condit Studio, Portland, Ore., Fig. 163; George Eastman House, Rochester, N.Y., Fig. 83; Edel-stein, H., Northampton, Mass., CL-123–25; Fortier, Norman, So. Dartmouth, Mass., Fig. 214, CL-121; Frick Art Reference Library, New York City, Fig. 221, CL-173; Frohman, Louis H., Bronxville, N.Y., CL-183; Higgins, F. J., Highland Park, N.J., CL-148; Kelly, Frank, Manchester, N.H., CL-146; M. Knoedler & Co., New York City, Figs. 21, 97, 200; Lockwood Mansion, Norwalk, Conn., Fig. 119; Mates, Robert E., and Paul Katz, New York City, Fig. 77; Mattoon, Lon, Elmira, N.Y., Fig. 12; Mengis, Einars J., Shelburne, Vt., Fig. 11, CL-243, CL-244; Obert, Karl, Santa Barbara, Calif., CL-22; Phaidon Press Ltd. Pub-lishers, London, Fig. 30; Pollitzer, Eric, Garden City Park, N.Y., half-title photo, Figs. 85, 86, 124, 150, 168; Jack Richards Studio, Cody, Wyo., CL-250–75, CL-278–80; Roy Robinson Studios, San Diego, Calif., Fig. 1; Stockmeyer, Lewis F., Upper Nyack, N.Y., Fig. 164; Szaszfai, Joseph, New Haven, Conn., CL-49; Union Dime Savings Bank, New York City, Fig. 192; Victor's Photography, Piscataway, N.J., CL-149, CL-150; Vose, Herbert P., Wellesley Hills, Mass., Fig. 25, CL-81; Whaling Museum, New Bedford, Mass., Fig. 210; Witt, Bill, Montclair, N.J., CL-147; University of Wyoming, Laramie, Fig. 15.